Reader's Guide
to
JANE AUSTEN

Reader's Guide to JANE AUSTEN

S. Dorsch

CENTRUM PRESS
NEW DELHI-110002 (INDIA)

CENTRUM PRESS
H.O.: 4360/4, Ansari Road, Daryaganj,
New Delhi-110 002 (India)
Ph.: 23278000, 23261597

B.O.: No. 1015, Ist Main Road, BSK IIIrd Stage
IIIrd Phase, IIIrd Block,
Bangalore - 560 085 (India)
Tel.: 080-41723429
Visit us at: www.centrumpress.com

Reader's Guide to Jane Austen

First Edition, 2009

ISBN 978-93-80106-54-0

PRINTED IN INDIA

Printed at Salasar Imaging Systems, Delhi-110035 (India)

Contents

Preface

Jane Austen was a major English novelist, who first gave the novel its modern character through the treatment of everyday life. Although Austen was widely read in her lifetime, she published her works anonymously. Jane Austen was great because she was honest, and dealt with nature nearly a hundred years ago as realism deals with it to-day. Realism is nothing more and nothing less than the truthful treatment of material, and she was the first and the last of the English novelists to treat material with entire truthfulness. Because she did this, she remains the most artistic of the English novelists, and alone worthy to be matched with the great Scandinavian and Slavic and Latin artists. It is not a question of intellect, or not wholly that.

The English have mind enough; but they have not taste enough; or, rather, their taste has been perverted by their false criticism, which is based upon personal preference, and not upon, principle; which instructs a man to think that what he likes is good, instead of teaching him first to distinguish what is good before he likes it. The art of fiction, as Jane Austen knew it, declined from her through Scott, and Bulwer, and Dickens, and Charlotte Bronte, and Thackeray, and even George Eliot, because the mania of romanticism had seized upon all Europe, and these great writers could not escape the taint of their time; but it has shown few signs of recovery in England, because English criticism, in the presence of the Continental masterpieces, has continued provincial and special and personal, and has expressed a love and a hate which had to do with the quality of the artist rather than the character of his work.

Author

Chapter 1

Introduction

Jane Austen (16 December 1775 – 18 July 1817) was an English novelist whose realism, biting social commentary and masterful use of free indirect speech, burlesque and irony have earned her a place as one of the most widely read and most beloved writers in English literature. Austen lived her entire life as part of a small and close-knit family located on the lower fringes of English gentry. She was educated primarily by her father and older brothers as well as through her own reading. The steadfast support of her family was critical to Austen's development as a professional writer. Austen's artistic apprenticeship lasted from her teenage years until she was about thirty-five years old. During this period, she wrote three major novels and began a fourth.

From 1811 until 1815, with the release of *Sense and Sensibility* (1811), *Pride and Prejudice* (1813), *Mansfield Park* (1814) and *Emma* (1815), she achieved success as a published writer. She wrote two additional novels, *Northanger Abbey* and *Persuasion,* both published after her death in 1817, and began a third, which was eventually titled *Sanditon,* but died before completing it. Austen's works critique the novels of sensibility of the second half of the eighteenth century and are part of the transition to nineteenth-century realism. Austen's plots, though fundamentally comic, highlight the dependence of women on marriage to secure social standing and economic security.

Like those of Samuel Johnson, one of the strongest influences on her writing, her works are concerned with moral issues. During her lifetime, Austen's works brought her little fame and only a few positive reviews. Through the mid-nineteenth century, her novels were admired only by a literary elite. However, the publication of her nephew's *A Memoir of Jane Austen* in 1869 introduced her life and works to a wider public. By the 1940s, Austen was firmly ensconced in academia as a "great English writer", and the second half of the twentieth century saw a proliferation of Austen scholarship that explored many aspects of her novels: artistic, ideological, and historical. In popular culture, a Janeite fan culture has developed, centred on Austen's life, her works, and the various film and television adaptations of them.

Biographical information concerning Jane Austen is "famously scarce", according to one biographer. Only some personal and family letters remain (by one estimate only 160 out of Austen's 3,000 letters are extant), and her sister Cassandra (to whom most of the letters were originally addressed) burned "the greater part" of the ones she kept and censored those she did not destroy. Other letters were destroyed by the heirs of Admiral Francis Austen, Jane's brother. Most of the biographical material produced for fifty years after Austen's death was written by her relatives and reflects the family's biases in favour of "good quiet Aunt Jane". Scholars have unearthed little information since.

FAMILY

Jane Austen's father, George Austen (1731–1805), and his wife, Cassandra (1739–1827), were members of substantial gentry families. George was descended from a family of woollen manufacturers which had risen through the professions to the lower ranks of the landed gentry. Cassandra was a member of the prominent Leigh family. From 1765 until 1801, that is, for much of Jane's life, George Austen served as the rector of the Anglican parishes at Steventon, Hampshire and a nearby village. From 1773 until 1796, he supplemented this income by farming and by teaching three or four boys at a time who boarded at his home. Austen's immediate family was large: six brothers—James (1765–1819), George (1766–1838), Edward (1767–1852), Henry Thomas (1771–1850),

Francis William (Frank) (1774-1865), Charles John (1779–1852)—and one sister, Cassandra Elizabeth (1773–1845), who, like Jane, died unmarried.

Cassandra was Austen's closest friend and confidante throughout her life. Of her brothers, Austen felt closest to Henry, who became a banker and, after his bank failed, an Anglican clergyman. Henry was also his sister's literary agent. His large circle of friends and acquaintances in London included bankers, merchants, publishers, painters, and actors: he provided Austen with a view of social worlds not normally visible from a small parish in rural Hampshire. George was sent to live with a local family at a young age because, as Austen biographer Le Faye describes it, he was "mentally abnormal and subject to fits". He may also have been deaf and dumb. Charles and Frank served in the navy, both rising to the rank of admiral. Edward was brought up by his second cousin Thomas Knight, eventually inheriting Knight's estate and taking his name.

LIFE AND EDUCATION

Austen was born on 16 December 1775 at Steventon rectory and publicly christened on 5 April 1776. After a few months at home, her mother placed Austen with a woman living in a nearby village who nursed and raised Austen for a year or eighteen months. In 1783, according to family tradition, Jane and Cassandra were sent to Oxford to be educated by Mrs Ann Cawley and they moved with her to Southampton later in the year. Both girls caught typhus and Jane nearly died. Austen was subsequently educated at home, until leaving for boarding school with her sister Cassandra early in 1785. The school curriculum probably included some French, spelling, needlework, dancing and music and, perhaps, drama. By December 1786, Jane and Cassandra had returned home because the Austens could not afford to send both of their daughters to school.

Austen acquired the remainder of her education by reading books, guided by her father and her brothers James and Henry. George Austen apparently gave his daughters unfettered access to his large and varied library, was tolerant of Austen's sometimes risqué experiments in writing, and provided both sisters with expensive paper and other materials for their writing and drawing. According to Park Honan, a biographer of Austen, life in the Austen home was lived in "an open, amused, easy intellectual atmosphere" where the ideas of those with whom the Austens might disagree politically or socially were considered and discussed. After returning from school in 1786, Austen "never again lived anywhere beyond the bounds of her immediate family environment".

Private theatricals were also a part of Austen's education. From when she was seven until she was thirteen, the family and close friends staged a series of plays, including Richard Sheridan's *The Rivals* (1775) and David Garrick's *Bon Ton*. While the details are unknown, Austen would certainly have joined in these activities, as a spectator at first and as a participant when she was older. Most of the plays were comedies, which suggests one way in which Austen's comedic and satirical gifts were cultivated.

Perhaps as early as 1787, Austen began to write poems, stories, and plays for her own and her family's amusement. Austen later compiled "fair copies" of 29 of these early works into three bound notebooks, now referred to as the *Juvenilia*, containing pieces originally written between 1787 and 1793. There is manuscript evidence that Austen continued to work on these pieces as late as the period 1809–11, and that her niece and nephew, Anna and James Edward Austen, made further additions as late as 1814. Among these works are a satirical novel in letters entitled *Love and Freindship* [*sic*], in which she mocked popular novels of sensibility, and *The History of England*, a manuscript of 34 pages accompanied by 13 watercolour miniatures by her sister Cassandra. Austen's "History" parodied popular historical writing, particularly Oliver Goldsmith's *History of England* (1764).

Austen wrote, for example: "Henry the 4th ascended the throne of England much to his own satisfaction in the year 1399, after having prevailed on his cousin & predecessor

Richard the 2nd, to resign it to him, & to retire for the rest of his Life to Pomfret Castle, where he happened to be murdered." Austen's *Juvenilia* are often, according to scholar Richard Jenkyns, "boisterous" and "anarchic"; he compares them to the work of eighteenth-century novelist Laurence Sterne and the twentieth-century comedy group Monty Python. As Austen grew into adulthood, she continued to live at her parents' home, carrying out those activities normal for women of her age and social standing: she practiced the pianoforte, assisted her sister and mother with supervising servants, and attended female relatives during childbirth and older relatives on their deathbeds. She sent short pieces of writing to her newborn nieces Fanny Catherine and Jane Anna Elizabeth. Austen was particularly proud of her accomplishments as a seamstress. She also attended church regularly, socialized frequently with friends and neighbours, and read novels—often of her own composition—aloud with her family in the evenings. Socializing with the neighbours often meant dancing, either impromptu in someone's home after supper or at the balls held regularly at the assembly rooms in the town hall. Her brother Henry later said that "Jane was fond of dancing, and excelled in it".

In 1793, Austen began and then abandoned a short play, later entitled *Sir Charles Grandison or the happy Man, a comedy in 6 acts,* which she returned to and completed around 1800. This was a short parody of various school textbook abridgments of Austen's favourite contemporary novel, *The History of Sir Charles Grandison* (1753), by Samuel Richardson. Honan speculates that at some point not long after writing *Love and Freindship* [sic] in 1789, Austen decided to "write for profit, to make stories her central effort", that is, to become a professional writer. Whenever she made that decision, beginning in about 1793, Austen began to write longer, more sophisticated works.

During the period between 1793 and 1795, Austen wrote *Lady Susan,* a short epistolary novel, usually described as her most ambitious and sophisticated early work. It is unlike any of Austen's other works. Austen biographer Claire Tomalin describes the heroine of the novella as a sexual predator who uses her intelligence and charm to manipulate, betray, and abuse her victims, whether lovers, friends or family. Tomalin writes: "Told in letters, it is as neatly plotted as a play, and as cynical in tone as any of the most outrageous of the Restoration dramatists who may have provided some of her inspiration....It stands alone in Austen's work as a study of an adult woman whose intelligence and force of character are greater than those of anyone she encounters."

EARLY NOVELS

After finishing *Lady Susan,* Austen attempted her first full-length novel—*Elinor and Marianne.* Her sister Cassandra later remembered that it was read to the family "before 1796" and was told through a series of letters. Without surviving original manuscripts, there is no way to know how much of the original draft survived in the novel published in 1811 as *Sense and Sensibility*. When Austen was twenty-one Tom Lefroy, a nephew of neighbours, visited Steventon from December 1795 to January 1796. He had just finished a university degree and was moving to London to train as a barrister. Lefroy and Austen would have been introduced at a ball or other neighbourhood social gathering, and it is clear from Austen's letters to Cassandra that they spent considerable time together: "I am almost afraid to tell you how my Irish friend and I behaved.

Imagine to yourself everything most profligate and shocking in the way of dancing and sitting down together." The Lefroy family intervened and sent him away at the end of January. Marriage was impractical, as both Lefroy and Austen must have known. Neither had any money, and he was dependent on a great-uncle in Ireland to finance his education and establish his legal career. If Tom Lefroy later visited Hampshire, he was carefully kept away from the Austens, and Jane Austen never saw him again. Austen began work on a second novel, *First Impressions,* in 1796 and completed the initial draft in August 1797 when she was only 21. (it would later become *Pride and Prejudice*); as with all of her novels,

Austen read the work aloud to her family as she was working on it and it became an "established favourite".

At this time, her father made the first attempt to publish one of her novels. In November 1797, George Austen wrote to Thomas Cadell, an established publisher in London, to ask if he would consider publishing "a Manuscript Novel, comprised in three Vols. about the length of Miss Burney's Evelina" (*First Impressions*) at the author's financial risk. Cadell quickly returned Mr. Austen's letter, marked "Declined by Return of Post". Austen may not have known of her father's efforts. Following the completion of *First Impressions*, Austen returned to *Elinor and Marianne* and from November 1797 until mid-1798, revised it heavily; she eliminated the epistolary format in favour of third-person narration and produced something close to *Sense and Sensibility*.

During the middle of 1798, after finishing revisions of *Elinor and Marianne*, Austen began writing a third novel with the working title *Susan*—later *Northanger Abbey*—a satire on the popular Gothic novel. Austen completed her work about a year later. In early 1803, Henry Austen offered *Susan* to Benjamin Crosby, a London publisher, who paid £10 for the copyright. Crosby promised early publication and went so far as to advertise the book publicly as being "in the press", but did nothing more. The manuscript remained in Crosby's hands, unpublished, until Austen repurchased the copyright from him in 1816.

In December 1800, Rev. Austen unexpectedly announced his decision to retire from the ministry, leave Steventon, and move the family to Bath. While retirement and travel were good for the elder Austens, Jane Austen was shocked to be told she was moving from the only home she had ever known. An indication of Austen's state of mind is her lack of productivity as a writer during the time she lived at Bath. She was able to make some revisions to *Susan*, and she began and then abandoned a new novel, *The Watsons*, but there was nothing like the productivity of the years 1795-1799. Tomalin suggests this reflected a deep depression disabling her as a writer, but Honan disagrees, arguing Austen wrote or revised her manuscripts throughout her creative life, except for a few months after her father died.

In December 1802, Austen received her only proposal of marriage. She and her sister visited Alethea and Catherine Bigg, old friends who lived near Basingstoke. Their younger brother, Harris Bigg-Wither, had recently finished his education at Oxford and was also at home. Bigg-Wither proposed and Austen accepted. As described by Caroline Austen, Jane's niece, and Reginald Bigg-Wither, a descendant, Harris was not attractive—he was a large, plain-looking man who spoke little, stuttered when he did speak, was aggressive in conversation, and almost completely tactless. However, Austen had known him since both were young and the marriage offered many practical advantages to Austen and her family. He was the heir to extensive family estates located in the area where the sisters had grown up. With these resources, Austen could provide her parents a comfortable old age, give Cassandra a permanent home and, perhaps, assist her brothers in their careers.

By the next morning, Austen realised she had made a mistake and withdrew her acceptance. No contemporary letters or diaries describe how Austen felt about this proposal. In 1814, Austen wrote a letter to her niece, Fanny Knight, who had asked for advice about a serious relationship, telling her that "having written so much on one side of the question, I shall now turn around & entreat you not to commit yourself farther, & not to think of accepting him unless you really do like him. Anything is to be preferred or endured rather than marrying without Affection". In 1804, while living in Bath, Austen started but did not complete a new novel, *The Watsons*.

The story centres on an invalid clergyman with little money and his four unmarried daughters. Sutherland describes the novel as "a study in the harsh economic realities of dependent women's lives". Honan suggests, and Tomalin agrees, that Austen chose to stop work on the novel after her father died on 21 January 1805 and her personal circumstances resembled those of her characters too closely for her comfort. Rev. Austen's final illness had struck suddenly, leaving him, as Austen reported to her brother Francis, "quite insensible of his own state", and he died quickly. Jane, Cassandra, and their mother were left in a precarious financial situation. Edward, James, Henry, and Francis Austen pledged to make annual contributions to support their mother and sisters.

For the next four years, the family's living arrangements reflected their financial insecurity. They lived part of the time in rented quarters in Bath and then, beginning in 1806, in Southampton, where they shared a house with Frank Austen and his new wife. A large part of this time they spent visiting various branches of the family. On 5 April 1809, about three months before the family's move to Chawton, Austen wrote an angry letter to Richard Crosby, offering him a new manuscript of *Susan* if that was needed to secure immediate publication of the novel, and otherwise requesting the return of the original so she could find another publisher. Crosby replied he had not agreed to publish the book by any particular time, or at all, and that Austen could repurchase the manuscript for the £10 he had paid her and find another publisher. However, Austen did not have the resources to repurchase the book.

Around early 1809, Austen's brother Edward offered his mother and sisters a more settled life—the use of a large "cottage" in Chawton village that was part of Edward's nearby estate, Chawton House. Jane, Cassandra, and their mother moved into Chawton cottage on 7 July 1809. In Chawton, life was quieter than it had been since the family's move to Bath in 1800. The Austens did not socialise with the neighbouring gentry and entertained only when family visited. Austen's niece Anna described the Austen family's life in Chawton: "It was a very quiet life, according to our ideas, but they were great readers, and besides the housekeeping our aunts occupied themselves in working with the poor and in teaching some girl or boy to read or write." Austen wrote almost daily, but privately, and seems to have been relieved of some household responsibilities to give her more opportunity to write. In this setting, she was able to be productive as a writer once more.

During her time at Chawton, Jane Austen successfully published four novels, which were generally well-received. Through her brother Henry, the publisher Thomas Egerton agreed to publish *Sense and Sensibility,* which appeared in October 1811. Reviews were favourable and the novel became fashionable among opinion-makers; the edition sold out by mid-1813. Austen's earnings from *Sense and Sensibility* provided her with some financial and psychological independence. Egerton then published *Pride and Prejudice,* a revision of *First Impressions,* in January 1813. He advertised the book widely and it was an immediate success, garnering three favourable reviews and selling well. By October 1813, Egerton was able to begin selling a second edition. *Mansfield Park* was published by Egerton in May 1814.

While *Mansfield Park* was ignored by reviewers, it was a great success with the public. All copies were sold within six months, and Austen's earnings on this novel were larger than for any of her other novels. Austen learned that the Prince Regent admired her novels and kept a set at each of his residences. In November 1815, the Prince Regent's librarian invited Austen to visit the Prince's London residence and hinted Austen should dedicate the forthcoming *Emma* to the Prince. Though Austen disliked the Prince, she could scarcely refuse the request. She later wrote *Plan of a Novel, according to hints from various quarters,* a satiric outline of the "perfect novel" based on the librarian's many suggestions for a future Austen novel.

In mid-1815, Austen moved her work from Egerton to John Murray, a better known London publisher, who published *Emma* in December 1815 and a second edition of *Mansfield Park* in February 1816. *Emma* sold well but the new edition of *Mansfield Park* did not, and this failure offset most of the profits Austen earned on *Emma.* These were the last of Austen's novels to be published during her lifetime. While Murray prepared *Emma* for publication, Austen began to write a new novel she titled *The Elliots,* later published as *Persuasion.* She completed her first draft in July 1816. In addition, shortly after the publication of *Emma,* Henry Austen repurchased the copyright for *Susan* from Crosby. Austen was forced to postpone publishing either of these completed novels by family financial troubles. Henry Austen's bank failed in March 1816, depriving him of all of his assets, leaving him deeply in debt and losing Edward, James, and Frank Austen large sums. Henry and Frank could no longer afford the contributions they had made to support their mother and sisters.

Early in 1816, Jane Austen began to feel unwell. She ignored her illness at first and continued to work and to participate in the usual round of family activities. By the middle of that year, her decline was unmistakable to Austen and to her family, and Austen's physical condition began a long, slow, and irregular deterioration culminating in her death the following year. The majority of Austen biographers rely on Dr. Vincent Cope's tentative 1964 retrospective diagnosis and list her cause of death as Addison's disease. However, her final illness has also been described as Hodgkin's lymphoma. Austen continued to work in spite of her illness. She became dissatisfied with the ending of *The Elliots* and rewrote the final two chapters, finishing them on 6 August 1816.

In January 1817, Austen began work on a new novel she called *The Brothers,* later titled *Sanditon* upon its first publication in 1925, and completed twelve chapters before stopping work in mid-March 1817, probably because her illness prevented her from continuing. Austen made light of her condition to others, describing it as "Bile" and rheumatism, but as her disease progressed she experienced increasing difficulty walking or finding the energy for other activities. By mid-April, Austen was confined to her bed. In May, their brother Henry escorted Jane and Cassandra to Winchester for medical treatment. Austen died in Winchester on 18 July 1817. Through his clerical connections, Henry arranged for his sister to be buried in the north aisle of the nave of Winchester Cathedral. The epitaph composed by her brother James praises Austen's personal qualities, expresses hope for her salvation, mentions the "extraordinary endowments of her mind", but does not explicitly mention her achievements as a writer.

After Austen's death, Cassandra and Henry Austen arranged with Murray for the publication of *Persuasion* and *Northanger Abbey* as a set in December 1817. Henry Austen contributed a *Biographical Note* which for the first time identified his sister as the author of the novels. Tomalin describes it as "a loving and polished eulogy". Sales were good for a year—only 321 copies remained unsold at the end of 1818—and then declined. Murray disposed of the remaining copies in 1820, and Austen's novels remained out of print for twelve years. In 1832, publisher Richard Bentley purchased the remaining copyrights to all of Austen's novels and, beginning in either December 1832 or January 1833, published them in five illustrated volumes as part of his *Standard Novels* series. In October 1833, Bentley published the first collected edition of Austen's works. Since then, Austen's novels have been continuously in print.

CONTEMPORARY RESPONSES

Austen's works brought her little personal renown because they were published anonymously. Although her novels quickly became fashionable among opinion-makers, such as Princess Charlotte Augusta, daughter of the Prince Regent, they received only a few published reviews. Most of the reviews were short and on balance favourable, although superficial and cautious. They most often focused on the moral lessons of the novels. Sir Walter Scott, a leading novelist of the day, contributed one of them, anonymously. Using the review as a platform from which to defend the then disreputable genre of the novel, he praised Austen's realism. The other important early review of Austen's works was published by Richard Whately in 1821. He drew favourable comparisons between Austen and such acknowledged greats as Homer and Shakespeare, praising the dramatic qualities of her narrative. Whately and Scott set the tone for almost all subsequent nineteenth-century Austen criticism.

Because Austen's novels failed to conform to Romantic and Victorian expectations that "powerful emotion [be] authenticated by an egregious display of sound and colour in the writing", nineteenth-century critics and audiences generally preferred the works of Charles Dickens and George Eliot. Though Austen's novels were republished in Britain beginning in the 1830s and remained steady sellers, they were not bestsellers.

Austen had many admiring readers in the nineteenth century who considered themselves part of a literary elite: they viewed their appreciation of Austen's works as a mark of their cultural taste. Philosopher and literary critic George Henry Lewes expressed this viewpoint in a series of enthusiastic articles published in the 1840s and 1850s. This theme continued later in the century with novelist Henry James, who referred to Austen several times with approval and on one occasion ranked her with Shakespeare, Cervantes, and Henry Fielding as among "the fine painters of life".

The publication of James Edward Austen-Leigh's *A Memoir of Jane Austen* in 1869 introduced Austen to a wider public as "dear aunt Jane", the respectable maiden aunt. Publication of the *Memoir* spurred the reissue of Austen's novels—the first popular editions were released in 1883 and fancy illustrated editions and collectors' sets quickly followed. Author and critic Leslie Stephen described the popular mania that started to develop for Austen in the 1880s as "Austenolatry". Around the turn of the century, members of the literary elite reacted against the popularization of Austen. They referred to themselves as *Janeites* in order to distinguish themselves from the masses who did not properly understand her works. For example, James responded negatively to what he described as "a beguiled infatuation" with Austen, a rising tide of public interest that exceeded Austen's "intrinsic merit and interest".

During the last quarter of the nineteenth century, the first books of criticism on Austen were published. In fact, after the publication of the *Memoir*, more criticism was published on Austen in two years than had appeared in the previous fifty.

Several important works paved the way for Austen's novels to become a focus of academic study. The first important milestone was a 1911 essay by Oxford

Shakespearean scholar A. C. Bradley, which is "generally regarded as the starting-point for the serious academic approach to Jane Austen". In it, he established the groupings of Austen's "early" and "late" novels, which are still used by scholars today. The second was R. W. Chapman's 1923 edition of Austen's collected works. Not only was it the first scholarly edition of Austen's works, it was also the first scholarly edition of any English novelist. The Chapman text has remained the basis for all subsequent published editions of Austen's works.

With the publication in 1939 of Mary Lascelles's *Jane Austen and Her Art*, the academic study of Austen took hold. Lascelles's innovative work included an analysis of the books Jane Austen read and the effect of her reading on her work, an extended analysis of Austen's style, and her "narrative art". At the time, concern arose over the fact that academics were taking over Austen criticism and it was becoming increasingly esoteric—a debate that has continued to the beginning of the twenty-first century. In a spurt of revisionist views in the 1940s, scholars approached Austen more sceptically and argued that she was a subversive writer. These revisionist views, together with F. R. Leavis's and Ian Watt's pronouncement that Austen was one of the great writers of English fiction, did much to cement Austen's reputation amongst academics. They agreed that she "combined [Henry Fielding's and Samuel Richardson's] qualities of interiority and irony, realism and satire to form an author superior to both".

The period since World War II has seen more scholarship on Austen using a diversity of critical approaches, including feminist theory, and perhaps most controversially, postcolonial theory. However, the continuing disconnection between the popular appreciation of Austen, particularly by modern Janeites, and the academic appreciation of Austen has widened considerably. Sequels, prequels, and adaptations of almost every sort have been based on the novels of Jane Austen, from soft-core pornography to fantasy. Beginning in the middle of the nineteenth century, Austen family members published conclusions to her incomplete novels, and by 2000 there were over 100 printed adaptations. The first film adaptation was the 1940 MGM production of *Pride and Prejudice* starring Laurence Olivier and Greer Garson. BBC television dramatisations, which were first produced in the 1970s, attempted to adhere meticulously to Austen's plots, characterisations, and settings.

Starting with Emma Thompson's film of *Sense and Sensibility*, a great wave of Austen adaptations began to appear around 1995. Books and scripts that use the general storyline of Austen's novels but change or otherwise modernise the story also became popular at the end of the twentieth century. For example, *Clueless* (1995), Amy Heckerling's updated version of *Emma*, which takes place in Beverly Hills, became a cultural phenomenon and spawned its own television series.

Chapter 2

Literary Analysis on Character Technique

Clueless, the 1995 film interpretation of Emma by Amy Heckerling, and the 1996 Meridian Broadcasting Ltd movie version of Emma, both exhibit numerous parallels to the original Jane Austen novel which was first published in 1816. Despite its modern deliverance through film media and the fact that it was created over a century after Emma, Clueless purposefully posses a stunning resemblance to Jane Austen's novel in both plot and characterisation.

Main characters in Clueless: Elton, Tai Fraiser, and Cher Horowitz directly reference the respective main characters in Emma: Mr. Elton, Harriet Smith, and Emma Woodhouse. In her novel, Jane Austen employs the timelessly effective characterisation agents of dialogue, action, and point of view to cleverly manipulate readers' emotions towards the characters.

Austen is so successful in applying characterisation techniques that her story line and her influence on the reader's opinions easily transcend the passage of time and variation of deliverance to give Meridian Broadcasting Ltd's Emma and Heckerling's Clueless the same modern day appeal as its forerunner Emma. In many ways, Austen's Mr. Elton and Heckerling's Elton are comparable to one another in both their actions and dialogue.

In Emma, we esteem Mr. Elton to be highly respected and well established in the upper social circles of Highbury because of his station as the vicar and his public displays of polite behaviour. Similarly, Elton from Clueless is also quite revered by his peers. Elton *"is the social director of the whole crew"* (*Clueless*) and belongs to a group of *"the most popular guys on campus"* (*Clueless*). Superficially both Eltons are gentlemen, but Austen's style reveals true character and gives depth to the Elton characters through their actions.

The reader realises the improper behaviour and intentions of Mr. Elton when he professes his love for young Emma upon returning from the Westons' party. Not only does this go against Miss Woodhouse's social doctrines, but it also causes her to say that she was *"very sorry that you should have been giving way to any feelings"* (*Austen*, 150).

Heckerling also uses Austen's genius to reveal Elton's true character when he lewdly expresses his affections for Cher during the return home from a party in the valley and then discourteously abandons her in an empty lot.

Cher rejects Elton saying that she does not return his feelings of love, but his continual encroachment upon herself forced Cher to leave the car. In both instances, the inappropriate demonstrations of love reveal the lack of true nobility that lies beneath their seemingly brilliant exterior veneers.

Justifiably, disastrous repercussions of the ignoble actions ensue and the friendships between the respective parties in Emma and Clueless end abruptly thereafter. Except for the increased foolishness of Mr. Elton in the Meridian Broadcasting Ltd direct Emma interpretation, the character in the movie essentially behaves exactly Austen originally created his character in the book. Throughout most of the three similar story lines, the reader perceives the Eltons as self-absorbed, hypocritical, and insincere individuals.

Dialogue also betrays true character and often in an embarrassing manner. In Emma, Mr. Elton declares, *"I shall have great pleasure, I am sure - for though beginning to feel myself rather an old married man, and that my dancing days are over, it would give me very great pleasure at any time to stand up with an old friend like Mrs. Gilbert"* (*Austen* 324). He then contradicts himself shortly afterwards when offered a dance with Harriet

Smith and says, "Miss Smith! - oh! - I had not observed. - You are extremely obliging - and if I were not an old married man. -But my dancing days are over" (Austen 324).

This shows his hypocritical, self absorbed attitude towards those of lower social classes. Mr. Elton believes that despite Harriet's attraction to him, he boasts, *"everyone has their level: but as for myself, I am not, I think, quite at so much at a loss"* (*Austen* 151). In Clueless, Elton jilts Tai Frasier and remarks to Cher, *"Don't you know who my father is?"* (*Clueless*). Even in the movie Emma, the viewer observes that Mr. Elton conducts himself in comparable manner to the literary Mr. Elton and possibly in a more effective manner due to his snobbish attitude that can be expressed by the emphatic action of his body language. Jane Austen's superior uses of dialogue and character action are reflected in the insightful understanding that the reader acquires about Mr. Elton.

Harriet Smith and Tai Fraiser, her modern successor, resemble one another almost perfectly. In Emma, Harriet Smith is the bumbling protege of Miss Woodhouse, she *"is a new and temporarily absorbing interest"* (*Gooneratne* 136) as she lives at Miss Woodhouse's beck and call. She worships Emma to such an extreme that she cannot even make the simplest decisions with out consulting her mentor.

Tai Frasier, the Clueless version of the uncultured Harriet, can be similarly recognised by her thick New York accent and East Coast fashion style that stands apart from the dress of her popular classmates. Out of boredom and a hint of pity, Cher adopts Tai as their next *"project"* and tries to mould Tai into a young socialite in her own image. *"Jane Austen attempts to perpetrate Harriet Smith's simple-mindedness through the depiction of the Ford's scene"* (*Gooneratne* 154) and displays Harriet's flighty and dim-witted personality through dialogue.

Harriet utters, *"Yes - no - yes, to Mrs. Goddard's. Only my pattern gown is at Hartfield. No, you shall send it to Hartfield, if you please. But then, Mrs Goddard will want to see it. - And I could take the pattern gown home any day. But I shall want the ribbon directly - so it had better go to Hartfield - at least the ribbon. You could make it into two parcels, Mrs. Ford, could not you?"* (*Austen*

242) Dialogue uncovers Harriet's inability to speak eloquently and her inability to make a decision, and ultimately emphasises her simpleton and less cultured personality.

To further embellish the subordinate quality of Harriet's personality, Austen makes the reader aware that Emma makes all Harriet's decisions to which Harriet unquestioningly responds *"Aye that would be much best"* (*Austen* 243). In Clueless, the viewer perceives Tai Frasier as an mindless follower who relies on Cher for ultimate approval. Cher coaches Tai in all social corners while telling Tai what is acceptable and what is not acceptable.

For example, Cher mentions that, *"the slackers hang out on the grass over there"* (Clueless) and then points to another group saying, *"if your going to date someone, those are the only guys who are acceptable"* (*Clueless*). Tai dotes upon Cher's every word as if she would not be able to do anything without instruction. The reader sees that Harriet and Tai's lack of independent action makes them Emma and Cher's simple minded puppets.

Although many similarities remain between the characters, the Meridian Broadcasting Ltd movie version of Emma over exaggerates Harriet and bestows her with a more flitty and air headed quality than in the novel. Emma Woodhouse and Cher Horowitz share many similarities. Through dialogue and action the two women become the most comprehensively developed characters. Austen allows the reader to become intimately involved with Emma through her inner thoughts and incessant talking. Emma, an upper class snob, possesses an acute sense of social rank in Highbury where her family is first in consequence and large fortune. Emma derides those of lower social standing and plainly rejects any one below genteel.

The haughty attitude is evidenced when the spoiled Emma attempts to isolate herself from the yeomanry: *"A young farmer, whether on horseback or on foot, is the very last sort of person to raise my curiosity. The yeomanry are precisely the order of people with whom I feel I can have nothing to do. A degree or two lower, and a creditable appearance might interest me; I might hope to be useful to their families in some way or other. But a farmer can need none of my help, and is therefore in one sense as much above my notice as in every other he is below it"* (*Austen* 59). Emma proudly demonstrates her stuck up and elitist attitude while Jane Arden believes that *"Emma Woodhouse is by far the most egotistical character"* (*109*) in Emma and that Miss Woodhouse is *"addicted to admiration and praise"* (*109*). Austen also uses Miss Woodhouse's actions as a personality descriptor.

When Miss Taylor marries Mr. Weston, Emma initially isolates herself and then amuses herself by adopting a new friend, Harriet. The reader perceives that by choosing the feeble-willed Harriet Smith, Emma possess a forceful personality and always wants to always be in control. As described by Arden, Emma believes that tenderness *"means weakness, lack of will, a softness of character which allows itself to be controlled"* (*26*).

This compulsive perfectionist tendency is reinforced when Austen says of Emma, *"so always first and so always right"(84)*. Similarly, Cher Horowitz comments, *"I don't know why they go out with high school boys"*(*Clueless*) about her other less chic high school classmates. Even Cher's friends note the socially superior attitude when they say, *"Cher's got an attitude with high school boys"* (*Clueless*). Cher, akin to Emma, eventually develops a predicament when she discovers that her social prodigy, Tai, turns out to be the perfect image of herself.

Consequently, Tai becomes obsessive like Cher and laments, *"I felt impotent and out of control which I really hate!" (Clueless)*. Most importantly, Austen cleverly relays her story line entirely through the main characters' points of view to make the reader empathize with women whom would otherwise have been perceived as snobbish and self-centered. An alert reader realizes the shrewd quality in Austen's choice to use the main heroine's perspective to narrate the story. If the story were told from any other point of view, the reader might not have the same compassion for Emma or Cher's trivial and egocentric problems.

However, Austen and Heckerling powerfully narrate the stories from the snobbish point of view to evoke reader compassion and almost cause the reader to adopt the same aristocratic attitude of the heroines; irregardless of how ridiculous they might appear.

The Meridian Broadcasting Ltd interpretation of Emma Woodhouse translates quite closely to the original rendering of the story. We perceive Emma to be less high minded in the movie because we are exposed to fewer of her inner thoughts, but the production is ultimately more similar than different. Jane Austen's Emma is so well composed and her characterization techniques are developed so competently that there exist no appreciable differences between the original characters, motifs and their contemporary companions. Both succeeding translations of Emma are rare in that they each remain very true to the original author's novel and style.

Heckerling remains faithful Jane Austen's character portrayals because they are inherently illustrated in manner that easily translates in a modern setting. The Meridian Broadcasting Ltd also creates a world almost exactly parallel to the classic Emma in a movie version because Austen's creative genius requires the most minimal amount of retooling. Clearly, Jane Austen is so effective in utilizing actions to articulate intriguing characters that successive interpreters of Emma faithfully emulate her style to produce popular and modern portrayals of an otherwise ordinary story line.

Although not easy to discern, at least on first glance, Jane Austen's gentle comedies of manners contain their fair share of monsters. Some, indeed are almost gothic in their capacity to create trails of wreckage among the other characters. Mrs. Bennet, the irrepressible mother in Pride and Prejudice, leaps immediately to mind. How does she really feel about her daughters, other than wanting to see them all married? She is proud of Jane's beauty, and sensitive to her position as the eldest daughter. In a perfect world, her Jane would be the first one married, and of course, to an eligible, handsome, wealthy young man. Even so, she gives little or no thought to Jane's feelings. For instance, on p. 30 of P&P, Jane has just received a letter. Mrs. Bennet, tactless, as always, immediately begins badgering her:

'"Well, Jane, who is it from? what is it about? what does he

say?...." She assumes that it is from Mr. Bingley. Jane, with the forbearance of a saint, replies quietly that it is from MISS Bingley, and that she has been invited to Netherfield for dinner.

> *"Can I have the carriage?" said Jane.*
>
> *"No, my dear, you had better go on horseback, because it seems likely to rain; and then you must stay all night"....*
>
> *"I had much rather go in the coach."*
>
> *"But, my dear, your father cannot spare the horses, I am sure."....*
>
> *Jane was therefore obliged to go on horseback, and her mother attended her to the door with many cheerful prognostics of a bad day..... Jane had not been gone long before it rained hard. Her sisters were uneasy for her, but her mother was delighted.'*

To her second daughter, Elizabeth, Mrs. Bennnet is cold-hearted in the extreme, scolding her when she refuses to marry the repulsive Mr. Collins, and never showing the least maternal tenderness or solicitude.

Mary and Catherine, the next two daughters in line, suffer the fate now commonly called the "middle child" syndrome. Mrs. Bennet scarcely acknowledges their existence. On the other hand, she lavishly indulges her youngest daughter, Lydia, an empty-headed sixteen-year-old. Without sensible advice and direction, Lydia runs wild and gets into trouble. Even when Lydia enters into a bad marriage, Mrs. Bennet thinks mostly of wedding clothes, and complains about the brevity of the announcement in the paper.

Added to all this is the damage done by Mrs. Bennet's unbridled tongue. She cannot keep her mouth shut. and very nearly causes Jane to be rejected by Mr. Bingley. This is on the advice of his friend, Mr. Darcy, who thinks that marrying into such a family would be a disaster. Mr. Darcy eventually asks for Elizabeth's hand, but he makes it clear that he loves her against his better judgement. He certainly does not relish the prospect of Mrs. Bennet as a mother-in-law.

Aunt Norris in Mansfield Park is another "hideous creature," always utterly selfish and cruel. In many respects she is worse than Mrs. Bennet, who doesn't seem to have a clue to the pain and suffering she is causing. Aunt Norris' unkindness is deliberate.

She enjoys the virtuous glow of "doing something" for Fanny, the child of a sister who married unwisely, and not well. But in order not to be inconvenienced herself, she foists Fanny off on her other sister, the placid Mrs. Bertram, and her wealthy husband, Sir Thomas. They don't object to being thus imposed on, and Aunt Norris has things pretty much her way until almost the end of the story. She continually shoves Fanny into the background, telling her how insignificant she is, and how grateful she should be to be allowed to exist on the fringe of this fine family. She also uses Fanny, who doesn't seem to have a very strong constitution, as her personal slave.

Lady Russell, in Persuasion, is a different kind of character, but her influence is no less malicious and hurtful. Whereas Mrs. Bennet and Aunt Norris are principal characters, causing trouble before the reader's eyes, Lady Russell wields her influence offstage.

She hardly enters into the story at all, except in Anne's memory. Lady Russell was the older woman, the surrogate mother who persuaded nineteen-year-old Anne to break her engagement with the young sea captain, an adventurer of whom neither Lady Russell nor Anne's widowed father approved. This state of affairs continued sadly for eight years. The difference between the character of Lady Russell and the others is revealed when Anne and her sea captain are finally reunited. Lady Russell lacks the practiced cruelty of Aunt Norris, and has the grace and intelligence to become reconciled to the situation without carrying on in the manner of Mrs. Bennet.

We now come to Emma, heroine of the book by the same name, who narrowly escapes becoming one of those "hideous creatures." She certainly starts out creating disaster areas. Her unconscionable interfering with her friend Harriet's life nearly wrecks Harriet's chances of a happy marriage. Her ego, combined with her dislike of Miss Jane Fairfax causes her to fall in with Jane's fiance's plans, thereby giving Jane a great deal of pain. This makes her, through part of the story, at least, one of Miss Austen's most exasperating little monsters. But here the similarity ends. Although it doesn't happen until quite late in the book, Emma has the ability to learn from her mistakes and to change from a manipulator into a truly compassionate, mature woman. For this reason, the story has a deeper, more philosophic character than the others.

Of the four Austen female characters here described, Mrs. Bennet and Aunt Norris are clearly the most monstrous, for they never change. At the end of the book they are just as silly, stupid, and destructive as they were in the beginning. Lady Russell, who destroyed Anne's young life, at least eight years of it, is not silly or stupid, but sadly, a product of her time and station in life.

Emma, unlike Aunt Norris, does not have a cruel or selfish bone in her body, but at one time or another, she is silly, stupid, destructive, and all too conscious of her station in life. With a lot of help from her wise friend and eventual husband, Mr. Knightly, she finally makes it through to become a really good person, - something for which we who love happy endings must be truly thankful.

The Romantic era is generally thought of as a period which reacted against the Age of Reason and against the drastic changes that were being brought into the daily lives of the people. In literature, subjective and private themes became increasingly popular and the once preferred public and general themes faded away. The popularity of novels, still relatively new as a form of literature, continued to rise. However, it wasn't until forty years into the Romantic era that a real fictional masterpiece was published. This masterpiece was written by one of England's best novelist of the era, Jane Austen.

Jane Austen was born in 1775 at Steventon, Hampshire, a small town in southwest England, where she spent the majority of her life. She was the seventh of eight children of her father, a clergyman and was raised in the middle class society. Like other young women of her social class, Jane and her sister Cassandra were educated mostly at home in subjects of music, drawing, painting, needlework, and social behaviour. Her father's encouragement and her own enjoyment in reading led Jane to became very well read.

Jane's middle class existence greatly influenced her writing. In her novels, Jane expressed her contempt for the superficiality of the upper class and usually made them her most comical characters. Most of Jane's writing was done during social engagements. Jane would spend the majority of the evening in the corner of the room with her manuscript and blotter observing the world surrounding her. She would write when the room was quiet and if she were interrupted, she would cover her manuscript with a blotter and continued when the room was silent again. Pride and Prejudice, one of Jane's earlier novels was written in this manner.

The most famous event of Jane Austen's life would have occurred in 1815 when she become known everywhere for her books which had one the favour of the Prince of Wale. This led Jane to dedicate her next novel, Emma, to the Prince. Other then this, there is little evidence of influence in Jane's work by events happening in England. As her brother, Henry Austen, once said in a "Biographical Notice" of Jane, "A life of usefulness, literature, and religion, was not by any means a life of events." The significant events in England during this time included the American Revolution of 1775, the Napoleonic Wars, and the industrial revolution. The remoteness of Jane's village also contributed to Jane's isolated life.

Before Jane Austen died of cancer in 1817 at Winchester, she had already published six successful novels: Sense and Sensibility, Pride and Prejudice, Northanger Abbey, Mansfield Park, Emma, and Persuasion, respectively. Jane Austen is now buried in the ancient cathedral in Winchester of her native Hampshire.

Jane Austen began her second novel, Pride and Prejudice, before she was twenty-one. It was originally titled First Impression because the appearances of the characters created the plot of the novel. However, because the novel is also concerned with the effects of the character's first impressions, that is their prejudice, Jane found the title Pride and Prejudice more appropriate.

Pride and Prejudice, similar to other Jane Austen's novels, is written in gentle or Horacian satire. The main object of Jane's satire in the novel is the mercenary and the ignorance of the people, a common criticism of the 18th century. Characters in the novel which best carries these qualities are Mrs. Bennet, a foolish woman who talks too much and is obsess with getting her daughters married; Lydia Bennet, the youngest of the Bennet daughter who is devoted to a life of dancing, fashions, gossips and flirting; and Mr. Williams Collins, the silly and conceited baboon who is completely stupify by Lady Catherine in every aspect of his life that he has forgotten his own morals and duty. The tone of the novel is light, satirical, and vivid.

A scene such as Mr. Collins proposal to Elizabeth, and Lady Catherine visits to Lizzy at Longbourn, provides comic relief to the reader while at the same time revealing certain characteristics of the characters.

For example, Lydia's lack of common sense and responsibility is revealed when she takes pride in being the first Bennet girl to be married. Lydia does not take into consideration the circumstance of her marriage, the personality of her husband, or the prospects of their marriage for the future. Elizabeth Bennet's ability to laugh off her misfortunate and to continue to be optimistic, considering her situation, also contributes to the tone of the novel. The point of view in Pride and Prejudice is limited omniscient; the story is told through Elizabeth, but not in first person. As a result, the mood of the novel lacks dramatic emotions.

The atmosphere is intellectual and cold; there is little descriptions of the setting. The main actions of the novel are the interactions between opinions, ideas, and attitudes, which weaves and advances the plot of the novel.

The emotions in the novel are to be perceived beneath the surface of the story and are not to be expressed to the readers directly. Jane's powers of subtle discrimination and shrewd perceptiveness are revealed in Pride and Prejudice; she is able to convey such a complex message using a simple, yet witty, style. The main subject in the novel is stated in the first sentence of the novel: "It is a truth universally acknowledged, that a single man in possession of a good fortune, must be in want of a wife."

In this statement, Jane has cleverly done three things: she has declared that the main subject of the novel will be courtship and marriage, she has established the humorous tone of the novel by taking a simple subject to elaborate and to speak intelligently of, and she has prepared the reader for a chase in the novel of either a husband in search of a wife, or a women in pursuit of a husband. The first line also defines Jane's book as a piece of literature that connects itself to the 18th century period. Pride and Prejudice is 18th century because of the emphasis on man in his social environment rather than in his individual conditions. The use of satire and wit, a common form of 18th century literature, also contributes to label the book as 18th century.

However, because Jane Austen had allowed personal feelings of the characters to be expressed in her work, she can also be classified as Romantic. In the figure of Elizabeth, Jane Austen shows passion attempting to find a valid mode of existence in society. Passion and reasons also comes together in the novel to show that they are complementary of marriage. There are seven different marriages presented in the novel. Excluding the Gardiner and the Lucas, the remaining five marriages contrasts each other to reveal Jane's opinions and thoughts on the subject of marriage.

The marriage between Darcy and Elizabeth reveals the characteristics which constitutes a successful marriage. One of these characteristics is that the feeling cannot be brought on by appearances, and must gradually develop between the two people as they get to know one another. In the beginning, Elizabeth and Darcy were distant from each other because of their prejudice. The series of events which they both experienced gave them the opportunity to understand one another and the time to reconcile their feelings for each other. Thus, their mutual understanding is the foundation of their relationship and will lead them to a peaceful and lasting marriage. This relationship between Elizabeth and Darcy reveals the importance of getting to know one's partner before marrying. The marriage between Jane Bennet and Bingley is also an example of successful marriage. Jane Austen, through Elizabeth, expresses her opinion of this in the novel:

"....really believed all his [Bingley] expectations of felicity, to be rationally founded, because they had for basis the excellent understanding, and super-excellent disposition of Jane, and a general similarity of feeling and taste between her and himself." (Chapter 55) However, unlike Darcy and Elizabeth, there is a flaw in their relationship. The flaw is that both characters are too gullible and too good-hearted to ever act strongly against external forces that may attempt to separate them:

"You [Jane and Bingley] are each of you so complying, that nothing will ever be resolved on; so easy, that every servant will cheat you; and so generous, that you will always exceed your income."

Obviously, Lydia and Wickham's marriage is an example of an bad marriage. Their marriage was based on appearances, good looks, and youthful vivacity. Once these qualities can no longer be seen by each other, the once strong relationship will slowly fade away. As in the novel, Lydia and Wickham's marriage gradually disintegrates; Lydia becomes a regular visitor at her two elder sister's homes when "her husband was gone to enjoy himself in London or Bath." Through their relationship, Jane Austen shows that hasty marriage based on superficial qualities quickly cool and leads to unhappiness.

Although little is told of how Mr. Bennet and Mrs. Bennet got together, it can be inferred by their conversions that their relationship was similar to that of Lydia and Wickham - Mr. Bennet had married a woman he found sexually attractive without realizing she was an unintelligent woman. Mrs. Bennet's favouritism towards Lydia and her comments on how she was once as energetic as Lydia reveals this similarity. Mr. Bennet's comment on Wickham being his favourite son-in-law reinforces this parallelism.

The effect of the relationships was that Mr. Bennet would isolate himself from his family; he found refugee in his library or in mocking his wife. Mr. Bennet's self-realization at the end of the novel in which he discovers that his lack of attention towards his family had lead his family to develop the way they are, was too late to save his family. He is Jane Austen's example of a weak father. In these two latter relationships, Austen shows that it is necessary to use good judgement to select a spouse, otherwise the two people will lose respect for each other.

The last example of a marriage is a of a different nature than the ones mentioned above. The marriage between Mr. Collins and Charlotte is based on economics rather than on love or appearance.

It was a common practice during Austen's time for women to marry a husband to save herself from spinsterhood or to gain financial security. However, Jane Austen viewed this as a type of prostitution and disapproved of it. In Pride and Prejudice, Jane Austen dramatizes this form of women inequality and show that women who submits themselves to this type of marriage will have to suffer in tormenting silence as Charlotte does:

"When Mr. Collins said any thing of which his wife might reasonably be ashamed, which certainly was not unseldom, she [Elizabeth] would involuntarily turned her eye on Charlotte. Once or twice she could discern a faint blush; but in general Charlotte wisely did not hear."

These five marriages contributes to the theme that a happy and strong marriage takes time to build and must be based on mutual feeling, understanding, and respect. Hasty marriages acting on impulse, and based on superficial qualities will not survive and will lead to inevitable unhappiness.

In Pride and Prejudice, Jane has denounced the elements of marriage and society that she found distasteful. These are the conclusions of her observation of the people in her world. However in her writing, Jane has also reflected her own enjoyment in life among these people with and without their faults.

"Satire is a sort of glass wherein beholders do generally discover everybody's face but their own." This statement is interesting and

excites my curiosity to find my own faults in a novel. Thus, this lead me to do a research project on Jane Austen.

Jane Austen tended to write in gentle satire which I prefer. I find that sever mockery is rude and can sometimes deeply hurt someone. Jane Austen's writing also appealed to me because of its simplicity. I do not mean to say her work is easy to understand, but that it uses the "ordinary language of man" or *"simple"* English.

I choose to read Pride and Prejudice because it was the first Jane Austen book to be introduced to me. It is humorous and whenever I think of my favourite character, Mr. Collins, I can not stop myself from giggling. Mr. Collins is the most foolish and ignorant person I can ever encounter. His ability to propose to Lizzy one day and Charlotte the next is absurd and ridiculous. It is also shows to me the infidelity of men. His connections to Lady Catherine can hardly be admired. His inability to perceive this only makes his character more comical.

The subject of the novel also interests me. It is a common event which happens daily and may someday happen to me too! Reading up on the topic will expand my picture of all the different type of marriages that exists and will prepare me for the one I may someday be a victim of.

After reading Jane Austen's works (I read Emma too because Pride and Prejudice was so good.) I have concluded that Jane Austen is my favourite author. However, I must disagree with Jane Austen when she refers to her own fiction as "the little bit (2 inches wide) of ivory on which I work with so fine a brush, as produces little effect after much labour." She has certainly produced everlasting masterpieces that will always survive the constantly changing demand of the literature world.

In Jane Austen's Sense and Sensibility, the two main characters, Elinor and Marianne Dashwood, represent sense and sensibility, respectively. Webster's Dictionary defines sense as practical intelligence; reasonable thought; something sensible or reasonable. Elinor Dashwood fits into the definition of the word perfectly. She is down-to-earth, sensible, practical, and rational. The dictionary defines sensibility as capacity for feeling; mental susceptibility; capacity for being affected emotionally or intellectually. Like her sister, Marianne Dashwood fits into this definition quite well. She is ruled by her emotions and has delicate and sensitive feelings. As sisters, the two girls are very close, and sometimes very much alike, but more often than not, as different as night and day.

Elinor Dashwood is the eldest of the two sisters. She fits the common stereotype of the eldest being the practical and rational sibling. She doesn't often let her emotions show and often has to make up for Marianne's shortcomings, caused by her overactive emotions.

Marianne is a very emotional girl, who has a dramatic opinion on every thing. She lets her emotions and her heart lead her, instead of her mind. Upon leaving their dear home, Norland, Marianne exclaims "'Oh! Happy house, could you know what I suffer in now viewing you from this spot, from whence perhaps I may view you no more!'". Although Elinor is also saddened at having to leave Norland, she quietly keeps it to herself, while her sister bursts forth a sorrowful goodbye.

The flighty emotionality of Marianne can be instantly seen upon the arrival of John Willoughby. She instantly falls in love with him and becomes obsessed with everything that has anything to do with him. She has no qualms about expressing the fact that she very much enjoys spending time with him, for she "abhors all concealment where no real disgrace could attend unreserve". She heartlessly laughs at the affections of Colonel Brandon, to which Elinor responds that he "'is a sensible man; and sense will always have attractions for [her]'". Here we see a sharp contrast between the two sisters. Marianne wildly loves the charming and handsome Willoughby, while Elinor likes the Sensible, quiet Colonel Brandon.

So in love is Marianne, that she abandons all her common sense. When Willoughby offers her a horse, she immediately accepts, not taking into account all that goes into the ownership of a horse. And even when the sensible Elinor points out the complications of accepting such a gift, Marianne is "most unwilling... to comprehend all the unhappy truths which attend the affair".

When Willoughby suddenly and abruptly leaves the Dashwoods and goes to London, Marianne is heartbroken and shows her sorrowful emotions quite freely. Being the emotional girl that she is, "Marianne [is] in all probability not merely giving way to... violent sorrow... as a relief, but feeding and encouraging it as a duty". She mopes around, doesn't eat much, and cries a lot. She thinks it would be "very inexcusable had she been able to sleep at all the first night after parting from Willoughby". Not only does she feel genuine sorrow on Willoughby's departure, but she also thinks it's her duty to feel that way.

Marianne knows how much her sister likes Edward Ferrars. But Elinor acts differently around him than Marianne acts around Willoughby. She remains composed and keeps her thoughts and feelings to herself. She notices that when Edward comes to visit at Barton, he is not himself, but she says nothing and doesn't obsess and worry over it as Marianne would. And when Edward must take his leave of them, Elinor remains calm and (outwardly) unemotional. She busies herself with other matters and doesn't shut herself off from the family. But Marianne doesn't understand her sister's lack of concern, for "such behaviour as this, so exactly the reverse of her own, appeared no more meritorious to Marianne, than her own had seemed faulty to her".

Elinor again shows her calm rationality when she hears of Edward's secret engagement to Lucy Steele. She is angry and saddened but quietly listens to all that Lucy tells her regarding the engagement. Afterwards, she carefully considers all that Lucy has told her, and she endeavors to discover more by engaging Lucy in private conversation once again. Elinor cleverly and carefully extracts from Lucy the information she wants to know. Unlike Marianne, she doesn't fly into a passion over the matter but ponders in her heart all that she has recently learned.

Marianne can't stand Mrs. Jennings, but when Mrs. Jennings invites the Dashwood sisters to town with her,

Marianne immediately declares she will go and that she can easily put up with the woman. However, her only desire and goal, is to be closer to Willoughby.

Elinor cannot ignore the "rapture of delightful expectation which fills the whole soul and beams in the eyes of Marianne". Marianne is very much excited about seeing Willoughby and doesn't try to hide it. But tremendous is her grief when Willoughby ignores her and then acts as if he had never had any affection for her.

His cold-hearted note to her breaks her heart and for many weeks she is sick with grief. She, somewhat selfishly, refuses to participate in various affairs with Elinor and is sad and downtrodden. She doesn't leave the house for several weeks, both because she has no desire to seek amusement and because she doesn't want to accidentally run into Willoughby. So sensitive is she that she wallows in her grief for a long period of time before beginning to return to herself.

When Elinor and Marianne meet Mrs. Ferrars, she is quite rude to Elinor and very nice and polite to Lucy Steele. But Elinor refuses to be bothered by it, for it is not in "Mrs. Ferrars power to distress her by it... and the difference of her manners to the Miss Steeles... only amuses her".

However, Marianne will not stand for this, and she honourably defends her sister against the subtle remarks against her. "Urged by a strong impulse of affectionate sensibility, she moved... to her sister's chair... and said 'Dear, dear Elinor, don't mind them. Don't let them make you unhappy'". At which point she bursts into tears. If their roles had been reversed, Elinor would have sensibly defended her sister by steering the conversation to another point, instead of retorting back and then becoming overwhelmed with emotion. This is a perfect example of how the two sisters are so different. While Elinor bears the criticism silently and calmly, her sister must react passionately.

Fanny is quite distressed by the news that her brother Edward is going to marry Lucy. Being related to her, Elinor sees it her duty to go and see how she is doing, even though she can't stand the woman. This is typical, practical Elinor, dutifully doing what is right. Marianne, however, who is "not contended with absolutely refusing to go herself, is very urgent to prevent her sister's going at all". Marianne doesn't see the point of visiting a woman whom she despises, be she relative or not. Again, Marianne is following her emotions and sensibilities rather than her duties and common sense.

At Cleveland, Marianne again abandons her senses by walking around in the damp and cold and then sitting around in wet clothes and shoes. As a result, she becomes quite ill. Elinor is very worried about her, but keeps her head and dutifully attends to her sister night and day. While Marianne is ill, Willoughby unexpectedly shows up. He tells Elinor all the particulars of why he broke Marianne's heart and how much he regrets what he had to do.

He begs forgiveness and asks Elinor to tell Marianne the whole story. Elinor doesn't cry for her sister, as Marianne would have done, but she does feel a little more compassionate for Willoughby. At the end of the novel, there are two instances when the sisters reverse rolls, when Marianne acts as Elinor would and vice versa. Upon finally returning home to Barton, Marianne tells Elinor that she is finally at peace with herself and can move on and forget Willoughby. After hearing what Willoughby told Elinor, she can finally leave the past behind and forgive him for what he did. This is the kind of sensible action that we would normally see in Elinor. But just as we see a little sense in Marianne, we also see a little sensibility in Elinor.

She had been struggling for quite some time with the distress of Edward's engagement to Lucy. But Edward visits Barton and informs the Dashwoods that Lucy has married his brother Robert and that he is no longer engaged. So incredibly happy is Elinor, that she runs out of the room, "and as soon as the door [is] closed, bursts into tears of joy, which at first she thought would never cease". This is just as Marianne would react in such a situation. This proves that though the two sisters are very much different in their thoughts and actions, they are also very much the same.

Marianne Dashwood is a sensitive, emotional, and

compassionate girl. Elinor Dashwood is a practical, rational, and sensible girl. These two sisters each have their own personalities, all their own. As a result, the two girls are good complements to each other. Elinor's sense balances Marianne's sensibility. And while Marianne will always be the sister with the strong sensibilities, and Elinor will always be the sister with the strong sense, they will always have a little bit of the other sister in themselves.

Chapter 3

Jane Austen and her Readers' Response

Marilyn Butler, in her introduction to the novel, suggests that; "Northanger Abbey,... from its first paragraph... moves to characterise the naïve romantic private reader as a beginner; it flatters and shames her into becoming more ambitious. In this educative process Catherine the heroine shows the way." However, Catherine learns more in the course of the novel than simply realizing the naïveté of her reading habits.

We see Jane Austen's 'anti-heroine' grow up, fall in love, and, through various strong betrayals of her unquestioning trust, learn to view human nature from a more realistic point of view. Throughout this maturing process Jane Austen's reader is invited to feel every emotion with Catherine, while maintaining a certain detachment which allows us to recognise Catherine's foibles and touching innocence.

34Many of the mistakes that Margaret Oliphant talks about in her description of Catherine in the title above come from Catherine's extreme innocence.

Jane Austen's heroine arrives in Bath as a young debutante and, entirely inexperienced in the ways of the world, is immediately impressed by the more sophisticated Isabella. After their first meeting this is clear as she watches her leave; "(she) admired the graceful spirit of her walk, the fashionable air of her figure and dress, and felt grateful, as well she might, for the chance which had procured her such a friend." Jane Austen's interjection here, ("as well she might"), expresses the reader's feelings at this point.

Up to now we have had few clues as to Isabella's less desirable character traits, and so we are guided, along with Catherine, into feeling grateful for her patronage of our heroine. No direct comment is required, however, when she displays her innocence to more amusing effect. Isabella having affected to not want the attentions of two young men who are watching her, Catherine characteristically takes her at her word, and so, 'with unaffected pleasure', she 'assured her that she need not be longer uneasy, as the gentlemen had just left the Pump Room.'

This 'unaffected pleasure' is in stark contrast to the affected way in which Isabella does almost everything. Catherine is, as Jane Austen says, entirely 'artless' in everything she does, and we are invited to delight in her slightly naïve, entirely genuine approach to life throughout the novel.

This innocence, however, does not always produce feelings of delight in the reader. When Catherine has been tricked into missing an engagement with the Tilneys, she goes to apologize to them. However, the servant who answers the door says that they are out. Moments later, though, she sees Miss Tilney leaving the house. Her response to this is 'deep mortification', and we feel extremely sorry for her as she reflects on her innocence. "She knew not how such an offence as hers might be classed by the laws of worldly politeness, to what a degree of unforgiveness it might with propriety lead, nor to what rigors of rudeness in return it might justly make her amenable."

Here Catherine not only displays her innocence but, as a result of this and her strong humility, she almost manages to blame the snub on herself. Had she reacted with indignation, our sympathy for her may have been reduced, however Jane Austen's presentation of Catherine as so self deprecating as to automatically put the blame for others' actions on herself increases immeasurably our sympathy and liking for the young girl. When this turns out to not have been a snub at all, but a result of General Tilney's obsession with time-keeping, we are as relieved as Catherine, as well as delighting in her unfettered enthusiasm as she considers herself 'one of the happiest creatures in the world'.

This enthusiasm is another of Catherine's endearing traits. Often, when presented with an enjoyable or pleasing situation, Catherine does not react with the controlled sense of decorum that we might expect from any other character in the novel. Her response is entirely natural and, in its clear honesty, very likeable. For example, when Miss Tilney suggests they take a country walk together, Catherine replies; "I shall like it... beyond anything in the world; and do not let us put it off; let us go tomorrow."

There is a childish enthusiasm to almost everything she enjoys and, as a result, as here, her language often seems gushing and simplistic. However, amongst the etiquette-ruled, almost stuffy atmosphere of the book's era, this comes as light relief, and the honesty of her responses increases her likeable air. Henry Tilney describes her as bringing 'fresh feelings of every sort' to Bath, and it is this sort of reaction that he must be referring to.

Catherine is different. She is the antithesis of the scheming, cruel Thorpes whose every word and action has some unstated intention, and yet she tries incredibly hard to think the best of them and help them until Isabella's final, unforgivable betrayal. When, in chapter 26, Isabella suggests that Catherine's father is mean, she is understandable 'hurt by these insinuations'. However, she tries not to think badly of her, and, rather than believe that Isabella is greedy, 'endeavored to believe that the delay of the marriage was the only source of Isabella's regret.'

Her growing maturity tells her otherwise, but her goodness of heart strives to see the best in people. Soon after this, when she sees Isabella and Captain Tilney flirting, she comments; "It seemed to her that Captain Tilney was falling in love with Isabella, and Isabella unconsciously encouraging him; unconsciously it must be, for Isabella's attachment to James was as certain... as her engagement." Here we not only see Catherine's automatic positive judgement of Isabella, but also her naïve view of human relationships. In believing that

Captain Tilney feels anything close to love for Isabella, she displays her romantic views of relationships in general, as well as a lack of understanding of the two people involved.

Catherine again shows a misunderstanding of Isabella's penchant for saying things that she does not mean in chapter 16. Isabella having said that dancing was 'quite out of the question, her being so preoccupied with thoughts of her fiancé, Catherine takes her at her word, telling Captain Tilney that she will not dance with him, and telling Henry; "Your brother will not mind it, I know,.... Because I heard him say before that he hated dancing; but it was very good-natured of him to think of it. I suppose he saw Isabella sitting down, and fancied she might wish for a partner;". Here Catherine displays two further misunderstandings - the first that Captain Tilney truly does not like dancing, and the second that he is asking Isabella to dance purely out of concern for her.

The latter comes from her judging others by her own, hidden motive-free standards, and Henry comments on this; *".... Your attributing my brother's wish of dancing with Miss Thorpe to good-nature alone, convinced me of your being superior in good-nature yourself to all the rest of the world." This huge, unprompted compliment from Henry is a reflection of his growing affection for her refreshing innocence, and the blush and 'modest disclaimer' serve to 'verify' 'the gentleman's predictions'. This good nature is seen in a different light in chapter 18. Isabella having told her that her brother has designs on Catherine, she is shocked. However, her rejection is very carefully framed so as to not upset Isabella; "I would not speak disrespectfully of a brother of yours, Isabella, I am sure, but you know very well that if I could think of one man more than another, he is not the person."*

The qualification preceding her rejection, coupled with the nature of the rejection, speaking positively of another rather than negatively of John Thorpe, give us a clear sign that Catherine is chiefly concerned with Isabella's welfare and reaction. This is confirmed in Catherine's next sentence; "I cannot suppose your brother cares so very much about me; and, you know, we shall still be sisters." The selflessness of this attitude, especially given the odiousness of John Thorpe, and the intentions of Isabella which will render Catherine's final affirmation untrue, make this response extremely endearing. Catherine is too good for her present company.

It is perhaps as a result of this concern for other people that Catherine at times lacks the courage of her own convictions. When meeting John Thorpe for the first time, for example, she frequently finds herself disagreeing with him, but does not have the courage to voice her opinion. Instead, she changes the subject, often only to be contradicted once more. For example; "Catherine,... with all the civility and deference of the youthful female mind, fearful of hazarding an opinion of its own in opposition to that of a self-assured man,... ventured at length to vary the subject." It comes as a relief, then, to see Catherine standing up for herself. The clearest example of this comes in chapter 13, when Isabella, John Thorpe and her brother James are trying to persuade her to replace an engagement with the Tilneys in going out with them. Catherine is determined not to, and, despite many insults and much pleading from the other three, she sticks to her guns; "If I am wrong, I am doing what I believe to be right."

This strength of character is a side to Catherine not seen before, and it comes as a sign of her slowly growing maturity. We feel pride as, after a trick form John Thorpe, Catherine remains determined; "If I could not be persuaded into doing what I thought wrong, I never will be tricked into it." This maturing process is as pleasing as the innocence that it replaces, and we are given many signs of it occurring. In chapter 8, Catherine begins to see Isabella's main fault - her affected feelings that are far from genuine.

When Isabella forgets her curiosity about Henry to flirt with James, Catherine; "... could not avoid a little suspicion at the total suspension of all Isabella's impatient desire to see Mr Tilney." The ironic tone which Jane Austen lends to this observation maintains Catherine's complete lack of cynicism, but it still a pleasing sign of Catherine's growing insight into human nature.

In chapter 18, she seems to be 'growing out' of Isabella, Jane Austen remarking; "Catherine was hardly aware that two or three days had passed away without her seeing Isabella for more than a few minutes together." This is a relief to the reader, who is by this time growing tired of Miss Thorpe's fatuousness. It would be a great disappointment, though, if such changes in Catherine brought a reduction in her genuine, fresh approach to life and a touch of cynicism. They don't and Catherine maintains too the tendency to romance that led her to be so enamoured with Henry Tilney's "mysteriousness" in chapter 5. When invited to Northanger Abbey, her imagination takes her into the world of the books she loves so much, and she dreams of "long, damp passages,.... narrow cells and (a) ruined chapel,.... within her daily reach."

The delightful frivolity contained in her "hope of some traditional legends, some awful memorials of an injured and ill-fated nun," not only helps Jane Austen's gentle satire of the gothic, but also reassures us that Catherine still has that youthfulness that caused Margaret Oliphant to call her 'captivating'. However, once at Northanger Abbey, this romanticism causes many of the mistakes about which Oliphant also writes. From the chest which she finds in her room, which she opens 'with trembling hands' to find that it contains spare linen, Catherine's gothic fancies becoming more and more ridiculous.

The embarrassment that this discovery causes her only deters her briefly, and it is not long before she suspects General Tilney of murdering or holding captive his wife. Catherine's assumptions on the way to this conclusion often seem a little unkind. On one occasion she takes his aversion to taking his wife's favourite walk as a sign that he did not love her, and moves quickly to remark; "His cruelty to such a charming woman made him odious to her."

Here, perhaps for the first time, the reader is a little ashamed of Catherine, seeing her take this gothic obsession too far. Eventually, however, she is brought back to her senses by what can only be described as a reprimand from Henry Tilney, and the 'tears of shame' that this prompts erase much of our displeasure with Catherine's actions and replace it with sympathy.

In an essay on Northanger Abbey, Norman Sherry remarks; "Catherine has first to learn to distinguish between literature and life, and then to learn the difficulties of ordinary life". The first sentence of chapter 25, "The visions of romance were over.", marks the end of the first learning process to which Sherry refers.

Throughout the rest of the novel we see how Catherine endures the second, through betrayal by friends and help from Henry. She recognizes that her mistake about the General was all her own doing, remarking; ".... it had been all a voluntary, self-created delusion, each trifling circumstance receiving importance from an imagination resolved on alarm." This is mature self-analysis, and soon afterwards she goes so far as to think; "she would not be surprised if even in Henry and Eleanor Tilney some slight imperfection might appear hereafter."

Her black-and-white innocent view is lost, and this goes a step further when, having betrayed her brother by breaking off their engagement, Isabella writes to her. It seems that Captain Tilney is no longer interested in her, (though she does not say so), and she wants to return to James.

Catherine will not be fooled, though; "Such a strain of shallow artifice could not impose even upon Catherine. Its inconsistencies, contradiction and falsehood, struck her from the very first." The strength of the language here assures us that Catherine holds no illusions that Isabella's actions may be forgivable.

So, we now have a heroine who, while still believing in the existence of perfection, (she remarks of Henry's home, "Fullerton had its faults, but Woodston probably had none"), recognizes true human nature and has grown into a delightful young woman. Having seen her grow up we feel a bond with her, and cannot help being moved when the General sends her home so ignominiously.

Her polite acceptance of this, still endeavoring to save Eleanor's feelings, ("But do not be unhappy Eleanor"), and perhaps most surprisingly, still endeavoring to see the best in the General. This is seen when she tries to blame her fate on herself; "Catherine could not believe it possible that an injury or any misfortune could provoke such ill-will against a person not connected... with it."

After all this, then, after all Catherine's dreadful experiences of her fellow man, betraying her innocence, trust and honesty, we feel very protective of our heroine. That she should end in 'perfect happiness' with Henry is a great pleasure to the reader.

Catherine, then, displays all of the traits that Oliphant describes in the title. Jane Austen shows them to us through Catherine's own thoughts and her reactions to others. By maintaining a narrow detachment from our heroine we can make an objective judgement of her which is thus all the more favourable. However, as well as Oliphant's qualities, Catherine gains maturity from her experiences which, untainted by cynicism, makes her all the more 'captivating'.

Jane Austen is one of the few novelists in world literature who is regarded as a "classic" and yet is widely read. As the contemporary novelist Fay Weldon puts it, for generations of students and the educated reading public in many countries, Austen's novels represent literature with a capital "L." On the other hand, Austen is the only novelist before Charles Dickens who still has a significant popular readership, and her fictional world—seen as an idyllic bygone time and place unlike, and preferable to, the present—has entered into popular literary culture.

Jane Austen was born into the rural professional middle class. Her father, George Austen (1731-1805), was a country clergyman at Steventon, a small village in the southern English county of Hampshire. He had risen by merit from a Kentish family in trade and the lower professions. Jane Austen's mother, Cassandra Leigh Austen (1739-1827), was from a higher social rank, minor gentry related distantly to titled people, but once she married the Reverend Austen in 1764 she entered wholeheartedly and with humour into the domestic life and responsibilities of managing a household economy by no means luxurious, bearing eight children—six sons and two daughters.

In this setting the Austens mingled easily with other gentrified professionals and with local gentry families.

Yet they were also linked, though tenuously in some ways, with the larger world of fashionable society and of patronage, politics, and state. George Austen owed his education at Oxford University to his own merit as a student at Tonbridge School, but he owed his clerical position, or "living," at Steventon to the patronage of a wealthy relative, Thomas Knight of Godmersham Park, Kent, who held the appointment in his gift.

Later the Knights, who were childless, adopted one of the Austens' sons, Edward, as their own son and heir to their estates in Kent and Hampshire. One of Jane Austen's cousins, Elizabeth (Eliza) Hancock, married a French aristocrat—Jean Capotte, Comte de Feuillide. The comte was guillotined during the French Revolution, and Eliza later married Jane Austen's brother Henry.

Local friends of the Austens included the Reverend George Lefroy and his wife, Anne, sister of an eccentric, novel-writing, obsessively aristocratic Kentish squire, Sir Samuel Egerton Brydges. "Madam Lefroy," as she was known locally, was lively and energetic, wrote verses (some of which got published), enthusiastically embraced the contemporary literature and culture of Sensibility, and engaged in fashionable philanthropy among the local poor.

She "took up" the young Jane Austen and encouraged her intellectual development. The closest friends of Jane Austen and her sister, Cassandra, were Elizabeth, Catherine, and Alethea Bigg, whose parents were local gentry and whose brother, Harris Bigg-Wither, later proposed marriage to Jane Austen. Other close friends were Mary and Martha Lloyd, daughters of a neighboring clergyman, whose mother was the daughter of a royal governor of South Carolina.

Austen's brothers, apart from Edward, went in for genteel but demanding professions. Her eldest brother, James (1765-1819), who had literary tastes and intellectual interests, followed his father's path to St. John's College, Oxford, and eventually became his father's successor as rector of Steventon.

Her second brother, George (1766-1838), was born handicapped and did not play a part in the family life. The third son was Edward (1767-1852), who was adopted by the Knights and took over the Knight estates in 1797. The fourth child, Henry (1771-1850), was the liveliest, the most adventurous and the most speculative of the Austens. Like James, he went to St. John's College, Oxford, but instead of taking orders upon graduation he joined the army, gave that up for the relatively ungenteel line of banking, and married his glamorous widowed cousin, Eliza de Feuillide.

When his bank failed in 1816 during the economic crisis following the Napoleonic Wars, he fell back on his father's profession and became a clergyman. The next child, Cassandra (1773-1845), was Jane's closest friend throughout her life and was known in the family for her steady character and sound judgment. Like Jane, she never married. Her fiancé, the Reverend Thomas Fowle, died while serving as a military chaplain in the West Indies in 1797. The two youngest Austen boys, Francis (1774-1865) and Charles (1779-1852), were trained at the Royal Naval Academy at Portsmouth, became officers, served in the French wars, and rose to the rank of admiral.

Though the issues and interests of the wider world may have come from afar somewhat muffled, they did flow through the rectory at Steventon, and later—less muffled—through the other habitations and homes of Jane Austen as well. But the rectory at Steventon with its lively, frank, and intimate yet open family life was her first and formative home. Her parents had a close and happy marriage. Her mother was thoroughly domestic yet commonsensical and humorous; her father was kind, loving, and encouraging to his daughters as well as his sons. Jane, known as "Jenny" in the family, was well liked by her brothers, who were often at home even while students at Oxford or Portsmouth, and who visited their sisters when they were away briefly at school.

The family members were readers, though more in literature of the day than abstruse learning. There was also a great deal of reading aloud in the Austen household. Many families at the time would have one of their members read to the others while they carried out small tasks. Reading aloud was considered a highly valuable professional and social skill, and the Reverend Mr. Austen, not surprisingly, excelled at it. The topic was later made a major point in *Mansfield Park* (1814). Jane Austen was helped by her father to select from his five-hundred-volume library, and there were, of course, books from circulating libraries.

These rental libraries, greatly varying in extent of stock and luxury of appointment, specialized in lighter reading. They were the main way that middle-class people, who made up most of the reading public, got access to books and magazines of the day, which were otherwise quite expensive. For example a typical three-volume novel of the kind Austen wrote cost the equivalent of about two weeks' wages for a rural laborer (about half of the laboring class could not read, however).

Like other families with literary interests, the Austens also enjoyed putting on plays. There was a vogue for such amateur domestic theatricals in the latter part of the eighteenth century. It was not surprising in such a family for Jane Austen to take to writing before she was even in her teens, and for her to amuse her family throughout her adolescence with burlesques of various kinds of literature. This early domestic writing shows a firm grasp of the current literary genres as well as literary styles, conventions, and clichés. Prose fiction was the major but not the only object of Austen's parody. "The Visit" and "The Mystery" burlesque popular late-eighteenth-century sentimental comedy.

"The History of England from the Reign of Henry the 4th to the Death of Charles the 1st" burlesques the objectivity, factuality, and authoritativeness of historiography, then considered a male discourse, by deliberately inserting attributes that would then have been considered "feminine," such as open prejudice, frank admission of ignorance, and occasional expressive passages, while making fun of the conventions of cause and effect and displaying a prominent interest in the sufferings of historical "women of feeling" such as Mary, Queen of Scots. "A Collection of Letters," with its letter "from a young lady crossed in love to her freind [*sic*]" and letter "from a young lady in distress'd circumstances to her friend," burlesques another kind of desultory sentimental text of the time. Other fragments parody sentimental didacticism and sentimental travel writing.

Austen's main interest, however, was in the varieties of prose fiction. For example "Frederic and Elfrida: A Novel" burlesques the contemporary sentimental novel, with its ideal hero and heroine, interspersed letters and verses, elegant dialogue, noble feelings, pathetic incidents, and plot of delayed courtship.

"Jack and Alice: A Novel," "Edgar and Emma: A Tale," "Henry and Eliza: A Novel," and "The Beautiful Cassandra: A Novel in Twelve Chapters" burlesque such novel conventions as the opening in medias res, the use of short racy chapters, names taken from *Burke's Peerage*, scenes of fashionable dissipation, extensive use of correspondence, inset narratives, fatal attractions, and glamorously distressed protagonists. "The Generous Curate: A Moral Tale," "The Adventures of Mr Harley," "Sir William Mountague," and "Memoirs of Mr Clifford" burlesque the newly popular form of the tale, or brief narrative, often packed with incident and characters lightly sketched, in contrast to the more extended treatment of "sentiment" in novels.

The epistolary novel, still much in vogue and the most obviously "sentimental" form of fiction by the 1780s, is burlesqued in "Amelia Webster," "The Three Sisters: A Novel," "Love and Friendship: A Novel in a Series of Letters," and "Lesley Castle: An Unfinished Novel in Letters." The last two, along with "Evelyn" and "Catherine; or, The Bower" are more extended satires on novelistic "heroinism," and several of these burlesques suggest a connection between sentimentalism, which was a common object of criticism in the Austen family, and other kinds of social and even political transgression.

A fragment of a burlesque apparently to be called "The Female Philosopher" indicates that Austen was familiar with the increasing tendency in the 1790s to associate

Sentimentalism, female appropriation of "philosophy" or social criticism from the period before the French Revolution, and the feminism of writers such as Mary Wollstonecraft and Mary Hays, inspired by the egalitarian doctrines of the Revolution.

Austen's main techniques of satiric undermining are familiar ones. Simply by drastically abbreviating some forms she achieves a burlesque effect, for example packing material that could fill out a three-volume novel into a ludicrously rushed few pages. Other devices are the exaggeration of heroic language into purple patches, mixing vulgar colloquialisms with such language, terminating heroic incidents with bathos, the adoption of a nonchalant and provocatively unprofessional narrative character, and flagrantly disregarding conventions of narrative continuity and plotting. These devices reappear, toned down, in her later, full-length novels. Austen's burlesques are minor but amusing pieces and show excellent familiarity with generic and stylistic conventions of many kinds. Perhaps more important, Austen's will to parody was an acceptably feminine exercise of critical thought, especially applied to the culture of writing. In her time such critical thought was seen as primarily an activity for men, especially in the professions.

Furthermore, critical response to classic and contemporary literature was no mere aesthetic diversion at that time, but a major way of participating in civic culture. "Literature of the day," as it was called, included novels, plays, light verse as well as more serious poetry, magazines, and so on; this literature expressed and reflected the interests and concerns of those who wrote and read it, and these writers and readers were, like the Austens, mainly professional middle-class people. They condemned what they saw as aristocratic snobbery, upper-class decadence, and the patronage system that spread from the royal court and government through the rest of society.

They also condemned middle-class emulation of their social "betters" and upper-class cultural domination of society through the fashion system, or "the *ton*." During the 1780s and

1790s, for example, middle-class observers were repeatedly scandalized by the moral misconduct and abuse of social position by the Prince of Wales and his brothers, supposedly the leaders of society. At the same time, the middle classes were becoming increasingly concerned about the condition and the culture of the lower classes. Much middle-class social criticism warned against contamination from the "vulgar." Such warnings became more urgent during the "Revolution Debate" of the 1790s, when the middle and upper classes had to take sides on the nature and significance of the French Revolution for Britain.

At the same time, many social critics complained that "literature of the day" contributed to what it attacked—that it was part of the very "fashion system" it condemned. "Fashionable novels," "indecent plays," and "sentimental" writing of various kinds were condemned for spreading decadent upper-class values and practices to eager middle-class—and especially female—readers. The Austen family kept up with "literature of the day" and was aware of its important and controversial place in civic life. Some of the Austens were even willing to contribute to this literature.

James and Henry Austen had literary tastes, and at Oxford University they published a literary magazine called *The Loiterer* in 1789-1790. In genteelly satirical style it promotes the professionalization of culture, attacks decadent court culture and emulation of it by the middle classes, and criticizes the fashionable literature of Sensibility as a form of aristocratic culture in disguise. Yet *The Loiterer* also advances thoroughly Tory, loyalist politics and defends the established Church. These themes, not unusual for the time, illustrate the way interconnections of politics, religion, and culture were taken for granted. Austen herself probably contributed an ironic letter to the editors from "Sophia Sentiment," purporting to complain about the magazine's neglect of feminine literary interests.

The education of Austen and her sister was not nearly as thorough and systematic as that offered their brothers. While the men would have to prepare for a profession and therefore spend their formative years accumulating intellectual and moral capital for the future, the only career open to women of the Austens' class was that of wife and mother. The sisters were prepared accordingly with some training in "accomplishments," that is, "elegant" skills such as music, drawing, dancing, and comportment. Too close emotionally to be separated for schooling, despite their difference in age, the sisters were taken to study with Ann Cooper Cawley, the widow of a head of an Oxford college, in 1783. She then took her charges and their cousin Jane Cooper to Southampton, where the three girls caught typhus and were taken home by their mothers; unfortunately Mrs. Austen's sister caught the fever and died.

In 1784 the sisters were sent to the Abbey School in Reading, where intellectual training was little emphasized. In December 1786 the girls returned home, where they received the majority of whatever education they ever had and largely educated themselves. Jane Austen acquired a good knowledge of the literature and culture that were thought valuable at the time, she had a modest talent for music, and she loved dancing. She especially admired the writings of Samuel Johnson and the poetry of William Cowper.

With the rest of her family, she shared Johnson's Tory politics, practical piety, Anglican theology, fine sense of language in everyday as well as literary use, and commitment to emergent national cultural institutions. Cowper was the great poet of middle-class sensibility and gave epic scope and even heroic grandeur to middle-class life before the Romantic poets also attempted to do so. All the Austens were novel readers and, as Jane Austen herself later boasted, were unashamed of the fact, unlike many of their contemporaries. The Austens realized and appreciated the potential of the novel for social criticism and moral discourse at a time when most critics condemned novels as immoral, disseminators of decadent court culture, and subliterature fit only for women (though dangerously seductive for the supposedly weak female intellect and strong female imagination).

Austen admired the novels of Samuel Richardson,

especially *Sir Charles Grandison* (1754), which she reread many times in her lifetime; with her niece Anna Austen she even tried adapting it into a play for performance by children of the family sometime after 1812. She and her family, with their gentry connections and professional standing, probably appreciated Richardson's portrayal of a landed gentleman thoroughly imbued with middle-class virtues. Richardson's novel not only argues for a fusion of gentry and professional middle-class cultures—a fusion that appealed strongly to the largely middle-class reading public; it also develops new techniques of "realism," or artistic persuasiveness, for representing the individual who is meritorious inwardly—intellectually and morally—rather than merely socially—by birth and rank.

As the Austens would have known well, the "Richardsonian revolution" in the novel was developed from the 1760s to the 1780s by women writers, especially Frances Burney, whose *Evelina* (1778) and *Cecilia* (1782) represent the novelistic version of the middle-class discourse of merit through a heroine rather than a hero. In *Cecilia* Burney also shifts from the Richardsonian epistolary form to authoritative third-person narration, using the new technique of "free indirect discourse," the narrator's filtered reporting of the character's inward thoughts and feelings.

This device sustains the reader's sympathetic identification with the character while retaining distance, control, and "objectivity" for the narrator. The forms of the novel used by Burney were those taken up by Austen when she began seriously to write novels in the 1790s, and though she abandoned the epistolary form, letters do have important functions in her novels. Not surprisingly, when Burney published her third novel, *Camilla,* by subscription in 1796, Austen's father signed up for a copy for his literary daughter. Once again the Austens' response as a family to the literary culture of the day, including its social and political implications, was decisive in Austen's formation as a writer.

Until 1801 Austen lived in her family home at Steventon, reading the literature of the day, rereading her favourite authors, maintaining her local visiting network, discussing the characters and vicissitudes of new acquaintances and old friends, visiting her brother Edward and his family in Kent, dancing at balls given by the local gentry, accompanying her family to Bath for the recreations and social life of an elegant spa town, and keeping up with issues of the day, such as the long trial (1788-1794) in the House of Commons of Warren Hastings, first governor general of British India, on charges of corruption and abuse of office. (The Austens were pro-Hastings.) Austen closely followed the careers of her brothers, especially the naval officers, who were at war from 1793 until the final defeat of Napoleon in 1815.

She shared the happiness, occasional bereavements, and disappointments of brothers and friends as they married, began families of their own, and lost their loved ones. In December 1795 she fell in love herself, with Thomas Langlois Lefroy, a graduate of Trinity College, Dublin, who was visiting his uncle and aunt. Recognizing that the young man would be disinherited if he married the daughter of a penniless clergyman, Madam Lefroy cut short the courtship by sending her nephew away. All the while Austen observed the successive feasts and holy days of the established Church, from quiet, but firm, personal conviction and not just from family duty.

In the 1790s she also left behind writing the spirited literary satires with which she had amused her family from about the age of eleven to the age of eighteen. At first without her family's knowledge, she began to write novels that were meant to be full-length and seriously literary, if still humorous and even satirical. Yet there is continuity between Austen's "juvenilia" and her maturer works. Both grew out of a family literary culture. As Lord David Cecil puts it, "Many authors start writing in order to relieve their private feelings; Jane Austen began in order to contribute to family entertainment.

Her early works were examples of a family activity and expressions of a family outlook." But it was a family outlook confident in being representative of the reading public at large, a reading public dominated by the values and culture of the middle classes, led by the professionals and in many ways linked to the progressive elements of the landed gentry. Austen's novels continued to reflect and advance this outlook. The novel was being used extensively in the Revolution debate of the 1790s: the struggle to lead the "political nation" and its immediate supporters and dependents (which could be equated with the reading public) into coalition either with politicized artisans and the lower-middle classes or with the landed gentry.

In the late 1790s and early 1800s, however, writers turned to representing the reconciliation of social differences and conflicts that had threatened to take Britain, like France, over the brink of revolution in the early and mid 1790s and that continued to cause concern for the preservation of Britain's unity and empire against challenge from Napoleonic France.

Women, conventionally seen as social mediators, were quick to take up the theme of national reconciliation in their writings, while avoiding overt discussion of the "unfeminine" subject of politics. Yet such writers wanted to continue the longstanding, middle-class critique of upper-class decadence, lower-class unreason, and middle-class social emulation of either.

Austen's novels participate in this post-Revolutionary literary movement. Austen began several novels in the latter half of the 1790s, though they were not published for some years, and then they were much altered. An epistolary novella, published after her death by her nephew as *Lady Susan,* in the second edition of his *Memoir of Jane Austen* (1871), depicts a selfish and witty courtly coquette. The text is partly a satirical exaggeration of the fashionable novels that portrayed such characters with apparent disapproval for fascinated and scandalized middle-class readers. In 1795 she wrote, again probably in epistolary form, a story titled "Elinor and Marianne," and began to revise it two years later in third-person narrative form as the novel that would be published in 1811 as *Sense and Sensibility.*

In 1796 and 1797 she worked on a novel titled "First Impressions," probably also in letter form; this novel was later revised and published in 1813 as *Pride and Prejudice.* Late in 1797 Austen's father offered "First Impressions" as a novel "comprised in three Vols. about the length of Miss Burney's *Evelina*" to the prominent London publishers Thomas Cadell and William Davies.

He hinted at willingness to pay the expense of printing if the novel were accepted, but it was turned down. In 1798 and 1799 Austen wrote most of a novel that was later revised, bought by the publisher Richard Crosby, and advertised in 1803 as "In the Press, SUSAN; a novel, in 2 vols."

It remained unpublished, however, and was later revised again and brought out at the end of 1817, after Austen's death, as *Northanger Abbey*. Austen's mother was in poor health, and in 1800 her father suddenly decided to retire, hire his son James as his curate, and settle in Bath. Austen fainted when told of the decision, but when she moved to Bath with her parents in May 1801 she determined to like the place.

It was still an important health spa, holiday centre, and place of fashionable resort for the gentry and well-to-do middle classes. While the Austens vacationed on the coast at Sidmouth in Devon in summer 1801, Austen seems to have met and fallen in love with a young clergyman. The Austens apparently expected that he would propose marriage and be accepted, but he died suddenly. More than a year later, while visiting her close friends the Bigg sisters, Austen was proposed to by their brother.

Because his fortune would insure her against a fate she feared—spending her old age in poverty—she accepted him even though he was younger and temperamentally unsuited to her, but she broke off the engagement the next morning and returned immediately to Bath. It was at this time that Austen began a novel depicting sisters apparently condemned to the fate Austen feared for herself, though in the novel eventually a marriage of true minds and sufficient means would avert this. The novel was never completed and the surviving fragment was published after her death as *The Watsons* in the second edition of her nephew's *Memoir of Jane Austen*.

One reason for Austen's failure to push a book through

to publication during these years may have been a series of personal losses and the anxiety of living near the edge of socially degrading circumstances. In December 1804 her close friend and early encourager, the lively Madam Lefroy, died from a concussion sustained in a riding accident.

In January 1805 Austen's father died. Since his clerical income ended with his death, his widow and daughters were faced with relative penury, but the Austen brothers pooled resources to maintain their mother and sisters, joined by their friend Martha Lloyd, in solid middle-class comfort at Bath. Although Austen had enjoyed the varied social scene at first, she eventually grew to dislike the place and its people. She continued to follow the career, both at sea and ashore, of her brother Frank.

In 1805 he just missed participating in the Battle of Trafalgar, an experience he much regretted because he lost not only an opportunity to increase his "professional credit" but also "pecuniary advantage" from the sale of any French ships he might have helped capture.

He married in 1806 and invited his mother and sisters to share his house at Southampton. They joined him there after a stay at Clifton near Bristol and a visit to the great country house of Stoneleigh Abbey, Warwickshire, just inherited by their relation the Reverend Thomas Leigh. When Frank was again away at sea the Austen women were left to a quiet and retired existence, visiting little, using the local circulating library, gardening, visiting Edward Austen and his large family (who took the surname Knight in 1812) in Kent and Henry Austen in London, and following news of the war in Spain. Austen became especially close to Edward's daughter Fanny, then in her teens; it was a lifelong friendship.

When Edward's wife died in late 1808, his mother and sisters comforted the family. Edward offered them the choice of a comfortable house on one of his estates, in Kent and Hampshire, so that they would be closer. They chose a house at Chawton, in Kent, not far from their early home at Steventon. In summer 1809 they moved to Chawton, where Austen would live until her final illness. Life at Chawton was simple and neither mean nor grand. The Austen women and Martha Lloyd kept one indoor and one outdoor servant. Austen and her sister managed the household economy with great efficiency and thoroughness. Since they could not afford to keep a carriage, their local social life was limited to places within walking distance and their larger social life was mainly in their brothers' households.

Jane Austen was less interested and involved in general socializing than her mother and sister. Mary Mitford, herself an ardent admirer of Austen's novels, recorded the report of a friend that Austen had "stiffened into the most perpendicular, precise, taciturn piece of 'single blessedness' that ever existed," and until *Pride and Prejudice* came out she was "no more regarded in society than a poker or a fire-screen, or any other thin, upright piece of wood or iron that fills the corner in peace and quietness." Cassandra Austen did some philanthropic and educational work among the local poor, but Jane Austen deliberately took second place to her sister, whom she regarded as her superior, and limited herself to affairs in and about Chawton Cottage. She kept up her music, practicing the piano before breakfast so as not to disturb the others. The Austens subscribed to the circulating library in the nearby village of Alton, and Austen also subscribed to a local literary society.

This group was a common way of sharing the cost of new books, which would be given to each member of the society for a specified period, after which the book had to be passed to the next member on the list. Austen looked after the household meals and in the evening joined in cards, needlework, games of skill, and conversation. She also read aloud to her companions, an interest and talent she inherited from her father. She interested herself in the doings of the large Austen family, especially her many nieces and nephews. In the morning she read and wrote apart from the others. This thoroughly feminine, supportive domesticity was not then regarded as degrading, but in fact had gained greatly in prestige in the aftermath of the Revolution debate.

Austen's way of life was represented by many writers—

and Austen would be prominent among them—as the proper sphere of woman, as repository and reproducer of the "national" culture, not in the sense of high culture but as the moral and ethical practices in local, daily existence that together constituted the nation, especially the political nation. Austen may have been sequestered in a small village and a household of women, but she was well aware of contemporary political and social thinking and would have realized that her life at Chawton in fact resembled the emergent ideal of romantic femininity, rooted in the "domestic affections" and the source of the national character.

Not surprisingly, then, she turned once again and with renewed purpose to writing. The novels that she began during this period were developed from the pre-Revolutionary novel of manners, sentiment, and emulation, but they were conceived in the latter part of the Revolutionary decade and rewritten to address the interests and concerns of a post-Revolutionary age, not directly or explicitly but obliquely. Indeed, their obliqueness was essential to their rhetorical effect, for the reading public was disgusted with direct ideological and political warfare in print, perhaps especially in novels. A further dimension to this obliqueness was Austen's secrecy about her writing as an activity, linked to her profound and genuine aversion to acquiring a public character and life as what would then have been called an "authoress."

It does seem likely that, in general, the balance between psychological and social being encourages the development of either a rich domestic life or a dominant social identity. Furthermore, the ideal of domestic woman formulated in the late eighteenth century was accompanied by ambiguity or even hostility toward women appearing in public characters, such as that of a published writer. More particularly, the Revolutionary aftermath saw an aggressive remasculization of literary culture along with an energetic appropriation by male writers of the themes of subjectivity and domesticity that female writers had exploited in order to build professional careers in the decades before 1800. Austen's secrecy about her writing and her rejection of a public character were responses to all these forces rather than what Cecil calls "the nearest thing to an eccentricity in her otherwise well-balanced character."

At Chawton Cottage she wrote away from the others at first, in a chamber that served as both a hallway and a dining room. The room had a squeaky door that Austen prevented from being repaired because it gave warning of anyone approaching. She worked on a writing desk placed on top of a small table and used small slips of paper that could quickly be put out of sight if someone did enter. (Later in her career she would sometimes write in the common sitting room when others were present.)

When she wrote to the publisher Crosby in 1809 to ask for the return of the still-unpublished manuscript of "Susan" she used the pseudonym "Mrs Ashton Dennis." The title page of her first published novel, *Sense and Sensibility*, states that it was "By A Lady," and such of her relations as knew of her authorship were enjoined to keep the secret. The title page of her next novel, *Pride and Prejudice*, attributed the work to "The Author of 'Sense and Sensibility,'" and this practice continued with each successive novel.

By the time she returned to novel writing at Chawton, Austen was an experienced novelist, if still an unpublished one, and had strong views on the art of fiction. She expressed these opinions only desultorily, however, in letters to her family. Austen read her niece Anna Austen's manuscript novel "Which Is the Heroine?" and offered detailed comments in letters of May or June, 10 August, 9 and 28 September, and December 1814.

Her criticisms were directed to maintaining plausibility in the representation of manners and social conventions and to establishing a clear focus of social relations—"3 or 4 Families in a Country Village is the very thing to work on." Cassandra Austen disliked "desultory novels," Jane Austen advised Anna, or ones with "too frequent a change from one set of people to another" and "circumstances" of "apparent consequence" that actually "lead to nothing." Such structure was in fact fairly common in the Burney type of novel that Jane Austen practiced, and she said that she herself allowed "much more Latitude" in this matter than Cassandra; at least she allowed it to other novelists, for her own novels have an economy of elements and tightness of construction that would have pleased Cassandra very much.

Austen was also conscious of the way genres and styles were seen as either "masculine" or "feminine." For example, the novel was widely regarded as a "woman's" form of writing though certain kinds of novels were seen as more appropriate for male writers. To her nephew James Edward Austen, who was trying to write a "man's" novel, Jane Austen protested: What should I do with your strong, manly, spirited Sketches, full of Variety and Glow?—How could I possibly join them on to the little bit (two Inches wide) of Ivory on which I work with so fine a Brush, as produces little effect after much labour? (16 December 1816)

Two years earlier, she had complained, tongue in cheek, against Walter Scott's taking up novel writing after a career as best-selling Romantic poet, because he "should not be taking the bread out of other people's mouths." She also made fun of novelists who padded out their works with extraneous matter, such as sermons, travelogues, and literary criticism.

As for the practicalities of composition, Austen fully realized the conflict between sustained creativity and domestic responsibility. Admiring the productivity of the novelist Jane West, who managed a farm, Austen wrote to her sister on 8 September 1816, "Composition seems to me Impossible, with a head full of Joints of Mutton & doses of rhubarb." Nevertheless, in 1809 the promise of domestic security at Chawton seems to have renewed her interest in novel writing and her determination to publish. She began by returning to her earlier work. In April 1809 she asked Crosby to publish "Susan," which he had bought for ten pounds in 1803, or to return it to her. The publisher insisted on retaining his rights, and Austen let the matter drop. Eventually she reacquired the manuscript in 1816 but died before it was published, as *Northanger Abbey*, in 1817.

Since she probably did little to revise the manuscript during the short time it was back in her hands, *Northanger*

Abbey is generally regarded as her earliest substantially completed novel.

Furthermore, since it satirizes the naive reader of popular Gothic "romances" as well as the conventions of that genre, it is usually seen as more closely linked than her later works to her early burlesques and parodies of literary genres and conventions, designed to entertain her family rather than for publication. Nevertheless, as Austen's family would have realized, parody of literary themes, genres, and conventions might be amusing and still have implications of national importance.

Northanger Abbey certainly deals with the politics of literary discourse in ways that would have been recognized in the mid 1790s or early 1800s, when it was first designed or written, as issues more vital than ever. Unlike such overtly political novels as William Godwin's *Things As They Are* (1794) or Mary Wollstonecraft's *The Wrongs of Woman* (1798), *Northanger Abbey*—like most of its contemporaries—works out issues of immediate political moment at the local level of individual lives; the oblique representation is the more rhetorically effective.

Northanger Abbey is clearly in the line of the Burney novel of a young woman's first entrance into the world—or rather "World," the common self-designation of narrow fashionable society as if it were to be equated with the whole of society. This narrow world is in fact the "political nation"—those of property or incomes sufficient to give them a voice in national affairs, however indirect. This world overlaps with the world of the "reading public"—those who can afford to rent or buy novels.

This overlap is what gave novels such as *Northanger Abbey* their importance. Like a Burney novel, though in much shorter compass, with far fewer characters, incidents, and complications of plot, *Northanger Abbey* sets a young protagonist in society peopled by both the fashionable and the vulgar. It follows her trials and errors in "reading" this world and negotiating through it to successful "establishment" there, as a woman married or about to be married to a "proper" man and thus with her otherwise hidden intellectual and moral merit recognized by and instrumental in the "World."

Though such novels usually have a female protagonist, she serves as a symbolic device rather than a representation of actual women. There is evidence that as many men as women read novels, and the socially inexperienced novel protagonist may stand for either a man or woman of merit faced with a seductive social reality dominated by considerations other than intellectual and moral merit—especially inherited wealth, rank, and power—and operating by courtly intrigue and patronage. Furthermore, this protagonist's situation must have been common to many novel readers at the time; thus such novels spoke to their real material interests and had powerful significance for them.

The protagonist of *Northanger Abbey*, Catherine Morland, is typical in these respects. Still in her teens and taken from her childhood home to stay with relatives in the fashionable spa of Bath, she and her brother James are taken up by Isabella and John Thorpe, social climbers who affect the fashionable cultures of female sensibility and male gallantry respectively. The Thorpes represent familiar types of upper-middle-class social emulation of their betters, resorting to deception and intrigue to advance their own interests. While Isabella sets her cap at James, John Thorpe hurries Catherine into a semblance of courtship. Catherine's genuine personal merit, despite her lack of worldly experience, is noticed by Henry Tilney, younger son of the socially ambitious General Tilney.

John Thorpe's attempt to impress the general by greatly exaggerating Catherine's fortune induces the general to consider her a suitable match for his son and to invite her to his estate, Northanger Abbey. The name is suggestive in several ways. Most obviously it echoes the titles of "Gothic romances." These are novels of description and place, in which residues of medieval culture intrude secretly into the present to exert power over the protagonist. Middle-class readers found these romances intensely interesting.

In the imaginary world of Gothic romance such readers could feel, if not consciously perceive, an analogy between the plight of the protagonist and their own situation in a society and culture dominated by what seemed an "alien," semifeudal system of court government, a system operating not through brute force but through the invisible agency of ideology and culture. In the 1790s, "English Jacobin" novelists such as Godwin and Wollstonecraft made the analogy between Gothic romance and the real world more explicit, borrowing elements of such romances to argue that "Gothic" (that is, medieval and feudal) oppression and tyranny were neither in the past nor mere fictional devices, but present political reality.

Austen's novel rejects "English Jacobin" political Gothicism. In the unfamiliar setting of Northanger Abbey, Catherine does make a mistake in interpretation. As often occurs with such protagonists, her inner strength becomes her weakness.

Lacking the worldly experience to chasten and direct her subjective power, her "natural" sympathy and imagination, she relies on what she has learned in reading novels and "reads" her present world as if it were that of a Gothic romance. She sees General Tilney as a domestic tyrant and Northanger as a facade for secret horrors. Henry Tilney recognizes her error and reminds her of the present social and political reality:

Remember the country and the age in which we live. Remember that we are English, that we are Christians. Consult your own understanding, your own sense of the probable, your own observation of what is passing around you—Does our education prepare us for such atrocities [as she has imagined]? Do our laws connive at them? Could they be perpetrated without being known, in a country like this, where social and literary intercourse is on such a footing; where every man is surrounded by a neighbourhood of voluntary spies, and where roads and newspapers lay every thing open? This speech asserts a particular view of the present constitution of Britain and thus of British society.

It is characteristic of Austen's rejection of novelistic excess of all kinds that Henry's perception of Catherine's error does not diminish the value of her character in his eyes, let alone lead him to reject her as a prospective wife—that would be too characteristic of a mere novel. As Henry soon discovers, Catherine's imaginings about his father have some truth. If not a Gothic tyrant, General Tilney is a modern equivalent, an ambitious squire aiming to advance his position by courtly intrigue and manipulation of the marriage market. When he learns that Catherine is not the great heiress John Thorpe has led him to believe, he sends her packing. Meanwhile, Catherine's brother has been thrown over by Isabella Thorpe in pursuit of the better material prospects offered by Captain Tilney, the general's older son and heir to Northanger Abbey. Austen retains the reformist criticism of courtliness and emulation as real social evils while rejecting the reformist global condemnation of "things as they are." This double move is characteristic of post-Revolutionary literature.

The move is formalized in the novel's plot by Catherine's disillusionment with the Thorpes and dismay at the general's inhumanity, Henry Tilney's confrontation with his father and decision to choose Catherine as a wife, and Catherine's prospective re-creation, with subjective merit intact and even enhanced, as wife of a man able both to school her further in the ways of the "World" and to confer on her, as married woman, social validation of her subjective merit. Austen's social criticism in *Northanger Abbey* is executed not only in the novel's "story," or structured sequence of incidents and related characters, but also in its "discourse," or composition and manner of telling. As with her political argument, Austen links critical reflection on the novel as a genre to the development of the individual's critical thought in general and thus to strengthening of domestic relations and society at large.

It is no accident that *Northanger Abbey* includes the best-known comment in English on the novel. Imagining a "miss" apologizing, when caught reading a book, that it is "only a novel," the narrator comments sarcastically that it is "only" Frances Burney's *Cecilla* (1782) or *Camilla* (1796) or Maria Edgeworth's *Belinda* (1801), "or, in short, only some work in which the greatest powers of the mind are displayed, in which the most thorough knowledge of human nature, the happiest delineation of its varieties, the liveliest effusions of wit and humour are conveyed to the world in the best chosen language." This comment could in fact be a reply to Edgeworth's prefatory remarks in *Belinda*, notifying the reader that the work is called a "tale" because "novel" has come to be associated with extravagant and seductive forms of fiction.

Readers in her day would probably think of two different forms of fiction—on one hand the fashionable novel glamorously depicting courtly decadence and on the other "English Jacobin," especially Revolutionary feminist, novels depicting emotional extravagance and social and political transgression. Both these kinds of fiction, it was increasingly felt, disseminated false ideology and impractical models, undermining individual morality and thus the "domestic affections," the foundation of the state. The fact that these false fictions were associated with either French courtliness or French Revolutionary culture indicates the importance of the novel as an instrument of political communication.

Austen's move to correct the excesses of the 1790s novel is similar to Edgeworth's. Austen reduces the scope and variety of incidents and characters, avoids narratorial expressivity—in fact adopting narratorial irony—eliminates characters that are mere "humors" or caricatures, as well as any hint of melodrama in incident, and in plotting takes a middle course between mere novelistic coincidence and "English Jacobin necessitarianism," that is, the tight connection of "circumstances," individual character, and the character's ethical action. She aims for a plausible though not inevitable outcome, thereby suggesting that "destiny" is a result of free will operating in a particular social and material horizon of possibility. Not surprisingly, such plotting accords with an Anglican theology of salvation through both true faith (or understanding, in secular terms) and good works (or ethical action in accordance with informed and accurate moral judgment).

Throughout her career, Austen followed this same pattern of correcting excessive novel conventions, at times alluding to specific bizarrenesses in particular novels of the day but otherwise cutting against generally well known novel devices. In *Northanger Abbey* this criticism by "rewriting" is especially obvious, as the narrator repeatedly draws the reader's attention to ways in which this novel is not like a common "novel of the day." In her later novels Austen's narrators are less obtrusive in this respect, but the same work is carried on. Rewriting is to effect rereading—not just reading again but reading as a critical and reflective activity. This activity produces true knowledge, a secular version of that "true faith" that is the basis of ethical action necessary to win salvation.

As much as her father or her clergymen brothers, Austen addresses a secular life in the light of eternity. Since women in her day could not do this from the pulpit they often chose to do so in the genre assigned to them by social, cultural, and literary convention. Narrative method plays a central role in this process of reformative reading.

The omniscient narrator represents a model consciousness, a figure for the "author," implicitly on the same level as the reader, representing the world of the novel from a superior position, whereas the protagonist is clearly fallible and limited, whether sympathetically or ironically treated by the narrator. As a character in the text, the narrator implicitly arranges all other characters in a hierarchical order over a grid whose coordinates are knowledge and moral judgment. Structurally the narrator represents a level of understanding toward which the protagonist is headed, somewhere beyond the end of the novel. The reader's interest in this progress is underpinned by Austen's use of free indirect discourse, or reported inward thought and feeling. Other novelists who use this device, such as Frances Burney, Ann Radcliffe, and Maria Edgeworth, treat several or many characters this way; Austen focuses almost exclusively on her protagonist, thereby giving a centrality and importance to a character that most other characters regard as unimportant.

This device is one of Austen's favourites, used in *Sense and Sensibility*, *Mansfield Park*, and *Persuasion*. But Austen also uses free indirect discourse to encourage the reader to sympathize with the protagonist, to accept her interpretations and judgments of the world around her. In this way the reader is often tricked into going along with the protagonist's errors until brought up short by the narrator's irony or revelation of the "truth." This device creates an irony of reading by which the reader identifies with both narrator and protagonist. In experiencing this irony at certain moments of narratorial revelation the reader vicariously experiences the gap between the protagonist's imperfection and fallibility and the narrator's superior understanding.

All human understanding, except the godlike narrator's, is conditional and relative. The narrator's irony reminds us of this mortal fallibility. This reading would be serious matter indeed were it not for the fact that it is presented in what is "only a novel." In political terms, the point does implicitly counter "English Jacobin" ideas of the "perfectibility of man."

Northanger Abbey, substantially completed by 1803, is thus very much a novel of its time, of a particular moment in the evolution in the novel as vehicle of ideological and cultural conflict. At the same time it includes the basic elements of the Austen novel, rapidly developed with greater sophistication and subtlety from Austen's settling at Chawton in 1809 to a few months before her death in 1817.

Through 1809 and 1810 Austen worked on revising "Elinor and Marianne," her epistolary novel of 1795, into *Sense and Sensibility*. When it was complete Henry Austen again served as intermediary between his sister and the publisher, this time Thomas Egerton, who may have been chosen because he had participated in the distribution of James and Henry Austen's Oxford magazine, *The Loiterer*. Jane Austen offered to pay the costs of printing and, not expecting to break even on the book, had saved some money for that purpose. She was to retain copyright, and the publisher was to get a commission for distributing the book.

In April 1810 she went to stay with Henry in London to correct proofs and wrote to her sister, "I am never too busy to think of S. & S. I can no more forget it, than a mother can forget her sucking child." It was published in the fall, and the first edition sold out in less than two years, making Austen £140, in those days a sum sufficient to support someone in comfort for a year or more. *Sense and Sensibility: A Novel* —the generic designation is important and was in the title of all Austen's novels published in her lifetime—is a more ambitious novel than *Northanger Abbey*.

Austen doubles the plot by representing the courtship of two sisters, Elinor and Marianne Dashwood, and by increasing the number of characters and incidents. In scope *Sense and Sensibility* is more like a full-blown Burney novel. Nevertheless, the narrator-protagonist relationship remains focused for the most part on one character, the unglamorous Elinor. In fact, in Elinor and Marianne, Austen foregrounds in one novel the two character types that she preferred to alternate in the later novels—the quiet but right-thinking heroine such as Fanny Price and Anne Elliot and the more outgoing and somewhat quixotic heroine such as Elizabeth Bennet and Emma Woodhouse. *Sense and Sensibility* brings into play another set of issues that were prominent in the Revolution debate and the post-Revolutionary quest for reform with renewed social stability—issues of property, patronage, and gender in the reconstruction of British society. The widowed Mrs. Dashwood and her three daughters are required to leave their home when the new heir, Mrs. Dashwood's stepson, John, assumes his inheritance with his fashionable and selfish wife, Fanny. Such is the lot of wives and daughters under the system of male primogeniture that was common at the time—and much criticized by feminists such as Mary Wollstonecraft. The Dashwood women are given a home at Barton Cottage on the Devonshire estate of a distant relation, Sir John Middleton, whose family is unfortunately a disorder of snobbery, vulgarity, and mere sociability. One visitor, Colonel Brandon, is interested in the middle daughter, Marianne, but he does not fit her romantic idea of a hero, constructed from her novel reading.

She makes no secret of her preference for the dashing Willoughby, who is also visiting in the neighborhood. The eldest daughter, Elinor, is disappointed, however, that Fanny Dashwood's brother Edward Ferrars, a young clergyman with a good estate in prospect, does not visit, for she has fallen in love with him and the feeling has seemed mutual. Other guests at the Middletons' include Charlotte Palmer and her husband, the one silly and the other aloof, and the obsequious Misses Steele, the younger of whom, Lucy, confidentially divulges to Elinor her secret engagement with Edward Ferrars. The Steeles, like the Dashwood women, are dependent on others to prevent a slide from comfort and gentility to poverty and social insignificance. Unlike her mother, Elinor Dashwood is prepared to deal with her situation with conventional feminine virtues of fortitude and forbearance.

Her sister Marianne indulges in romantic fantasy. Lucy Steele has evidently taken the worst course, practicing the courtly arts of coquetry to inveigle Edward Ferrars into an imprudent engagement. When the scene shifts from the country to London the destinies of the Dashwood sisters seem to take a further turn for the worse. Marianne learns that Willoughby is a fortune hunter and is about to marry for money. Fanny Dashwood's mother, old Mrs. Ferrars, suspects her son Edward of being in love with Elinor and snubs the Dashwood women in favour of the Steeles, until Lucy reveals her secret engagement to Edward, who is then disinherited in favour of his younger brother, Robert, a mere man of fashion. Returning to Barton, the Dashwoods stay with the Palmers, where Marianne falls ill.

Alarmed, Willoughby arrives and confesses to Elinor that he did love Marianne and must now live out an unhappy marriage. Back at Barton the last movement of the plot unfolds. Marianne recovers, but Elinor is further distressed when told that a Mr. Ferrars, whom she takes to be Edward, has recently married Lucy Steele. But the new husband turns out to be Edward's brother, whom Lucy has turned to as now the better prospect. Edward is freed from his engagement and proposes to Elinor; Colonel Brandon has offered the young clergyman a living in his gift; eventually Marianne comes to see the colonel's quiet domestic and social virtues and marries him.

There is an obvious post-Revolutionary argument in *Sense and Sensibility,* indicated in its title. "Sensibility" as indulgence of personal absolutes, such as romantic love, regardless of social conventions and even laws, was widely seen as a major ideological source of Revolutionary transgression. In the Revolution debate "sense," or "common sense," was often opposed to Revolutionary theory, speculation, and enthusiasm. In Austen's novel the evident triumph of sense over sensibility, and the confinement of sensibility, as domestic and social sympathy, though enacted on the level of common life, would have had political and public implications for readers at the time the novel was published, in part because moral, religious, and educational writers insisted that there was a close connection between small, apparently insignificant transgressions and more serious ones.

Furthermore, *Sense and Sensibility* clearly establishes the value of "feminine" passive virtues of the kind possessed from the outset by Elinor and acquired through error and suffering by Marianne. These virtues were proclaimed by numerous writers of the Revolutionary aftermath, beginning at least as early as Hannah More's *Strictures on the Modern System of Female Education* (1799), as central to social order and even to national survival. At the same time it is clear that *Sense and Sensibility* registers the desperate situation of genteel women deprived of the wherewithal to sustain social dignity or even nobility of mind and feeling. Mary Wollstonecraft argued in *A Vindication of the Rights of Woman* (1792) that this plight drove many women of the middle and upper class to coquetry and courtly intrigue, to the ruin of the domestic affections and thus the corruption of society as a whole.

Austen does not explicitly make this kind of protest in *Sense and Sensibility* or elsewhere, but her reticence accords with a post-Revolutionary programme of avoiding the explicitnesses that many thought had threatened to tear the country apart in the 1790s. Furthermore, the fact that her novel has a happy ending reflects her Anglican faith in a just and benevolent deity presiding over a universe that is comic in the sense that suffering and injustice have, finally, a beneficial effect. "Wise passiveness" is better in the long run than rebellion. If Austen was a feminist, she was a post-

Revolutionary one. Certainly the social criticism of *Sense and Sensibility* takes in a broad sweep of foolish and even vulgar emulation, by gentry and professional middle class alike, of a court culture increasingly seen as threatening ruin to the nation.

With *Sense and Sensibility* published, Austen turned again to "First Impressions," the novel she had completed in 1797 and tried to sell to Cadell. She revised it, gave it the title *Pride and Prejudice: A Novel,* and sold the copyright to Egerton for £110 late in 1812, having asked for £150. It was published early in 1813, anonymously, though Austen's authorship soon became known beyond the family circle. It was very well received; for example, Byron's future wife, Anne Isabella Milbanke, considered it to be "the fashionable novel" of the season. It seems to have been widely read and discussed in fashionable and literary society.

Pride and Prejudice takes another pair of sisters but puts the outgoing one, Elizabeth Bennet, more into the foreground, while keeping the silent suffering one, Jane, much more in the background. Property inheritance again becomes a major factor in the destiny of these two—along with their three younger sisters Mary, Kitty, and Lydia—for their father's small estate is entailed to the nearest male relative, the Reverend William Collins. Entailment was the kind of injustice against women that Wollstonecraft and other Revolutionary feminists had criticized sharply, for it forced women to make their fortune the only way open to them—by speculating on the marriage market.

Mr. Bennet has also committed an error attacked by feminists of the time—giving in to the influence of courtly erotic culture and marrying a woman who was merely beautiful and lacking in the intellectual and moral resources necessary to support her own social position with dignity and discretion, to be a true friend and companion to her husband, and to raise children—especially children themselves utterly dependent on such inner resources. Closed up in his gentleman's library for much of the time, Mr. Bennet does not even pass on his own knowledge and discrimination to his children, except to his favourite, Elizabeth. Fortunately, Elizabeth and Jane have also spent time with some cultivated relations, the Gardiners, who were formerly in the ungenteel mercantile middle class. Of the other sisters, Mary is a junior pedant, Kitty is impressionable, and Lydia is a mere ambitious coquette.

When Mr. Bingley, a wealthy young man also from an ungenteel background, rents a nearby manor and arrives with his sister and a friend, Mrs. Bennet's notion that well-managed intrigue will get her daughters husbands seems to have promise. Bingley seems to be falling in love with Jane, despite the condescending discouragement of his sister and the aloof disapproval of his friend, Mr. Darcy. Elizabeth resents their intrusion, especially Mr. Darcy's. The Reverend Mr. Collins shows up determined to marry one of the Bennet girls and thereby make some recompense for the harsh terms of the entail. For their part, Lydia and Kitty are delighted with the prospects offered by some officers quartered nearby.

A young militia officer, Mr. Wickham, seems especially attracted to Elizabeth, and she is more disposed to return his regard after he tells her Darcy has treated him unjustly. When the recently arrived Mr. Collins learns Jane is already in love he proposes immediately to Elizabeth, who refuses his offer because she cannot love him. Shortly thereafter, however, he is accepted by Elizabeth's friend Charlotte Lucas, whom Elizabeth knows to have too much sense not to see that Collins is a fool. Disillusioned, Elizabeth decides that Charlotte has merely sold herself on the marriage market. When Bingley and his party leave suddenly for London, she concludes that Darcy has talked Bingley out of proposing to Jane. Jane visits the Gardiners in London, where she is treated with mere formal politeness by Miss Bingley, who suggests that her brother is to marry Darcy's sister.

Learning that Wickham is courting an heiress merely for her money, Elizabeth is completely disillusioned: all except her sister Jane seem mere courtly and self-interested intriguers, and she can only congratulate herself on not being taken in. Elizabeth meets Darcy by accident, however, while visiting

Charlotte and Mr. Collins, who has a living on the estate of Lady Catherine de Bourgh, a haughty snob and Darcy's aunt. Elizabeth is dumbfounded when Darcy suddenly proposes to her, and angrily rejects him, accusing him of separating Bingley and Jane and of being unjust to Wickham.

The next day he gives her a letter explaining and justifying his conduct; at first Elizabeth believes it must be false, but gradually she comes to accept the truth of everything Darcy says. Ashamed, she admits that until this moment she never knew herself, and she now sees all the characters and incidents to this point in the story in a new light. Structurally, this scene is the centre of the novel. It is clear to the reader, if not entirely clear to Elizabeth, that she and Darcy would be a match, and the plot now turns to repairing the breach between them.

Against Elizabeth's advice, Mr. Bennet allows Lydia to visit the family of one of the officers, who are at the fashionable resort of Brighton, somewhat notorious at that time as the preferred haunt of the Prince of Wales. Elizabeth herself goes on a tour with the Gardiners through scenic Derbyshire. The Gardiners want to visit Darcy's estate of Pemberley, and when they learn that he is absent, Elizabeth agrees.

They are shown over the house, and the house-keeper gives them a glowing report of its master's character and conduct. The Gardiners are surprised, but Elizabeth has more reason than ever to regret her prejudice against the man. When Darcy returns unexpectedly he is all hospitality, and prospects for a new understanding seem to be opening. But these possibilities seem dashed when Elizabeth hears that her sister Lydia has eloped from Brighton with Wickham, who is unlikely to marry someone with little money. By the social conventions of the time the "ruin" of Lydia will affect the marriageability of all her sisters.

Distressed at this news, Elizabeth blurts it out to Darcy, and Mr. Gardiner leaves to help Mr. Bennet track down the couple. Later the Bennets learn that Wickham has agreed to marry Lydia and surmise that he has been bribed to do so by Mr. Gardiner. But Elizabeth learns that Darcy arranged everything.

When the Bingleys and Darcy return to the neighborhood, Bingley and Jane quickly resume their love for one another and become engaged. To Elizabeth's surprise, however, Lady Catherine de Bourgh arrives and haughtily tries to extract a promise from Elizabeth that she will not marry Darcy. As happens to such domineering intriguers, her aim is undermined by her own actions: Darcy learns of Elizabeth's standing up to his aunt, and to Elizabeth's further surprise—though not the reader's—he comes to propose again. This time he is accepted. In a characteristic final comic touch, Mrs. Bennet is ecstatic at the accomplishment of more than she could have imagined in her plans to marry off her daughters.

In its plot, incidents, and characters *Pride and Prejudice* is an interesting variation on the novel of manners and sentiment. But its originality—more obviously than in *Sense and Sensibility* or *Northanger Abbey*—is in its manipulation of the triangular relationship between narrator, protagonist, and reader. As in the earlier novels, the omniscient narrator retains the power to withhold information from the reader and restrict access to the consciousness of characters other than the protagonist. By being let fully into Elizabeth's mind but virtually excluded from all others, the reader is meant to develop a sympathetic identification with Elizabeth's character and judgments. Thus when Elizabeth realizes in the middle of the novel that she, who prided herself on her perspicacity, has been mistaken about all the main points, her confidence in her ability to "read" her world is seriously shaken. Similarly, the reader, who might feel confidently able to decode the story correctly but who has fallen in with Elizabeth's reading, will feel an analogous humiliation.

Chastened, though in different ways, Elizabeth and the reader continue their adventures in the text, but it becomes increasingly apparent to the reader that Elizabeth's abandonment of any hope for a return from Darcy is yet another mistake in her "reading" of him and herself. The narrator, too, who has been fairly non-committal about Elizabeth's "readings" in the early part of the novel, becomes more ironic in the later part. In short, the novel constructs an exercise in reading for both protagonist and reader, and manipulates narrative so as to make the reader conscious of the fallibility and precariousness of reading of any kind. Again, it would not be going too far to see this exercise in terms of Austen's deeply held Anglican faith and its theology of the imperfection yet improvability—though not perfectibility—of humankind.

In June 1813, five months after *Pride and Prejudice* was published, Austen completed a new novel, begun in February 1811. *Mansfield Park: A Novel,* which some scholars feel also had an earlier version, was published by Egerton, though Austen kept the copyright this time and made more than three hundred pounds by the first edition. In *Mansfield Park* Austen returns to a heroine who, like Elinor Dashwood, is right-thinking but socially disregarded from the outset. Fanny Price is one of a large and impecunious family at Portsmouth. Her mother is one of three once-famous beauties, though her sisters married better than she—one, Mrs. Norris, to a country clergyman and the other, Lady Bertram, to a baronet, the owner of the large estate of Mansfield Park.

After the death of her husband, Mrs. Norris, who resides near the Bertrams, persuades Sir Thomas Bertram to take in their niece Fanny. Separated from her family and especially her beloved brother William, Fanny remains an outcast at Mansfield, condescended to by her cousins Tom, Maria, and Julia, though her kind cousin Edmund protects her and guides her education. Not surprisingly, she comes to love him for it. Her uncle Sir Thomas leaves to attend to his plantations in Antigua. In the absence of the father the others in the family soon drift into one folly or another, abetted by Mrs. Norris, who dotes on her wealthy nieces and nephews while treating Fanny like a servant.

Maria becomes engaged to Mr. Rushworth, a wealthy neighboring gentleman whose name accurately represents his moral and intellectual value. All the Bertrams become intrigued by Henry and Mary Crawford, a fashionable brother and sister who are visiting their half sister Mrs. Grant, wife of the local vicar, himself an old-style clergyman more interested in the pleasures of the table than in the cure of souls. Together the young people visit Rushworth's estate of Sotherton Court, the name of which suggests the decadent, courtly, more "southern" or Mediterranean than English fashionableness (or ton) pervading the values of all but Fanny and Edmund. The outing is ostensibly to discuss Rushworth's planned "improvements," or ornamental additions to his estate, but new love interests and flirtations develop quickly in the symbolically sultry weather.

While the Bertram sisters become rivals in flirting with Henry, Edmund becomes fascinated by Mary, who is, however, dismayed to learn that as the second son he intends to take up a profession in the church. Fanny remains a silently suffering spectator. When Tom brings to Mansfield his vacuous friend Yates, the young people catch the contemporary fad for amateur theatricals and plan to perform *Lovers' Vows*, a translation of August von Kotzebue's *Das Kind der Liebe* (1791, The Lőve Child). The play is a dubious choice for several reasons. It represents illicit love; it celebrates romantic subjectivity in the face of social convention, in a way that had already given such "German plays" a bad reputation in respectable English society; and it will enable the young people at Mansfield to make love speeches to each other that social convention would prohibit them from making in their real characters. Fanny, significantly, wishes to decline any part in it.

Sir Thomas's sudden return from the West Indies puts a stop to these follies, though he allows Maria to marry Rushworth. The next movement of the story focuses on Fanny, who begins to be more noticed by everyone. Mary Crawford tries to make her a confidante regarding Mary's infatuation for Edmund, which she feels is impeded by Edmund's determination to become a "mere" country clergyman. Fanny is treated with consideration by Sir Thomas and with friendly solicitude by Edmund, all to Mrs. Norris's disgust. Even Henry Crawford now finds her interesting enough to wish that he could make her fall in love with him. Fanny's only real delight, however, is in a visit from her beloved sailor brother, whose career is being promoted by Sir Thomas. To Henry's surprise, he finds himself actually falling in love with Fanny, and persuades his uncle, an admiral, to arrange William's promotion to lieutenant. Henry then proposes to Fanny, and the connection between the two actions suggests the kind of leverage used in the patronage system rather than a disinterested courtship.

To Sir Thomas's anger and Mary's surprise, Fanny rejects Henry, whom she sees as merely a courtly seducer. To remind Fanny of the degrading life that awaits her if she does not change her mind and accept Henry, Sir Thomas sends her to her vulgar parents' home in Portsmouth. Henry visits her there, and despite his apparent sincerity she finds she still cannot love him, or will not. The denouement now unfolds, as the Bertram family seems to disintegrate. When Tom Bertram falls seriously ill, Mary writes to Fanny and reveals her true character by expressing the hope that Tom's death will clear the way for Edmund to become heir to Mansfield, and thus the kind of catch Mary wants. The recent bride Maria runs off with Henry, and Julia elopes with Yates. Mary's inability to see Maria and Henry's adultery as morally serious, rather than just socially damaging, shocks Edmund out of his fascination for her. When Fanny returns to Mansfield to lend what comfort she can, even the indolent Lady Bertram is relieved by her presence.

Fanny is still the shyly feminine person she has always been, but now, amid so many crises, her steadiness of character and moral authority begin to be recognized by all—she is indeed a woman of "price," in the sense of intrinsic value. Tom's brush with death sobers him into a greater sense of moral and social responsibility, and Fanny marries Edmund. They will continue to sustain Mansfield Park and will spread their wedded virtues through-local society from the nearby, and again aptly named, vicarage of Thornton Lacey—uniting the symbol of Christ's sacrifice with an ornament of upper-class dress.

Mansfield Park embodies the timeliest possible message for the novel-reading public of the early Regency and the late stages of the long struggle with Revolutionary and Napoleonic France. Mansfield Park is a figure for England or Britain as rural, leisured, and cultivated but with heavy social, economic, and imperial responsibilities that must be carefully tended and reinvigorated in each generation. It is also a "mansefield," a field for the inspiriting influence of the manse of domestic home of the established church and its theology of true faith, or ideological correctness, and good works, or social responsibility and leadership. This home is of course presided over by a woman, the heart of the nation according to an increasingly powerful ideology of domestic woman as repository and nurturer of the national soul, conscience, culture, and destiny.

Late in January 1814, four months before *Mansfield Park* came out, Austen began work on *Emma,* and she completed it fourteen months later, in March 1815. Here Austen again reverses the character of her heroine, for Emma Woodhouse is quite unlike Fanny Price, subjectively and socially. Emma is the belle of her neighborhood—beautiful, young, and wealthy, the younger and unmarried daughter of a querulous hypochondriac widower.

Emma's education was supervised by a kindly governess, Miss Taylor, now married to a neighboring gentleman, Mr. Weston. Miss Taylor was more of a friend than a preceptor, and Emma's mind is neither well stocked nor well trained. She has therefore become an "imaginist," a fictionist or romancer of real life, speculating incorrectly on the characters and intentions of others while presuming on her native talents and her social power to arrange their lives.

She prides herself, for example, on having brought about the marriage of Miss Taylor and Mr. Weston. Emma has been freer than ever to indulge in her brand of local patronage since the marriage of her older sister, Isabella, to John Knightley, a London lawyer and younger brother of a local landed gentleman. This gentleman, as his name suggests—Knightley is the knight's ley, or field—epitomizes the best of the rural landed class and its modern chivalric, moral-and-ethical culture. Not surprisingly, he is the only person who dares try to correct Emma's character and point out her errors.

He has his work cut out for him. Soon after the novel opens Emma is already planning another match, between the local clergyman Mr. Elton and Emma's new protégée, Harriet Smith. An impressionable boarding-school girl, Harriet is an illegitimate child of unknown parentage, and Emma imagines she must be the love child of some nobleman. Harriet is attracted to Mr. Martin, a yeoman farmer and tenant of Mr. Knightley's. Knightley thinks Harriet and Martin would make a good couple, but Emma insists on a higher destiny for her client and discourages the match, to Knightley's chagrin. (Yet he and Emma do work well together in smoothing relations between her father and Knightley's brother.)

Emma's plans for Harriet and Elton are disastrously—though comically—overset, however, when Elton mistakes Emma's interest as a sign of love for him. Emboldened by too much wine, he proposes. After Emma explains that she has intended him for the lowly Harriet, Elton is offended and goes off to Bath. Chastened, Emma resolves to give up matchmaking.

Yet her imagination is already at work on Frank Churchill, Weston's son by his previous marriage, long ago adopted by a wealthy, childless uncle and aunt. He is soon expected to pay a courtesy call to his father and new stepmother. Frank does not appear on schedule, apparently detained by his imperious aunt.

Another visitor arrives, however—the beautiful and talented, but impecunious, Jane Fairfax, orphan granddaughter of a clergyman's widow, Mrs. Bates, who lives in straitened circumstances with her unmarried daughter. While she recognizes her social and material superiority to Jane, Emma feels shamed by Jane's superiority of mind and evident discipline of character. When Frank arrives, Emma is attracted to him and realizes that the Westons hope she can be drawn into marriage with him, but Knightley finds Frank to be an extravagant and self-willed flirt. Emma is further chagrined when Elton returns with a bride who, as a married woman, takes social precedence over Emma.

When Elton rudely snubs Harriet at a ball, Knightley comes to the rescue, and when Harriet is later harassed by some gypsies she is rescued by Frank. Emma now projects a match between Frank and Harriet and encourages her young friend not to be deterred from falling in love with a man above her socially, but Knightley suspects some secret between Frank and Jane. Meanwhile, Mrs. Elton, a snobbish busybody, finds a situation as governess for Jane. When the company goes on an outing to Box Hill Frank flirts with Emma and, made careless by his attention, she insults Miss Bates, who dares not stand up to her. Knightley is shocked, and his reproof gives Emma real pain. She realizes she has abused her social position and responsibility, and in a characteristic act of self-abnegation calls on Miss Bates by way of apology.

The death of the dictatorial Mrs. Churchill seems to free her nephew to follow his own wishes in marriage. Emma now expects Frank may propose to Harriet, but a few weeks later she is amazed to learn that he and Jane have been secretly engaged for some time. Emma now fears the ill consequences of having again encouraged Harriet to love a man beyond her reach, but she is stunned to learn that Harriet thought Emma was encouraging her to think of Knightley, not Frank, and she has taken Knightley's kindness to her as a sign of love. With a sickening shock, Emma realizes that she herself loves Knightley and fears that Harriet's surmise may be right. When Knightley calls to console Emma, in case she has allowed herself to be taken in by Frank's flirtation, she at first prevents him from speaking because she thinks he is about to confess his love for Harriet. Then, in another act of self-sacrifice, she invites him to say what he had intended. With a third and even greater shock—Austen was playfully fond of the fairy-tale pattern of threes—Knightley confesses his love for Emma and hopes she can return his feeling.

Characteristically, the narrator draws away from Emma's joy with a sudden turn of amused irony. Emma now has the unpleasant duty of telling Harriet, but it soon transpires that

Harriet has been seeing Martin, with Knightley's encouragement, and is to marry him. It later turns out that Harriet's father is not a dashing aristocrat but a solid and unromantic tradesman. Emma's "novelizing" of those around her is completely exposed. If this book were a sentimental tale or a Gothic novel the consequences would be tragic; but in Austen's comic novel no real harm has been done. In fact, Emma's errors have helped to educate others, as well as herself, to their human fallibility, as one might expect in a novelistic universe ruled by a benevolent deity much like the one supposed by Austen's Anglican theology to preside over the natural universe.

Like its predecessor, *Emma* shows the centrality of domestic woman to a renewed nation led by a reformed professionalized gentry. Emma resembles heroines in other novels of the time, representing the socially divisive and destabilizing effect of a woman who lacks intellectual resources and moral discipline appropriate to her station and thus misuses her social power. Yet Austen characteristically gives a comic rather than pathetic or tragic cast to this story and greatly diminishes what is too commonly treated melodramatically by other writers. She also denies that extensive social reform is necessary to end the social evil caused by such vitiated female characters. In Austen's benign novelistic universe reform on the individual level is enough to effect social change, provided that a character can practice, in however small and local a way, the virtues of self-correction and self-abnegation, which are in fact, for Austen, Christian and Anglican virtues.

Further, the value of marriage, which is a sacrament as well as a property arrangement and legal contract, is shown in the fact that Knightley's more practiced ethical character will support Emma's continued spiritual growth and consequent social usefulness—a much subtler echo of the conclusion to Eaton Stannard Barrett's spoof *The Heroine; or, Adventures of a Fair Romance Reader* (1813), which Austen had read in March 1814. When she was ready to publish *Emma,* Austen decided to change publishers and offered the work to

Byron's publisher, John Murray. He referred it to a leading man of letters, William Gifford, editor of the Tory *Quarterly Review*. Gifford had published two verse satires, the *Baviad* (1791) and *Maeviad* (1795), attacking what he saw as signs of moral and cultural decline, including women authors.

He thought very highly of Austen's novel, however, and Murray offered her £450 for the copyright, along with those of *Mansfield Park* and *Sense and Sensibility*. Austen preferred to retain property in her work, however, and Murray published *Emma: A Novel* on commission, in December 1815. Following a suggestion from the Prince Regent's librarian, the Reverend James Stanier Clarke, Austen dedicated the novel, though with no enthusiasm, to the prince. She had met Clarke in autumn 1815 when he had been sent by the prince to invite Austen, then in London, to see Carlton House, his London residence. Clarke told her that the prince admired her novels and kept a set in each of his residences.

Austen was not overawed. Though she accepted Clarke's suggestion that she dedicate her next novel to the prince, she rejected Clarke's suggestion that she write a novel about a clergyman, evidently somewhat like Clarke himself, and declared:

The comic part of the character I might be equal to, but not the good, the enthusiastic, the literary. Such a man's conversation must at times be upon subjects of science and philosophy, of which I know nothing; or at least be occasionally abundant in quotations and allusions which a woman who, like me, knows only her own mother tongue, and has read very little in that, would be totally without the power of giving.

A classical education, or at any rate a very extensive acquaintance with English literature, ancient and modern, appears to me quite indispensable for the person who would do any justice to your clergyman; and I think I may boast myself to be, with all possible vanity, the most unlearned and uninformed female who ever dared to be an authoress. (11 December 1815)

Obviously if Austen desired, she could use to her own

advantage the conventional distinctions between "masculine" and "feminine" genres and styles.

Undeterred, Clarke then hinted that it might be in Austen's interest to write some "historical romance, illustrative of the history of the august House of Cobourg," in view of the impending marriage of the princess Charlotte, heir presumptive to the throne. Austen replied even more emphatically that she realized such a work "might be much more to the purpose of profit or popularity than such pictures of domestic life in country villages as I deal in." Then she added,

> But I could no more write a romance than an epic poem. I could not sit seriously down to write a serious romance under any other motive than to save my life; and if it were indispensable for me to keep it up and never relax into laughing at myself or other people, I am sure I should be hung before I had finished the first chapter. No, I must keep to my own style and go on in my own way; and though I may never succeed again in that, I am convinced that I should totally fail in any other. (1 April 1816)

The reply is less interesting for its apparent modesty than for its clear sense of generic distinctions and the commercialized nature of the literary marketplace.

A few months after she finished *Emma,* Austen did "go on in [her] own way," with *Persuasion,* begun in August 1815 and completed, though not finally polished, a year later. In this novel Austen returns to the silently suffering, stoical heroine disregarded by everyone who applies merely social criteria in judging others. Austen also presents more directly than before the problem, underlying *Mansfield Park,* of reconstructing Britain and its social leadership in the Revolutionary aftermath. Austen and a host of other writers were representing this reconstruction as a progressive dialectic of gentry and professionals, especially the elite professions to which Austen's brothers belonged. In *Mansfield Park* the estate (and state) dangerously divided within is purged of courtly and vulgar elements—or at least such elements are put in their place—and reinvigorated with merit "from below." In

Persuasion an estate dangerously overextended morally, socially, and financially is not so much reinvigorated as superseded by an estate acquired entirely on merit and able to take into itself the neglected best of the older estate (or state). Not surprisingly, the representatives of merit are, like two of Austen's brothers, navy men.

The novel opens with the vain and vacuous widower, Sir Walter Elliot of Kellynch Hall, contemplating retrenchment of his estate, which his proud extravagance has run into debt. Moreover the estate, like that of Mr. Bennet in *Pride and Prejudice*, is entailed on the nearest male relative. It will not go to any of Sir Walter's three daughters unless one of them marries the heir at law. Sir Walter's youngest daughter, Mary, who has inherited his merely social values, has married a neighboring gentleman, Charles Musgrove, son and heir of a wealthy squire. Sir Walter's other two daughters remain unmarried, but Sir Walter's projects are only for the elder, Elizabeth, who is as vain and superficial as her father.

The middle daughter, Anne, is taken for granted by everyone, though the narrator lets the reader see that she is the only one with real inner resources and character, partly thanks to her older friend and adviser, Lady Russell. Reluctantly accepting the advice of his estate agent, Sir Walter agrees to let Kellynch to Admiral Croft and his wife, who are looking for a home now that war with France is over. Sir Walter looks down on such mere men of merit, rushed to prominence and even wealth by the vicissitudes of war. In fact eight years earlier he had, with the help of Lady Russell, persuaded Anne not to marry Mrs. Croft's brother, Frederick Wentworth, a man unsuitable in rank and prospects for a daughter of a baronet. Fortunately the matter was kept secret from other members of both families at the time.

Sir Walter plans to take his family to Bath, where he can maintain his social standing without great expense and where his daughters will have enhanced prospects of finding husbands. He and Elizabeth leave for Bath first, while Anne spends time with her sister Mary's family, the Musgroves, mediating the differences and difficulties of various family members. When Wentworth, now a successful and wealthy man thanks to the fortunes of war, arrives to see the Crofts he evidently harbors resentment against Anne and gaily joins the circle of the sociable flirts Henrietta and Louisa Musgrove as Anne suffers in silence. Wentworth does her several small kindnesses, but he seems determined to value in a woman what he thinks Anne lacked by rejecting him, namely firmness of purpose.

The party visits the seacoast town of Lyme Regis, where they meet Wentworth's friends Captains Harville and Benwick. Benwick, who is staying with Harville and his family, is despondent over the death of his fiancée, Harville's sister. Anne continues to act as healer and counselor of other characters' upsets, such as Benwick's romantic grief, and while at Lyme Regis she finds herself being admired by a stranger, who turns out to be the heir to Kellynch, William Walter Elliot. After the impetuous Louisa Musgrove, to whom Wentworth seems drawn, suffers a serious accident because of her own careless folly, it is Anne who takes charge of the situation.

The next movement of the novel opens with Anne's arrival in Bath with Lady Russell to join her father and sister. There she finds William Walter Elliot paying court to her father, who still hopes a marriage between the heir and Elizabeth will keep Kellynch in his line. Anne also finds the insinuating Mrs. Clay, a vulgar older woman who seems determined to marry Sir Walter. Anne visits an old friend, Mrs. Smith, now ill and living at Bath in straitened circumstances. Mrs. Smith seems to know a good deal about William Walter Elliot, whom Anne finds hard to read and suspects of having a double character. Then the Crofts and Wentworth arrive at Bath, and Anne hears with surprise that the apparently heartbroken Benwick has become engaged to Louisa Musgrove. In the great set piece of the novel the various principal characters encounter each other at a concert, where Anne as usual devotes herself to the comfort of others.

Later she learns from Mrs. Smith that William Walter Elliot has a vicious character. He has come to Bath to head off Mrs. Clay's designs on Sir Walter because he fears that a marriage between them might result in the male heir needed to keep Kellynch in Sir Walter's line. The Bath party is enlarged when the Musgroves and Harvilles arrive.

During one meeting Wentworth appears to be writing a letter for Harville while Harville discusses with Anne the differing perseverance of men and women in loving someone who has been lost to them. Against Harville's claim that women easily turn to new love, Anne protests that men—with their public duties and professional interests—have greater aid in overcoming loss, while women can only silently suffer and endure. When the party leaves, Wentworth comes back and puts a letter in Anne's hand; overhearing her talk with Harville he has realized that he has to ask once more for her love.

Anne is afraid she will find no chance to reassure him, but a chance meeting in the street affords the opportunity. This time Sir Walter and Lady Russell approve of the match; William Walter Elliot and Mrs. Clay leave Bath together. The novel closes not on a note of narratorial irony and detachment but with a sense that despite present happiness, with Anne having to fear only some future outbreak of war, some years of conjugal joy and social usefulness have already been needlessly lost because of social prejudice and a feminine weakness in face of merely social persuasion.

As Jane Austen was writing *Persuasion* her brother Henry and his partners found their bank threatened by their overoptimistic speculation and some rather questionable business practices. The postwar economic slump soon brought the bank down, and in March 1816 Henry was bankrupt; worse still, his speculations had involved large sums of his brothers' money. He decided to become a clergyman and became assistant at Chawton. At this time he regained the manuscript for Austen's unpublished novel "Susan" from Crosby, who had held it since 1803. Austen first wanted to publish immediately, but then decided to put it aside. Early in 1816 she began to show symptoms of what was probably Addison's disease, a malfunction of the adrenal cortex resulting in imbalance of the body's mineral metabolism, with symptoms such as physical weakness, skin discoloration, as well as abdominal and back pain.

Though the disease progressed steadily, Austen enjoyed increased contact with her family, including her young nieces and nephews, especially her brother James's son Edward, who, like his sister Anna, had aspirations to be a novel writer. Austen's brothers Francis and Charles, freed from constant naval duty with the ending of war, came with their families to Chawton.

In January 1817 Austen began drafting a new novel and worked at it until March, when she was too ill to continue; extracts were published in 1871 by her favourite nephew Edward in the second edition of his *Memoir of Jane Austen*. He called it *Sanditon*, though a family tradition held that Austen herself intended it to be called "The Brothers." It opens as Mr. Parker, an entrepreneur developing a seaside health spa named Sanditon, is seeking a physician to serve his new resort. When Parker's coach is overturned on a country road, he is looked after by a local family, the Heywoods.

He takes young Charlotte Heywood as his guest to Sanditon, where she meets a variety of individualists seemingly tainted by the new culture of Romanticism, including Parker's brothers and sisters and the literary man of feeling, Sir Edward Denham. Another visitor to Sanditon is the rich West Indian, Miss Lambe. Austen did not get much farther than setting the scene and cast of characters, but her intention was clearly to continue her exploration of class, gender, and culture in post-Revolutionary Britain. Austen became seriously ill in March 1817, and in May she was taken to consult a surgeon in Winchester, where she stayed in lodgings in College Street. Attended by her faithful sister, Cassandra, she rallied from time to time, and even wrote a comic poem to mark St. Swithin's Day, 15 July, but she died three days later, early in the morning. She was buried in Winchester Cathedral on 24 July. In her will Austen left the remainder of her estate after funeral expenses, £561 and two shillings, to Cassandra.

"Susan" was published as *Northanger Abbey* with

Persuasion and a "Biographical Notice" of Austen by her brother Henry, at the end of 1817, though it is dated 1818. She was much missed in her family, but her passing caused little stir in the literary world, and her novels were soon virtually forgotten by the reading public. It was not until 1833, when they were republished in the Bentley's Standard Novels series, that her novels began a steady rise in their status to become both commercially successful and recognized as "classics." Of the thousands of novels published in the late eighteenth and early nineteenth centuries, they are among the few to survive their own time. Bentley reprinted the Standard Novels editions into the 1880s; other publishers started putting out their own editions soon after the copyrights began to expire in 1839. By the late nineteenth century, in response to Austen's emergent status as a "popular classic," editions were appearing with introductions by leading men of letters and illustrations by fashionable artists. In 1906 Austen's novels began to be published in the Everyman Library; in 1907 they began to appear in the Oxford World's Classics series; and in 1938 Penguin books began publishing them.

In addition to these various popular editions, R. W. Chapman's critical edition was published by the Clarendon Press of Oxford University Press in 1923; in the 1970s Oxford University Press had this edition reedited for the Oxford English Novels series and later republished them in the new Oxford World's Classics series. Other editions are legion, and there are numerous film and television adaptations. Studied in English classes around the world, yet still read by thousands just for pleasure, Austen is now one of the world's most widely read authors.

In Austen's own time her works were praised by the few critics to review them, but not so as to distinguish them in any extraordinary way from other novels of that time. Yet Walter Scott recognized Austen's achievement. He wrote approvingly of her novels in the *Quarterly Review* (October 1815), and ten years later he reread *Pride and Prejudice* "for the third time at least" and confided to his journal:

That young lady had a talent for describing the

involvements and feelings and characters of ordinary life which is to me the most wonderful I ever met with. The Big Bow wow strain I can do myself like any now going but the exquisite touch which renders ordinary common-place things and characters interesting from the truth of the description and the sentiment is denied to me. What a pity such a gifted creature died so early. (14 March 1826)

Mary Mitford at first found Austen's novels lacking in "elegance" and "taste," but by the early 1820s she enlisted them, along with Gilbert White's *Natural History of Selborne* (1789), for her book *Our Village* (1824-1832), her own middleclass appropriation of rural England—one of the most powerful influences on the cultural imagination of the nineteenth and twentieth centuries. Nevertheless, for much of the nineteenth century Austen remained, in Brian C. Southam's words, "a critic's novelist."

The modern construction of Austen as a literary *and* popular classic—popular with the educated middle-class reading public—was spurred by the publication in 1870 of James Edward Austen-Leigh's *Memoir of Jane Austen*. Its portrayal of Austen as a feminine and domestic sage simply recording a real world of rural felicity clearly had considerable cultural and political use in an age of ever deeper social, national, and imperial conflicts, of horrific industrial blight and social problems that seemed or were made out to be beyond the power of the state to remedy. Austen, like Mary Mitford, Gilbert White, and many other earlier writers, was brought to serve what Martin Wiener has described as the attack of an upper-middle-class English culture against the industrial spirit, an attack only decisively rebutted, according to Wiener, by Margaret Thatcher.

The late-nineteenth- and early-twentieth-century "Janeites," the uncritical devotees of Austen and the world she was thought to represent, saw Austen's supposed limitations of social scope and psychological depth to be strengths, something peculiarly "English." More important, such devotees often held important positions in governmental, cultural, and educational institutions. They found in Austen a vision of "Englishness" they were looking for and applied to Britain and its empire. Reaction against this complacent late-imperial, anti-industrial culture generated new approaches to and understanding of Austen, especially after the unprecedented horror of World War I and with the rise of professionalized, university-based criticism.

In broad terms social historians were exploding the popular myth of an idyllic, preindustrial, Austenian world. R. W. Chapman's critical editions of Austen's novels, early writings, and letters made available materials for better understanding Austen in her own time as well as critical analysis that was more searching than the "appreciations" characteristic of earlier, "Janeite" criticism. J. David Grey and Deirdre La Faye's forthcoming, revised and expanded edition of Austen's letters will make still more information available. Mary Lascelles, Q. D. Leavis, D. W. Harding, and others showed Austen as a determined, conscious artist and social critic.

After World War II and the further democratization of education, especially at the higher levels, Austen and her work were interpreted in the light of new social issues, including class conflict, feminism, and anti-imperialism. Austen has even become one of the few novelists to have a concordance to her works. Meanwhile, Austen's fiction had served for some time as one model for an emergent form of popular novel known as the "Regency romance." Enterprising writers undertook to "complete" Austen's unfinished works such as *The Watsons* and *Sanditon*. It is true that Austen has not yet been fully accepted as a "Romantic" writer, and as recently as 1975 Alistair M. Duckworth could write, "In spite of a staggering amount of critical attention Jane Austen can hardly be said, in her bicentennial year, to be understood better than she understood herself" ("Prospects and Retrospects," in *Jane Austen Today*). At the same time, as Duckworth goes on to illustrate, Austen's work has been profitably explored in light of recent critical and literary theory, and determined exploration of Austen's relation to her contemporary novelists and contemporary issues is making possible new understandings of her and her work in her time, thus providing new ways of understanding her importance in the present.

The Plenary this morning featured Claudia Johnson, on Can We Ever have Enough of Jane Austen? Professor Johnson, chairman of Princeton University's English Department and author of several books of Austen scholarship (and especially appreciated by this blog writer for her "Jane Austen: Women, Politics and the Novel"), is always a delight at the AGMs and she did not disappoint in Chicago! Focusing on textual criticism, Dr. Johnson told of her experience in editing a new edition of Mansfield Park and the "dilemma of a comma" – in the two editions of MP published during Austen's lifetime in 1814 and 1816, there is a discrepancy in the placement of a comma – is this the publisher's handiwork, a printing error, or more importantly an editing change by Austen herself? In comparing this textual analysis to one of the many variants in Shakespeare's Hamlet, Johnson showed us the process of editing and the importance of a misplaced comma in the comprehension of a single sentence. Eventually Johnson "conjures" Austen herself, when in the quiet of her study, she hears "an intake of breath," a ghostly Jane telling of the errant comma's intended placement.

Johnson went on the discuss this "channeling Austen" and how the various biographers – Constance Hill in Jane Austen's homes and haunts, Oscar Fay Adam's view that Austen's characters are alive, and how Janeites are often referred to as being "possessed" or "manical" and PROUD OF IT!, and how we strive to "collapse the distance" between us and Austen with our gatherings, our Regency balls, banquets and the making of reticules.

So much humour in this talk! – lost in translation I am afraid, but the packed house was nearly rolling in the aisles at some of her allusions! I was a tad spooked because my daughter had just left me phone message doing a little "channeling' of her own – Austen in heaven most appreciative that I was at her conference and babbling on about her lively discussions with Shakespeare (in and out of bed I might add, though I shouldn't!) and how heaven was indeed a grand place for these literary giants – (my daughter is a middle school English teacher and thus goes to great imaginative lengths!) – so how timely and unnerving to head into Johnson's talk on conjuring Austen! Yikes! Next up another Breakout Session, this time to the talk on Shades of Jane Austen in Ian McEwan's *Atonement* by Juliette Wells.As many of you might not know, the epigraph to *Atonement* is Henry Tilney's "voluntary spies" speech to Catherine in Northanger Abbey.

McEwan has said he has an affinity to Austen but cites no specifics in his works, so Wells tellingly does it for him: the likeness of Briony as Austen herself, the precocious child writer; the family theatricals; the play "The Trials of Arabella" had similar versions in Austen's juvenilia; the name of "Tilney's Hotel;" etc. Wells then discussed aspects of the film that also invoke Austen, and though there are no specific references, Austen pervades the movie in a number of ways, both visually and thematically: Joe Wright directed this and the 2005 P&P; Kiera Knightly stars in both; James McAvoy starred as Austen's "boyfriend" in Becoming Jane; Brenda Blethyn as Mrs. Bennet and as Robbie Turner's mother; both productions had the same costume designer and the same soundtrack composer (Dario Marianelli); similar kissing scenes; the appearance of the PIGS...all these visuals are very powerful with their oblique references.

I loved Atonement, both book and movie, and found this talk most interesting...I hope it is published in Persuasions, so those not there can enjoy it as well. Off next to Poster Session 2 (I missed Session 1 due to meetings) – this is a new feature at the AGMs and quite wonderful. I visited several of the presentations: delighted to meet Maggie Sullivan of Austenblog, who had a board filled with Blogging Jane; Elaine Bander of Montreal had posted a series of thoughts on comparing Susanna Clarke's 2004 fantasy novel Jonathan Strange & Mr. Norrell to Austen's world (this book had been sitting on my bedside table for way too long- indeed because it IS way too long!...I now have the incentive to pick it up finally, despite its "dark forces of Magic"); loved the How Not to Write an Austen-Inspired Novel (see photo) by Karen Doornebos; and a pleasure to meet and discuss Persuasions and Persuasions On-Line with editor Susan Allen Ford; tons of photos to-be-adored of Colin Firth et.al in Mr. Darcy as an Actor by Katherine Zimolzak; and several others. I very much liked this poster session idea, though I quibble that the presenters had to get it all up and down within a 3-hour period...I realise there was a space problem, so for future AGMs it would be nice to have these set up and left for perusal during the 3 days with their creators needing to be there for only a few hours.

They were too interesting a visual treat (not to mention a lot of work!) to not be enjoyed for longer (and so sorry that I completely missed the first group.) I understand that this was William Philips's idea, so kudos to him for a very informative addition to the meeting!

Henry's speech in NA (one of my favourites!) and Edward Ferrars in S&S on his ignorance of the Picturesque (Edward at his funniest and I think often overlooked in the general view that Edward is a bore); in P&P, Elizabeth's journey to Derbyshire exactly follows Gilpin's; how the description of Lyme Regis in Persuasion reads almost like a travelogue and so unlike Austen; how Austen's character's view of nature and the landscape conveys to the reader who they are almost as much as their dialogue; and finally, how all the successful proposal scenes are all OUTSIDE in the open air All was presented with visuals of the various landscapes, with back and forth talk and citing passages from the novels. Again, hoping this will appear in print!

Phew! On to the next...with barely a moment for a breath or lunch, but cannot miss a Plenary with the crowd-pleasing Joan Ray! Like Johnson, Ray never disappoints, and today she was a hoot! Fully dressed in Doctor garb, " Doctor of Austenology" embroidered on her white coat, Ray launched into an update of the old board game "Operation" and in a play on her own book Jane Austen for Dummies, she regaled us with Jane Austen for Smarties! Working through some of the earliest writings on Austen, both biographical and critical,

Ray singles out those who most understood Austen: George Lewes (whose blurb for *Sense & Sensibility* in an 1897 Bentley's publisher ad was erroneously attributed to George Eliot); Margaret Oliphant, author of 98 novels and a foresighted feminist critic; Richard Simpson who early on detected Austen's humour, irony and mockery and her emphasis on rational love over romantic love; Mrs. Humphey Ward; and of course Mark Twain, though often quoted for disliking Austen with a vengeance, does say how "every time I read P&P...". Ray ends with summarizing her five points that if you understand this about Austen you will officially be a JA Smartie:

- Her skill in creating life-like characters
- Dramatic presentation: her characters are revealed through dialogue
- Her feminine cynicism her social criticism through satire – irony and humour
- Her self-restraint: she never wrote a throwaway line

and all this presented with the naked (though discreetly-covered!) "Operation" doll peering at us through the joys of Power-point!

Another breakout session (are you completely exhausted yet?...and my son always questions me "whatever can you talk about for 4 days when she only wrote SIX books?")...can people not know that you can have a very powerful discussion on the mere placement of a COMMA?

So off to hear one of my favourites Elaine Bander from Montreal. I have attended Elaine's talks at every AGM I have gone to because she is so accessible...she says what I am thinking, but so much better! Her talk today on The Challenge of Reading Jane Austen Reading posits that Austen's genius as a writer was due to her being a reader, and understanding her works presumes a familiarity with those traditions. Austen's books challenge us and either a careless reading of the novels or any of the film adaptations do not and cannot meet this challenge (excepting perhaps "Clueless" which succeeds in reimaging Emma.)

Austen came of age with the English novel and while

invoking the conventions, she then undermines them: Northanger Abbey is her obvious teasing take on them all and introduces Catherine at the outset to undercut the expected work featuring the "beautiful modest heroine, the recognized hero, the obstacles in their way, the fall of the suitor, the melodramatic rescue, and the requisite happy ending." The narrator reminds the reader that Catherine is not going to fulfill any of these conventions, all the while introducing them in part.

We are given Willoughby, Frank Churchill, Henry Crawford and Wickham in her other works and are led to believe that they are the heroes, only to have romantic expectations played with (but even in S&S Elinor is still left feeling a pang for the cad Willoughby after his late-night confessing his love for Marianne); Emma is reading everyone's lives but her own in a romantic cliché, with Harriet as the burlesque of the heroine – as Bander says so well, "Austen cuts her cloth on the bias."

And then finally, as everyone seems to do because they are so much with us, Bander refers to the films and their inability to convey this: with the loss of the narrative voice and the putting of these novel clichés back in to the visual telling, the films become standardized versions and we lose our own view of the story and the author's intention. Bander references here Austen's Plan of the Novel, her complete spoof on what she will not put to paper though all around her clamor for these traditions.

One of course is missing so many other sessions, equally interesting...a perfect example of needing to clone oneself. My friend Sara and I try to go to different sessions at these meetings so we can share our notes, but alas! at this AGM we found ourselves wanting to go to almost all the same sessions, and in the end a useless exercise as Sara does not take notes! So the evening awaits! The Banquet and the Ball, a walk down Michigan Avenue and an Evening talk on Romance!

There were more costumes at this AGM than ever seen before (there were rentals available and many took advantage)... last year I promised that I would make a dress and pelisse but got only as far as purchasing the pattern, so perhaps next year?

So off to dinner, a lovely event with all the details of setting up an AGM all around us: the table settings, centerpieces, place-cards, etc... with the hours of work behind it all most appreciated... I scouted out Lorraine Hanaway, former JASNA president and lately at one of our Vermont meetings to share about the beginnings of the Society...I was so pleased to see her honoured for being the "fourth" founding member of JASNA.

After dinner chat with seat mates, always a treat to reconnect and make new friends, and then off for the walk down Michigan Avenue. If anything could stop traffic in Chicago, it would be hundreds of Regency-costumed, Austen-crazed attendees promenading along this main thoroughfare, walkers and drivers all agape...it was quite the scene! And I was lucky enough to spot the lovely "Jane Austen Addict" Laurie Viera Rigler!

Jane Austen was born in the village of Steventon, Hampshire in 1775, within five years of Wordsworth and Scott. She was the seventh of eight children. Her father, George, had been a Fellow of St. John's College, Oxford and lately Rector of Steventon. Her mother, Cassandra, nee Leigh, came from an ancient family, linked to the Leighs of Stonehill Abbey in Warwickshire. Jane and her sister, also Cassandra, were sent to school in Oxford and Southampton, before attending the Abbey School in Reading, and were encouraged to write from an early age. Jane started writing novels in 1790, at the age of only 14, while she was living in Steventon, although her first novel to be published, *Sense and Sensibility*, did not appear until 1811.

Although her early life appeared secure enough, it was touched by tragedy. Her cousin, Eliza Hancock, married a French nobleman, who was arrested and guillotined on his return to Paris soon after the French Revolution. Her aunt, Mrs. Leigh Perrot, was arrested when falsely accused of stealing a card of lace, and suffered eight months imprisonment with the threat of the death penalty, before she was able to prove her innocence.

On her father's retirement, in 1801, the family moved to Bath. Jane's years at Bath were not happy. The family made acquaintances, but few friends. Their stay at Bath was broken up by annual excursions to the seaside: to Sidmouth, Dawlish and Lyme Regis. As was the custom, the sons of the family pursued careers (two of Jane's brothers joined the Navy), while the daughters stayed at home, awaiting marriage and involving themselves with domestic affairs.

A neighbour from their Hampshire days, Harris Bigg-Wither of Manydown Park (Wootton St. Lawrence) asked Jane to marry him in the Winter of 1802. Though she initially accepted, a sleepless night saw the poor man turned down the following morning.

In several of Jane's letters from Bath to her sister, Cassandra, one senses her frustration at this sheltered existence.

Tuesday, 12 May 1801. "Another stupid party...with six people to look on, and talk nonsense to each other".

Some time after the death of Jane's father in 1805, the family left Bath to stay with Jane's brother, Frank, who was stationed at the Naval Dockyard, in Southampton. Jane's brother, Edward, had been formally adopted by a rich and childless relative, which led to his elevation as a country gentleman. Cassandra had been sent to assist with his domestic arrangements at Godmersham Park, near Canterbury. He also owned Chawton House, Hampshire and in 1809 offered a home to his mother and sisters on the estate there. The family settled happily and it was here that Jane was to enjoy the success of the publication of her first novel. Initially, the secret of their authorship was kept, the author being referred to only as "a lady", but later, her proud brother, Henry, let it be known and she became instantly famous.

Her last completed novel, *Persuasion,* was not published until after her death. By the time of its completion, she was seriously ill and not expected to live. During the last few weeks of her life, she lived in College Street, Winchester, to be close to her physician. She died in Cassandra's arms in Winchester at the age of 41. The family exercised the right, as members of a clergyman's family, that she should be buried in Winchester Cathedral.

Today, the museum at Chawton is visited by Jane Austen admirers from across the Globe. There are many mementoes of her life on display. Jane's mother and her beloved sister, Cassandra are buried in the churchyard.

The Novels

"Sense and Sensibility":published 1811
"Pride and Prejudice": published 1813
"Mansfield Park": published 1813
"Emma":published 1816
"Persuasion":published 1818
"Northanger Abbey":published 1818.

Jane Austen started to write at a time when the Romantic Movement was expressing its passionate involvement with the landscape, in particular, the melancholic aspects of gothic ruins, and the natural world in general. She was one of the few writers to adopt an irreverent attitude to this obsession. Edward Ferrars, speaking to the impressionable Marianne, in *"Sense and Sensibility"*, admits his confusion when attempting to describe a picturesque landscape and when Henry Tilney decides to lecture on the picturesque to Catherine, in *"Northanger Abbey,"* she "was so hopeful a scholar that when they gained the top of Beechen Cliff, she voluntarily rejected the whole city of Bath, as unworthy to make part of a landscape".

In many ways, Jane Austen's detached, ironic style was an antithesis of the Romantic ideal. Many people have commented on the modernity of her novels. Elizabeth Bowen in *English Novelists* (Collins, 1946), suggests this comment is "an agreeable way of saying that she is still some distance ahead of us". She followed in the wake of the success of Fielding and Richardson and her sense of comedy and style has been likened to that of Fielding. She is noted for the precision of her observations. Her attention to detail is a means to enlighten a subject. As Elizabeth Bowen notes, "she applies big truths to little scenes".

Chapter 4

Cognitive Science to See Jane Austen Veiw

Something happened to the novel "around the time of Jane Austen" (vii) argues George Butte in his compelling reintroduction of Maurice Merleau-Ponty's discourse on phenomenology into contemporary literary and film studies, I Know That You Know That I Know: Narrating Subjects from Moll Flanders to Marnie. English writers began to portray a multiply-layered and mutually-reflecting subjectivity, deep intersubjectivity, a "change so subtle and fundamental that it has been difficult to conceive and describe", particularly as today we take its impact for granted in the prose of George Eliot, Henry James, James Joyce, Virginia Woolf, Vladimir Nabokov, Ian McEwan, and others.

Butte defines deep intersubjectivity as the web of partially interpenetrating consciousnesses that exists wherever perceiving subjects, that is, human beings, collect. [T]he process begins when a self perceives the gestures, either of body or word, of another consciousness, and it continues when the self can perceive in those gestures an awareness of her or his own gestures.

Subsequently the self, upon revealing a consciousness of the other's response, perceives yet another gesture responding to its response, so that out of this conversation of symbolic behaviours emerges a web woven from elements of mutually exchanged consciousnesses. For a vivid early example of deep intersubjectivity, Butte turns to the episode in Austen's Persuasion, in which Anne Elliot witnesses a silent but poignant communication between her former suitor, Frederick Wentworth, and her sister, Elizabeth, who run into each other in Molland's bakery shop:

It did not surprise, but it grieved Anne to observe that Elizabeth would not know [Wentworth]. She saw that he saw Elizabeth, that Elizabeth saw him, that there was complete internal recognition on each side; she was convinced that he was ready to be acknowledged as an acquaintance, expecting it, and she had the pain of seeing her sister turn away with unalterable coldness.

According to Butte, When Anne Elliot watches Wentworth and Elizabeth negotiating complex force fields of memory and protocol, the enabling strategy of her story is a new layering of human consciousness, or a new representation of those subjectivities as layered in a specific way. Deep intersubjectivity has made its appearance in storytelling in modern culture, and it has altered our sense of self and community and the discourses that construct and reflect them.

Was Austen the first English writer to construct deeply intersubjective passages? According to Butte, some of her eighteenth-century predecessors came close to but stopped short of exploring the rich possibilities opened by having a character perceive the reaction of another character to the first character's mental state. In the novels of Defoe, Richardson, Fielding, and Burney, the "encounter with the other never moves beyond a two-layer exchange to multiple negotiations and perceptions," whereas in Austen the scenes "about the observation of observations" give voice to a "new way of shaping narrative".

Butte's argument thus supports the critical view that Austen was profoundly innovative in her treatment of fictional consciousnesses, a view that gets obscured when her novels are treated as archetypes of the genre. Moreover, his exploration of mutually reflecting fictional subjectivities turns out to dovetail research in evolutionary psychology that focuses on cognitive challenges of processing multiple mental states embedded within each other. In other words, although Butte does not position himself as working within the new field known as cognitive approaches to literature, (1) his argument provides a crucial first step for recognizing Austen's prose as actively experimenting with readers' cognition. The goal of the present essay is to articulate this interdisciplinary potential of the concept of deep intersubjectivity and, more broadly, to demonstrate how a cognitive approach encourages us to see fictional narratives as engaging our evolved cognitive adaptations: playing with these adaptations and pushing them beyond their zones of comfort.

To speak of mental states in works of fiction, we need to borrow from cognitive science the concept of Theory of Mind. Cognitive psychologists and philosophers of mind use this term interchangeably with mind-reading to refer to our ability to explain observable behaviour in terms of underlying thoughts, feelings, desires, and intentions (for example, we see somebody reaching for a cup of water and immediately assume that she is thirsty).

We attribute mental states to others and to ourselves all the time. Our attributions are frequently incorrect (for example, the person who reached for the cup of water might have done it for reasons other than being thirsty); still, reading minds is the default way by which we construct and navigate our social environment. When Theory of Mind is impaired, as it is in varying degrees in the case of autism and schizophrenia, communication breaks down.

Cognitive evolutionary psychologists working with mind-reading adaptations think that they may have developed during the "massive neurocognitive evolution" that took place during the Pleistocene (1.8 million to 10,000 years ago). The emergence of Theory of Mind was evolution's answer to the "staggeringly complex" challenge faced by our ancestors, who needed to make sense of the behaviour of other people in their group, which could include up to two hundred individuals. As Simon Baron-Cohen points out, "attributing mental states to a complex system (such as a human being) is by far the easiest way of understanding it," that is, of "coming up with an explanation of the complex system's behaviour and predicting what it will do next". In other words, mind-reading is both predicated on the intensely social nature of our species and makes this intense social nature possible.

Lest this argument strike you as circular, think of our legs: their shape is both predicated upon the evolution of our species' locomotion and makes our present locomotion possible. Note that the words theory in Theory of Mind and reading in mind-reading are potentially misleading because they seem to imply that we attribute states of mind intentionally and consciously. In fact, it might be difficult for us to appreciate at this point just how much mind-reading takes place on the level inaccessible to our consciousness. For it seems that while our perceptual systems "eagerly" register the information about people's bodies and their facial expressions, they do not necessarily make all that information available to us for our conscious interpretation.

Think of the intriguing functioning of the so-called "mirror neurons." Studies of imitation in monkeys and humans have discovered a "neural mirror system that demonstrates an internal correlation between the representations of perceptual and motor functionalities". What this means is that "an action is understood when its observation causes the motor system of the observer to 'resonate.'" So when you observe someone else grasping a cup, the "same population of neurons that control the execution of grasping movements becomes active in [your own] motor areas" (Rizzolatti et al. 662). At least on some level, your brain does not seem to distinguish between your actions and a person you observe doing them.

In other words, our neural circuits are powerfully attuned to the presence, behaviour, and emotional display of other members of our species. This attunement begins early (since some form of it is already present in newborn infants) and takes numerous nuanced forms as we grow into our environment. We are intensely aware of the body language and facial expressions of other people, even if the full extent and significance of such awareness escapes us. Moreover, as I have argued elsewhere, the workings of our Theory of Mind make literature as we know it possible (Why We Read Fiction,

10.) The very process of making sense of what we read appears to be grounded in our ability to invest the flimsy verbal constructions that we generously call "characters" with a potential for a variety of thoughts, feelings, and desires and then to look for the "cues" that would allow us to guess at their feelings and thus predict their actions. Literature pervasively capitalizes on and stimulates our Theory of Mind adaptations that had evolved to deal with real people, even as on some level readers do remain aware that fictive characters are not real people at all.

Research and publications on Theory of Mind grow apace, but for the purposes of this essay, I want to focus on one particular line of that research, which explores our ability to process multiply embedded states of mind, as in, "I know that you know that I know that.... "Evolutionary psychologist Robin Dunbar and his colleagues have demonstrated that we have marked difficulties processing units of information that embed more than four recursive mental states. After the fourth level, our understanding plummets sixty per cent. For a brief illustration, look at the following three sentences (the words that describe mental states are italicized):

- I find Butte's argument compelling on its own terms and also full of exciting possibilities when considered in the context of recent research on Theory of Mind and its implications for literary studies.
- I thought that she wanted me to think that she liked what I was saying, so I pretended not to notice that her eyes glazed over now and then.
- I thought that she wanted me to think that she liked that I believed that she was interested in what I was saying."

It may be possible to do without dancing entirely. Instances have been known of young people passing many, many months successively, without being at any ball of any description, and no material injury accrue either to body or mind;—but when a beginning is made—when the felicities of rapid motion have once been, though slightly, felt—it must be a very heavy set that does not ask for more. (*Emma* 246)

Jane Austen was an enthusiastic dancer in her youth, and dancing forms an important part of all of her fictional heroine's lives. From her use of dance in the novels, we can obtain a better glimpse of how dances in middle class life in the late eighteenth and early nineteenth centuries were conducted, so that the six novels become an useful source document for the dance historian. In addition, when general readers learn more about the common dances of the period and the social conventions around them, they will be in a better position to understand some of the delicate nuances of the pivotal dancing episodes in each of the novels.

In eighteenth-century fiction, as well as in life, there was a wide range of venues for dances, several different types of dances and various social behaviours appropriate at or for each. Perhaps the highest was at Almack's of London, which Austen never described and probably never attended, since the tickets of admission were jealously guarded by the six lady patronesses. (One could imagine that Sir Walter and Miss Elliot would have loved to attend Almack's, but the Elliots would probably be considered too provincial to attend; only Mr. and Mrs. Darcy belong to the proper social sphere.)

Instead, Austen shows us private London parties and balls, such as those given by Sir John and Lady Middleton; public dances at the Bath Assembly Rooms, such as those that Catherine Morland attends; a gentleman's private country house ball, such as that given by Mr. Bingley at Netherfield; and informal family dances, held after dinner to the playing of one amateur musician, such as those held in the Musgrove's parlor. Certain dances might be performed more often at one event than another, and certain behaviours might be more or less desirable at each of these events, yet the same individual could—with the possible exception of visiting Almack's—feel comfortable dancing at each of them.

In order to understand Austen's use of dance in her novels, let us begin with some general statements about the ballroom in the last quarter of the eighteenth century. In the 1770s, a formal Assembly in London or Bath would open with a series of minuets, the French dance for one couple at a time.

The rest of the participants would sit on benches that lined the room and watch, as couple after couple would apply to the Master of Ceremonies for permission to dance. At Bath and other towns where older people congregated, a ball would continue to be opened by at least one minuet during even the early years of the nineteenth century. The dance was definitely antiquated, even in Austen's youth, however, and none of her heroines seem to know it. Instead, they enjoy the more social country dances. Country dances had had a peculiarly English character since the publication of John Playford's *The English Dancing Master* in 1651. Dances for two, three, four or more couples at a time, they were more lively and relaxed than the complex French dances like the minuet, the boure or the louvre. By the late eighteenth century, most country dances were performed in a "longways" set for five to eight couples, with partners standing opposite each other.

Dances were usually performed in what are today called "triple minor longways" sets. That is, the dance began with only the first couple starting at the top and dancing with couples two and three. At the end of one turn through the dance the first couple progressed to dance with couples three and four, while couple two waited or "stood out" at the top of the set for two more turns of the dance until they, too, had an opportunity to begin dancing.

Because so many couples stood relatively passively during the dance, they used this time as a welcome opportunity to talk and flirt—as many dancing masters, who preferred attentive silence, pointed out with indignation. The dance would continue until the original first couple had worked its way back to the "top" or the beginning of the set. Couples who danced down the set but then walked away to sit down rather than performing their social duty as inactive couples working up the set were considered selfish and disrespectful.

The romantic sensibilities embraced by Marianne Dashwood expressed themselves on the dance floor as well as in the music and literature she loved: angular lines were condemned and only curves were considered worthy of admiration. In fact, Mr. Wilson, a dancing master, criticized certain common country dance figures, such as "lead down the middle and up again" or "lead out to the wall and back" on the grounds that they were angular and dull. "Straight lines are useful," he noted, "but not elegant; and, when applied to the Human Figure, are productive of an extremely ungraceful effect".

On the other hand, curving movements such as the weaving hey or the "turn partner and then corner" figure were admired. "With persons of taste, and true judges of beauty, the gently flowing Serpentine and Curved Lines, form the *acme* of grace and have always been considered most beautiful," Wilson wrote. He further urged his readers and pupils to learn to present objects, such as a dropped glove, fan, ticket or card of address, with a beautiful and elegant curve to the arm, thereby affording the observer "ample means of drawing comparison between the accomplished and the uncultivated".

Over the two hundred or so years of their general popularity, country dances could be performed with or without steps, as the period, the venue, or the dexterity of the performer might call for. For example, we know that Fanny, in a state "approaching high spirits," "[practiced] her steps about the drawing-room as long as she could be safe from the notice of her Aunt Norris" (*MP* 273). With the addition of the steps (similar in this period to modern Scottish country dance steps) and with a spirited tempo, country dances could be quite vigorous and were suited mostly for the young and fit: "When [Fanny's] two dances with [Edmund] were over, her inclination and strength for more were pretty well at an end; and Sir Thomas having seen her walk rather than dance down the shortening set, breathless and with her hand at her side, gave his orders for her sitting down entirely. From that time, Mr. Crawford sat down likewise". The choice of the steps used, and the execution of them, was another test of the taste, skill—and character—of the performer.

For still in Regency as in former times, it was felt that the skill of a person's dancing expressed the quality of his or her soul or spirit. Today we do not measure our leaders of government or industry by their ability to dance—but a clearly traceable precept from Renaissance times through the Regency was this concept that one measure of determining whether a man was truly a gentleman was by his ability to dance with confidence, to stand well, to move easily without calling attention to himself, to enter a room gracefully. Clumsiness, haughtiness, and ostentatious display were to be avoided, as another dancing master, Mr. Barclay Dun, noted:

There are many who imagine that he is the best of dancers who can leap so high as to be able to cross his legs several times before he falls, and spring or bound to an amazing distance forward, backward, or to either side. That such a person may be the most powerful of men, I readily allow; but with no other qualifications than his strength and agility, he can never hope to obtain the suffrages of those who are skilled in the art: indeed, *people of refined and delicate feeling, would reject his exhibitions with disgust. To be regarded, he must possess that sensibility of soul which enables its possessor to distinguish the true from the false, and to trace out the way of perfection.* (8; emphasis added)

Austen demonstrated this precept that gentlemanly behaviour and style were both expressed in dancing several times. When the obsequious Sir William Lucas attempts to compliment Mr. Darcy, he says: "'I have been most highly gratified indeed, my dear Sir. Such very superior dancing is not often seen. *It is evident that you belong to the first circles*'" (*P&P* 92; emphasis added). While his words are silly and his timing poor, the expression of his gallantry would have been easily recognized by contemporary readers. Yet, by eighteenth century standards, Mr. Darcy by his haughty behaviour and previous refusals to dance has amply demonstrated that he considers himself above his company. The more amiable Mr. Bingley, who "danced every dance", has behaved in a more gentlemanly fashion.

Another example of this belief that one sure sign of a gentleman is his ability to dance and move well occurs in *Emma*, when the heroine (who has unaccountably reached her eighteenth birthday without ever having had an opportunity to see Mr. Knightly dance) observes his performance:

[Mr. Knightley] moved a few steps nearer, and *those few steps were enough to prove in how gentlemanlike a manner, with what natural grace, he must have danced, would he but take the trouble....* [Eventually he does dance, and] *His dancing proved to be just what she had believed it, extremely good....* (325-26, 328; emphasis added)

Assemblies or balls were conducted with great formality. The most important lady present—distinguished by rank, debutante, or bridal status—opened the ball by dancing at the top of the first set in the room. Thus we hear of Miss Elliot that "thirteen winters' revolving frosts had seen her opening every ball of credit which a scanty neighborhood afforded" (*P* 7). Austen shows us this common convention in several more dramatic episodes: for example, in one novel, the heroine expects to open the ball but doesn't, and in another, she doesn't but does. It is Emma, of course, who is foiled—"Emma must submit to stand second to [the newly-wed] Mrs. Elton, though she had always considered the ball as peculiarly for her. It was almost enough to make her think of marrying'—and it is Fanny who is honoured by standing with Mr. Crawford at the top of the room, to be joined by the rest of the dancers.

At more formal or more public balls, the ladies could "draw for numbers" upon entering the ballroom. As each dance began, the Master of Ceremonies would then call out the numbers and assign the ladies and their partners to places. The topmost lady in the first set would choose the dance. This meant that a couple could ask for the specific figures associated with a specific tune, such as Bath Assembly, Trip to Tunbridge or The Duke of Kent's Waltz. It also meant that a lady could announce a group of figures that she devised herself and ask for a tune of a certain length to accompany them. At the conclusion of the dance, the Master of Ceremonies would reshuffle the sets, and a new lady would request or "call" a dance. While this procedure may sound daunting, in any given evening, dances were probably chosen from a fairly small pool of what were considered to be the most fashionable dances for any given year. This practice was facilitated, or perhaps fostered, by the custom of music publishers to produce slim annual collections of dances, such as "Twenty Four Country Dances for the Year 17—."

These volumes all promised to include only the latest and most fashionable dances, though many of them did include reprints of earlier dances. These popular books were in fact a necessity: starting in about 1730 or so, country dances became less and less original and were attached or devised to go with a specific and easily recognizable tune. From 1730 to 1830 over twenty-seven thousand country dances with their tunes were published in England alone. The dances had increasingly become combinations and recombinations of a small number of figures so that the dances were not very easily differentiated from each other.

Although easy to learn just by watching the top couple (a characteristic which added to their popularity), they were hard to remember. Indeed, some dancing masters found it necessary to request participants not to dance the same dance more than once in an evening—a sure sign that this proscribed behaviour must have occurred frequently enough to be noticed and criticized. This very popularity of the country dance eventually contributed to its demise. Towards the end of George III's life, even the country dances were finally going out of fashion among the "smart set"; there were too many dull dances set to dull tunes and people were ready for something innovative.

Though the Regency ballroom was dominated by country dances, there were several other major categories of dance that could be seen there: the so-called "Scotch" dances, the quadrille, and the waltz. Starting in the 1780s, a wave of romantic enthusiasm for the culture of the Gaelic North swept over England. Scottish country dances were popular in England, as were the Scotch Threesome and Foursome Reels, which featured a weaving "hey" figure interspersed with points at which performers would perform showy steps. During the course of the dance the men (and occasionally) the ladies would raise one or both arms above their heads, snap their fingers together and give the distinctive yell or "heuch."

In *Pride and Prejudice* Austen shows Scotch dances twice: first at the Lucases, where a large party is assembled. After the ladies perform a few songs, and pedantic Mary bores everyone with a long concerto, she is "glad to purchase praise and gratitude by Scotch and Irish airs, at the request of her younger sisters" who, with some young officers, start dancing at one end of the room, to the indignation of Mr. Darcy. Later, Miss Bingley is playing at Netherfield while Elizabeth visits due to Jane's illness. She plays a "lively Scotch air" and Mr. Darcy draws near and in a clumsy attempt to make conversation asks Elizabeth: "'Do you not feel a great inclination, Miss Bennet, to seize such an opportunity of dancing a reel?'".

Late in the author's life, following the Peace celebrations of 1814, two other dance types became wildly popular which Austen, since her dancing years were behind her, hardly mentions in her novels. These were the quadrille and the waltz. Like the cotillon of Austen's youth, the quadrille was a dance for four couples in a square formation, but, unlike the cotillon, it consisted of, typically, five separate country dance figures, each with a distinctive name and music. Requiring balletic steps and a greater ability to remember the figures (one couldn't just watch the top couple as in a longways line), quadrilles taxed the skills of the dancer. None of Austen's fictional heroines dances a quadrille, though their author was apparently aware of at least the music for them.

The German waltz was known, but was not very popular until 1814, when Wellington's dashing young officers came back from the continent and the lively Countess Lieven, one of the patronesses of Almack's, performed it there. The waltz was considered "fast" because of the close embrace of the partners (a popular position had the partners stand face-to-face, one hand on the shoulder, one around the waist'), and some parents disapproved of it. Even Lord Byron had mixed feelings about the dance:

Endearing Waltz!—to thy more melting tune
Bow Irish jig and ancient rigadoon.
Scotch reels, avaunt! And country-dance, forego
Your future claims to each fantastic toe!
Waltz—Waltz alone—both legs and arms demands,

Liberal of feet and lavish of her hands;
Hands which may freely range in public sight
Where ne'er before—but—pray "put out the light".... (146-50)

The waltz appealed to adherents of the cult of romantic sensibility, as described by the eponymous hero of Goethe's wildly popular novel *The Sorrows of Young Werther*:

"Never had I danced more lightly. I felt myself more than mortal, holding this loveliest of creatures in my arms, flying with her like the wind, till I lost sight of everything else; and—Wilhelm, I vowed at that moment that a girl whom I loved, or for whom I felt the slightest attachment, should never waltz with another, even if it should be my end!".

Given these fervid expressions of romantic sensibility, it is perhaps a shame that Marianne and Willoughby never get the opportunity to enjoy the dance! In fact, Austen mentions the waltz only once, in *Emma,* where Mrs. Weston plays an "irresistible waltz," possibly an air or perhaps or perhaps a country dance in waltz time, which Mr. Wilson tells us he helped to popularize.

While the above section described the dances of the period, Austen's writings depict other conventions of ballroom conduct. For example, just as today, not everyone would dance at an assembly. From Frank Churchill's careful arrangements at the Crown we see that a card room needed to be provided so that the older people could play whist. Supper was an integral part of a ball evening, and a gentleman escorted the lady with whom he last had danced to the supper room where he attended to her needs.

As late as 1778, as seen in Frances Burney's novel *Evelina,* the choice of a partner was excruciatingly important, since one danced with him all evening. By the turn of the century, however, the convention had relaxed to one of standing up for two consecutive dances together. Typically, a gentleman was expected to engage a series of partners, rather than favouring one for the whole evening; however, the romantic and careless Whiloughby and Marianne Dashwood—of whose activities both Eleanor and Austen disapprove—flout this rule by standing up together half the night.

As should be clear by now, an assembly was more than just a dance; it was a prime area for young ladies and gentlemen to get to know each other. Young people were expected to have on hand a repertoire of light conversation, with which to pass the time during the dance while they stood inactive. Readers will remember the lengthy scene in *Pride & Prejudice* where Elizabeth forces Mr. Darcy to speak during the course of their first two dances: "'It is *your* turn to say something now, Mr. Darcy. *I* talked about the dance, and *you* ought to make some kind of remark on the size of the room, or the number of couples'".

Novels, plays, and poems of the past are often fruitful sources for a dance historian to learn more about the attitudes towards or conventions of the dance. Despite the fact that Austen never describes a specific dance, her novels are particularly useful sources, as we have seen. In addition, an understanding of the conventions of the period provides today's readers with a deeper understanding of the characterizations in Jane Austen's works, as illuminated by her dance episodes.

There's An Admirable Sort Of Reader for whom the above question doesn't need asking, since what's been happening to Jane Austen has been happening ever since Walter Scott assured readers that "Those... who delight in the study of human nature, may improve in the knowledge of it, and in the profitable application of that knowledge, by the perusal of such fictions as those before us."

Such general readers find it eminently natural and highly pleasurable to reread the six finished novels at regular intervals, always encountering something to make the latest reading a fresh one.

They may or may not pick up unfinished or unpublished (during her lifetime) works like Lady Susan or The Watsons or Sanditon, and they may or may not be moved to look at recent biographies, the best of which is by Claire Tomalin. But I suspect they will stay clear of the fearful parade of books and essays produced by academic critics of the writer, specialists in this or that area of Austen-work that, in one way or another, those critics will demonstrate to be very "problematic" indeed.

An even more recent biography of her is a mini one by the late Carol Shields, herself a skilled novelist, in the Penguin Lives series, and it may be a good place to begin for readers who never felt impelled to seek out a life of Austen (in my case the disinclination has been similar to not much caring about Shakespeare's life).

Carol Shields won my sympathy early on when she addressed the problem of deciding what to call her subject: The Novelist?; Ms. Austen? ("unthinkable"); Miss Austen (but her sister Cassandra deserves that title). "Jane" is also unsatisfactory, while "Austen on its very own possesses an indelicacy." So we're left with "Jane Austen"-or at least that's the form Shields applies, even though it's politically incorrect not to call her "Austen," since one speaks of "Dickens" or "Trollope." Shields's book puts forward nothing revelatory about her subject (she goes along with Claire Tomalin's suggestion that Jane Austen died of a lymphoma, rather than the Addison's Disease that had been earlier favoured). But I'm in her debt for directing me to Sanditon, the novelistic fragment Austen gave up on three months before she died, which Shields thinks not only "as vigorous and inventive as her earlier work," but also shows her on the verge of widening her scope as a writer. At any rate, to my fresh, untutored eyes Sanditon's twelve chapters contain some of the finest and funniest comedy in all of Jane Austen's work.

You would never gather that, however, from rereading the pages on Sanditon that conclude William H. Galperin's The Historical Austen.3 "The Body in Persuasion and Sanditon" (watch out for anyone writing about The Body these days) is the last of eight chapters written throughout in an absolutely jawbreaking idiom and a manner of nothing less than wall-to-wall solemnity. Mr. Galperin is intelligent, a scholar, has read every previous book about his subject and a good many besides, but his insights tend to get expressed in a style like the following from the Sanditon chapter:

In raising the spectre of the antireal, particularly as a

contestional mode where realism is concerned, I am not suggesting that probabilistic fiction maintains a referentiality independent of either contrivance or of the many complications that language as an arbitrary and figurative apparatus, brings to any verbal act. I am suggesting only... (etc.)

I worked hard at this book but kept breaking down at moments like the following, only part of a much longer sentence:

... so her project overall is virtually suspended between certain generic imperatives, the majority clustering around free indirect discourse as an armature of the realistic imagination, and a generic memory (for want of a better term) where, in modes ranging from allegory to epistolarity, reading and interpretation may ultimately supersede narrative authority.

"Project," by the way, is another of the dread overused words of which the armature of current literary commentary is enamored. Who would guess from reading such discourse, as the friends of Michel Foucault like to call it, that Sanditon contains perhaps the funniest sequence in all of Jane Austen, as its sensible heroine, Charlotte Heywood, takes tea with the hypochondriacal Parker sisters and their brother, observing the peculiar "enjoyments in Invalidisms" of Arthur Parker and his buttered toast:

... "I hope you will eat some of this Toast," said he, "I reckon myself a very good Toaster; I never burn my Toasts-I never put them too near the Fire at first-& yet, you see, there is not a Corner but what is well browned.-I hope you like dry Toast."-"With a reasonable quantity of Butter spread over it, very much"- said Charlotte-"but not otherwise.-" "No more do I"-said he exceedingly pleased-"We think quite alike there.- So far from dry Toast being wholesome, I think it a very bad thing for the Stomach. Without a little butter to soften it, it hurts the Coats of the Stomach. I am sure it does.-I will have the pleasure of spreading some for you directly-& afterwards I will spread some for myself.-Very bad indeed for the Coats of the Stomach-but there is no convincing some people.-It irritates & acts like a nutmeg grater.-" He could not get command of the Butter however, without a struggle; His Sisters accusing him of eating a great deal too much, & declaring he was not to be trusted; - and he maintaining that he only eat enough to secure the Coats of his Stomach;-& besides, he only wanted it now for Miss Heywood.- Such a plea must prevail, he got the butter & spread away for her with an accuracy of judgement which at least delighted himself; but when her Toast was done, & he took his own in hand, Charlotte c^sup d^ hardly contain herself as she saw him watching his sisters, while he scrupulously scraped off almost as much butter as he put on, & then seize an odd moment for adding a great dab just before it went into his Mouth.

If any literary commentary can rise to the challenge presented by the rich vein of comic humour evident throughout Sanditon, it certainly can't do so in language as employed by Galperin.

In his attempt to read "against the grain" (why is this a good thing to do?) and show how not-enough-noticed aspects of Austen's novels subvert or qualify the "normative momentum of the courtship plot," Galperin is ingenious to the point of absurdity. He discovers, for instance, that the real villain of Sense and Sensibility is Colonel Brandon, since Brandon withholds or "micromanages" information that might have averted particular unfortunate events. Remarkable that it has taken almost two hundred years and tons of writing about the novel for this discovery to have been made. In a like manner, who would have thought (until 2003) to title a chapter about the charming, touching, and earliest of her novels, "Narrative Incompetence in Northanger Abbey"? For Galperin the incompetence partly resides "in the narrator's obtuseness regarding same-sex relations among women in the novel, which variously circumscribe and direct Catherine's affective life." Reading this my eyes excitedly widened, wondering if I had missed something in the novel just reread.

The "obtuseness" partly resides in how the narrator pays insufficient attention to the fact that Catherine Morland and the new friend she meets at Bath, Isabella Thorpe, spend time reading novels together and sharing their enthusiasms for them. It seems that the narrator fails to recognize sufficiently the depth of this same-sex attachment. But according to Galperin it is in Catherine's fondness for Henry Tilney and his sister Eleanor, altogether more worthy figures than the vulgar and unpleasant Isabella Thorpe, that the narrator's (may we not say Jane Austen's?) narrative incompetence most clearly shows itself. Catherine's delight in Eleanor, and her anguish when Isabella arranges an outing that conflicts with Catherine's previously made engagement to go driving with the Tilneys, seems in Galperin's eyes to have little to do with Henry and everything to do with his sister.

He quotes Catherine's pained cry to Isabella: "'This will not do... I cannot submit to this. I must run after Miss Tilney directly and set her right'." For Galperin "there is little doubt that, by comparison to the other pursuit that has preoccupied Austen's narrative thus far, namely the pursuit of a 'single man... in want of a wife' [the allusion is to the opening sentence of Pride and Prejudice], Catherine's following of Eleanor marks an "alterity that the narrator seems unable or unwilling to recognize." It is fitting that this preposterous condescension to Austen's "incompetence" should issue in yet another critical buzzword-"alterity."

Although not his main concern in The Historical Austen, Galperin is happy to contribute to recent sexings-up of the novelist, referring in the Northanger Abbey chapter to "a treatment of the homoerotic bond uniting Mary and Fanny in Mansfield Park." There follows a quotation from the aptly-named Misty G. Anderson, whose article "The Different Sorts of Friendship: Desire in Mansfield Park" finds that this homoerotic bond "emerges as a protest against a narrative mandate of heterosexual closure as well as a social and political act countering the tyranny of the culturally prescribed ending of marriage." Galperin does not, but might well have referred in this "homoerotic" connection to two rather more publicized essays than Misty Anderson's: "Jane Austen and the Masturbating Girl," (in Tendencies, 1993) by Eve Kosofsky Sedgwick, and "Was Jane Austen Gay?" by Terry Castle.4 The vulgarity of Castle's title may perhaps be laid to those at the

London Review of Books where she published a review of Deirdre Le Faye's 1995 edition of Austen's letters.

Noting the intensity of the novelist's feelings for her sister Cassandra and for her niece Fanny Knight (whom Castle says she was infatuated with), Castle nevertheless draws back from making what she calls "the vulgar case for Austen's homoeroticism." In a postcript to the review, she is content only to claim that "the culture at large reinforced-far more than our own culture does today-same-sex intimacy of all kinds." No one is likely to attempt refutation of such a large and vague claim. Sedgwick's title-for which she is indeed responsible, and which surely provided her with a spasm of pleasure, since it would offend "conservative" admirers of Austen-promises much more than, so far as I can see, it performs. She cites a "a particularly devastating bedroom scene" from Sense and Sensibility in which Elinor Dashwood, roused from sleep, finds her sister Marianne in torment, writing a last letter to the Willoughby who has betrayed her.

After treating us to heavy doses of Foucault, Sedgwick compares the Elinor-Marianne scene to a nineteeth-century case history, "Onanism and Nervous Disorders in Two Little Girls," then concludes that "If what defines 'sexual identity' is the impaction of epistemological issues around the core of a particular genital possibility, then the compulsive attention paid by antionanist discourse to disorders of attention makes it a suitable point of inauguration for modern sexuality." Got that, reader? This reader, who didn't get it, lacks the desire even to begin "arguing" with such prose, and so it seems appropriate that eleven years after the essay was published no one to my knowledge has even bothered to "refute" Sedgwick's contention that Marianne Dashwood's "erotic identity" is "that of the masturbating girl."

After the linguistic contortions of Galperin and Sedgwick (Terry Castle, by contrast, writes clearly and wittily), it is a relief to open a book that begins, "All of us who read Jane Austen early-say, at eleven or twelve, the age when she began writing-were lost to the siren lure of her work." Although I don't know who belongs to that crowd of "us" (certainly not me) who began reading her at such an age, the siren voice of D. A. Miller has struck its first note.

Mr. Miller has written about Jane Austen previously-in the first chapter of his first book, Narrative and Its Discontents (1981)-about "narratability" and "closure" in the novels. One feels the presence in that book of Barthes and Foucault, who play a significant part in Miller's thinking about writing and other matters and who are heard from also in his lively and original essays on Dickens, Trollope, and Wilkie Collins in The Novel and the Police (1988).

Then Miller's books became more personal, less academic, indeed saucy, in Bringing out Roland Barthes (1992) and in Place for Us: Essays on the Broadway Musical (1998). The flavour of his increasingly "outrageous" prose may be conveyed by some sentences from the book about musicals-it is filled with the most inward lore about the genre-when he recounts his schoolboy habit of rushing home after classes to belt out musical comedy songs in the basement of the Miller house. (A full-page photo is provided of the young Miller, decked out in a toothy grin and playing the accordion.) He proceeds to affirm the connection between loving musical comedy and being gay, in a paragraph headed, as all the book's paragraphs are, with a bold-faced-type allusion to a song, this one from Carousel-"You're a queer one, Julie Jordan."

To recognize the Broadway musical for one of "the signs," the stupefied audience of network television has become as competent as the professionally trained psychiatrists and literary critics to whom Tennessee Williams once threw a subtly flavored bone when he conveyed the "latent homosexuality" of a character by the fact that as a youth the sweet bird had sung in the chorus of Oklahoma! In the admittedly monstrous case that he isn't gay, the aficionado of the Broadway musical must resign himself to being thought so, or work as hard as Frank Rich to establish his improbable but true sexual orientation.

This is good, strenuous fun, the product of someone who stakes everything on the clever unobvious moves of his original sentences, his Style. I capitalize the word because Miller, in speaking of Jane Austen, does so, calling her the epitome of Style or Austen Style or Absolute Style. In Austen, style is impersonal; No One speaks it; there is no enunciator, no person to be intuited from its matchless sentences.

For Miller and those others in the group of eleven-year-olds who discovered Austen Style in "the creative eye of daydream" we saw ourselves already wielding, already flashing the wondrous brand: saw its brilliant surface dazzle our enemies, and its sharp point, when they persisted in attack, pierce them to the quick: saw, to crown everything, its genius for detachment-for clean cuts-sever us once and forever from all the particulars of who and what we were, including of course those most responsible for the pain of our being thought peculiar.

Better, even, than musical comedy after school in the basement! But then this discovery of Style puts the "boy all wrong," at least so it happened to Boy Miller when he found that Austen Style had, as it were, "put him in a dress," leaving him to make an "asinine transvestite spectacle" of himself that would spell "the most awful social doom imaginable." As a capping anecdote for this "doom," he quotes Leo Bersani's "Is the Rectum a Grave?," an essay containing the "classic putdown" where one gay man exposes another's pretensions to manhood by finding, after having been picked up at the gay bar and taken home to the seducer's flat, the complete works of fane Austen gracing that flat.

Yet it is possible, even exercising the utmost sympathetic recognition for Miller's jouissance, to wonder exactly what it all has to do with the secret of Style in Jane Austen. Late in the short book's final chapter, Miller confesses to practicing "ever-necessary watchfulness" in the fear that his own literary style will betray itself, will commit some "scarlet illiteracy" or "ludicrous suggestion of the signifier" that, having caught such a lapse in himself, will make him feel "the full force of the shame I imagine I would have felt if I hadn't." But then the watchfulness in turn needs to be watched, since "where style is concerned, neither must one be too careful, nor the desired effect will rigidify into affectation, a manner that, like certain muscular spasms, chokes the underlying nerve."

From the sentences I've quoted thus far, it may be agreed that "arch" is a feeble word to characterize Miller's full-time effort at practicing a writing so "close" (he is in favour of close reading) that affectation (or archness) will be totally absent. Readers of the book will decide for themselves the degree of his success; but it (the style) does threaten more than once to usher, ever so elegantly, Jane Austen into a back seat.

From the outset, Miller is determined to go too far in his self-presentation as Austenphile ("Enough! or Too Much"- William Blake), and the following sentences seem wilfully determined to make his critical audience a very exclusive one indeed:

I have so far presented the feminizing shame of Style (a shame that Style at once incurs and inflicts) as a very narrowly distributed abjection, peculiar to the minuscule band of juvenile Austen readers by whom it is first sustained, or to the closed company of the gay subculture in which it is post-traumatically confessed and mimed. A vulgar psychological reading might even find it most relevantly peculiar to myself, whose interest in Austen and the question of (her) Style would be reducible to this "personal" history.

One wonders just how vulgarly psychological such an inference would be? (I must confess this "reading" occurred to me.) He continues:

One way or another, in short, this question must seem circumscribed within the already vehemently circumscribed social category of the male homosexual; it is his "thing" or not even that: his thingy. Miller's thingy receives most extended display in the twenty pages that follow this claim and provide a fiercely close reading of a scene in Sense and Sensibility where Elinor and Marianne (mainly Elinor) observe, in a London shop, a young man later identified as the despicable Robert Ferrars (brother to good Edward), who inspects at great length a number of toothpick cases while remaining impervious to the sisters waiting to carry out an errand of their own. But Robert does give them a few broad stares, enough to imprint on Elinor's mind a person and face "of strong, natural, sterling insignificance, though adorned in the first style of fashion."

Miller emphasizes the brutality of style with which Robert Ferrars is presented, then goes on at length to read the whole thing in sexual terms. Robert is "almost a gay man"; the "cause of Elinor's animus is the insignificance with which Robert afflicts one thing in particular: male heterosexuality"; his "fetishistic to-do over a mere toothpick... hints perhaps that he can't perform with a woman"; his attitude is "unheterosexual"; his manner is a "little bit of protohomosexuality." Summing up: "Having entirely given up virility, the various behaviours that give masculinity its content, he has nonetheless retained the phallus that gives them their ideal form." Where does all this come from? When a bit later Elinor is introduced to Robert Ferrars, his manner assures her "that he was exactly the coxcomb she had heard him described to be."

A good strong depreciatory word, coxcomb, but evidently not strong enough to bear the heavy freight Miller invests the scene and character with. This is not to disparage the effort, just to respond to Miller's boldly unqualified conviction that the secret of Austen Style can only be discovered through what looks to me like sex overkill. His book is at his best when it proceeds, as in the following passage, to show how Austen Style presupposes and enforces, its author's own under-representability, a condition I can describe most simply... by observing that the realism of her works allows no one like Jane Austen to appear in them. Amid the happy wives and pathetic old maids, there is no successful unmarried woman.... The social grounding is insufficient not of course for this woman to exist-she does, she is Jane Austen-but to entitle her existence to the same dignity of novelistic representation that she gives Elizabeth and Emma, or even Mrs. Elton and Lady Bertram. Like the Unheterosexual, the Spinster too resorts to Style, the Utopia of those with almost no place to go.

Excellently said, until perhaps the final sentence where the "like" induces a bit of discomfort. Miller's discussions of

Pride and Prejudice, Emma ("the melancholy of Austen Style"), Persuasion ("the sacrifice of the very essence of Austen Style") and Sanditon ("the formal ruination of the Austen novel") are fresh and provocative. (He shows how in the last named its signifiers go out of control-though to these eyes and ears that doesn't prevent it from being a fragment full of splendidly comic bits.) He is excellent on free indirect discourse in the writing, and his own identity as a "Stylothete" (he likes the word) means there's never a page without a lot going on in writing so dense as to make abstracting from it, as in the attempt above, virtually impossible.

Ten years ago, Miller began a short piece, "Austen's Attitude," as follows: "It is a truth universally acknowledged that a single man in possession of a good fortune, must be in want of a wife. Perhaps most attached to this commanding sentence is the frightened soul who has never recovered from the terrors whose reign in Austen's novel it pronounces. "Jane Austen and the Secret of Style enacts such a recovery on the part of D. A. Miller, even as the Absolute Stylist Herself remains unwrung.

Chapter 5

Rhetorical Conversation

Reading novels has always been a form of escapism for me. As a teenager, I had a passion for reading but no guidance, so I often left my local library with a stack of paperback romance novels that I would devour like candy, one piece a day. It wasn't until I entered college that I discovered pioneers of the genre such as Jane Austen and Charlotte Brontë. I also discovered a new depth to reading and escaping. Sitting on the couch with an afghan over my legs, a cat or two curled up next to me, and a good novel to read, which usually includes a strong, intelligent heroine, allows me even today to enter this other world. As someone who now studies as well as escapes through novels, I try to peel back the many layers that make up this sometimes academically dismissed form of writing.

One layer of the female novel that I uncovered appeared to me by chance while reading Walter Ong's *Orality and Literacy*:

> *A great gap in our understanding of the influence of women on literary genre and style could be bridged or closed through attention to the orality-literacy-print shift.... [E]arly women novelists and other women writers generally worked from outside the oral tradition because of the simple fact that women were not commonly subjected to the orally based rhetorical training that boys got in school.... Certainly, non-rhetorical styles congenial to women writers helped make the novel what it is: more like a conversation than a platform performance. (159-60)*

Because Ong suggests that an alternative, conversational form of rhetoric came from the efforts of early female novelists,

I begin my examination with Samuel Richardson, who is responsible for transforming the reputation of the novel. Jane Austen is my next puzzle piece since she creates humour from the established roles imposed on both men and women. Following Austen, the Brontë sisters lived and wrote about the limited experiences of women during the nineteenth century. Finally, Virginia Woolf provides insight into how the British female novel of the nineteenth century crossed over into a type of female-rhetorical genre. In her own writing, Woolf brings up many of the questions I would like to explore concerning how and why women became drawn to the novel, eventually using the female narrative voice to expose their views on the treatment of women, and thus, creating their own unique form of feminist rhetoric:

> The question is one not merely of literature, but to a large extent of social history. What, for example, was the origin of the extraordinary outburst in the eighteenth century of novel writing by women? Why did it begin then, and not in the time of Elizabethan renaissance? Was the motive which finally determined them to write a desire to correct the current view of their sex expressed in so many volumes and for so many ages by male writers? ("Women Novelists" 14)

In order to consider some of these questions, I begin with Ong's notion that this group was barred from following traditional forms of rhetoric. As a result, they created their own rhetorical voice to fit their abilities, and this is when we begin to see the development of the female novelist.

During the eighteenth century, the social stigma surrounding the novel started to change and, surprisingly enough, it began with a male writer, Samuel Richardson. In his novel *Pamela,* Richardson "demonstrated how fiction could deploy strategies that reorganized the country house around a woman who had nothing but a gendered form of literacy to offer" (Armstrong 98). While I believe Richardson's gender excludes him from writing feminist rhetoric novels, I think his part in the development of this genre is important because he is credited with making the novel respectable, and the eventual result allowed more women to write novels.

One way he accomplished this was by adhering to conventions outlined in conduct books, which were very popular at the time. By attempting to shape women in order that they follow predefined social roles, conduct books preached the importance of a limited female education, insisting that the fine arts and classical traditions be exclusive to the male sex (Armstrong 99-103). Richardson's *Pamela* was a mixture of both conduct book and female narrative.

More changes came to the novel and the female voice in the nineteenth century, and though a man is credited with altering the novel from a "vulgar form of writing" to a "safe" and "polite" form of fiction (Armstrong 96-97), the female novel made the final transition into what I consider true feminist rhetoric when women started to dominate this form of writing. Jane Austen is one author who is responsible for this transformation, for "placed as she is historically, [Austen] is perhaps most often seen as a pivotal figure, looking both backward and forward" (Morrison). She was raised on the restricting theory encouraged by conduct writings. Consequently, many of the themes in her novels understandably revolve around the socially assigned roles of men and women.

While I cannot prove Austen intentionally infused her writing with feminist ideas, the social parody she creates in such novels as *Pride and Prejudice* and *Persuasion* may be the result of prescriptions imposed through conduct books. Women were indoctrinated with advice on a wide variety of matters from how to spend their spare time to how they should care for the male members of their family, be they brother, father, or husband. Conduct writing advocated that "a woman's social environment presented her with too many forms of activity that smacked of amusement," and it was not considered appropriate for women to work, so "authors of conduct books generally insisted that the activities comprising the domestic arts – and therefore a women's duty – had to be carefully supervised" (Armstrong 99-100).

Austen's female heroines participate in many socially approved domestic activities. They are intelligent and well read but not overly bookish, even admitting to enjoying a scandalous novel such as *The Mysteries of Udolpho*. Accomplished at least at one form of the leisure arts such as drawing, needlework, or music, her heroines can play the piano, stitch a piece of fancy work, or sketch a portrait, but they are not showy with their talents.

Austen's characters are in accordance with the standards described in conduct writings and fit the role of the stereotypical female, but Austen also subtly comments on these stereotypes through characterization and direct narrative. Virginia Woolf discusses Austen's use of characterization in her essay "Jane Austen," suggesting that there is a "much deeper emotion than appears upon the surface," and though the "life scenes" that are so much a part of Austen's novels may seem "outwardly trivial," "always the stress is laid upon character".

One of her strongest female characters is Elizabeth Bennet from *Pride and Prejudice*. In most respects, Elizabeth fits the typical rôle of the English gentlewoman of the time, but she is by no means a passive female, nor is she shy about voicing her opinions whether or not they fit in with the social restrictions placed upon her. Pressured to marry well, Elizabeth, with decided frankness, turns down two offers of marriage from adequately suitable gentlemen. Austen exposes the non-conformist nature of Elizabeth by contrasting her to the character of Caroline Bingley, who like Elizabeth is of the gentry class but is her superior economically. On more than one occasion, both characters verbally spar or comment to other characters about one another's actions, which helps Austen create her subtle statements concerning the women's socially defined roles.

Elizabeth Bennet is the heroine of the novel, but Austen also uses her sisters and mother in a similar fashion. Mrs. Bennet, for example, is described as a "woman of mean understanding, little information, and uncertain temper". As with most women in her position, her goal is to make sure that all her daughters marry, and while it would be nice if they marry someone they love, this requirement is not of primary importance. Mrs. Bennet's character contrasts with Elizabeth's, and Austen uses their differences to develop the ironic humour of the novel. She creates the characters to be "her fools, her prigs, her worldings" for "no excuse is found for them and no mercy shown them".

Paula Marantz Cohen believes that "Austen responded to prevailing ideas concerning sexual stereotyping in a highly controlled and consistent fashion," so her humour is purposefully exercised. This is most evident when it seems as if Jane will not be married to Mr. Bingley as expected, and instead of consoling her daughter, Mrs. Bennet comforts herself with the idea that "'Jane will die of a broken heart, and then he will be sorry for what he has done'". Again, this is not "the kind of explicit message that we associate with more modern feminist writers" (Cohen), but the message is still evident. Austen plays with the roles of men and women, and this allows her to express her views about the limitations imposed on both sexes.

Characterization works in unison with narrative for "emergence of what can be called" Austen's "feminist perspective" (Cohen). Following the trend of most women novelists of the nineteenth century, Austen's narrative is akin to conversation. This connects back to the idea of women's limited exposure to formal rhetoric, and consequently, their experiences were based more in an oral rather than a literary culture, unlike that of men who had been sent away to school and had a wider range of life experiences.

A woman's life was centered around the home, and due to her sex, she was "excluded... from certain kinds of experience. Even their emotional life was strictly regulated by law and custom" ("Women and Fiction" 1258). Virginia Woolf goes on to explain that the result of this limited life experience is a uniquely feminine narrative voice. Authors such as Jane Austen were able to find their own style, which does not try to copy or impose a traditional, masculine structure.

Like someone who is sitting in a drawing room talking to her readers, Austen's direct narrative approach is combined with social satire. Jane Austen introduced the nineteenth century to this genre, and the Brontës continued into the middle part of the century, becoming bolder with their portrayal of the plight of women in novels such as *Jane Eyre* and *Wuthering Heights*. They often interwove personal experiences into their writing, and like their heroines, these authors were constrained economically and socially due to their gender. Like most women of their class, the Brontës spent their lives primarily at home in their father's parsonage. However, they managed to receive some exposure to the outside world through the reading materials, including books and newspapers, which filtered through their home.

The only other way to experience life outside the home for the Brontës and many of their heroines was through employment as a governess, and while Charlotte Brontë's novel *Jane Eyre* is best known as the tale of a young girl who is pushed out into the world to make her living through hard means, I believe Anne Brontë's novel *Agnes Grey* is more autobiographically close to the Brontës' true experiences.

One method used by Anne Brontë to create the appearance of autobiography rather than fiction is by directly addressing the reader in the opening paragraph:

All true stories contain instruction; though in some, the treasure may be hard to find....Whether this be the case with my history or not, I am hardly competent to judge; I sometimes think it might prove useful to some, and entertaining to others, but the world may judge for itself: shielded by my own obscurity, and the lapse of years, and a few fictitious names, I do not fear to venture, and will candidly lay before the public what I would not disclose to the most intimate friend.

Will Hale describes the style of narrative in *Agnes Grey* as lacking artistry but also insists that it "does seem real" and provides "all the actuality of a transcription of Anne's own life." To a certain extent, I believe Hale accurately describes Anne Brontë's intentions because she admits in the text that her purpose is to provide information rather than judgment. The details are culled from Anne Brontë's own horrible experiences. In order to inform the public about the pervasive abuse of women who must work as governesses, Anne Brontë creates a fictional adaptation of the events from her own life (Hale). Informal narrative and autobiography again relate to the notions put forth by Ong and Woolf: women of this century developed their own style of story telling, and due to the limited sphere they lived in, they often used incidents from their own lives.

Anne Brontë's character, Agnes Grey, is much like herself. She is the youngest child, daughter of a clergyman, and educated at home. Her family is considered middle class, despite the fact that they have little money, and this is one reason Agnes decides to become a governess. Also, like the Brontës, she wants the opportunity to explore more of the world because she has been exposed only to her immediate family and a few neighbors, rarely venturing more than a few miles from her home. Rather than be "made to stagnate in a parsonage mending stockings," she wants "to wander free over the world".

As one of three women in the Grey household, Agnes's role is strictly defined. The Grey women are to run the house and support the patriarch of the home, Mr. Grey. Though well-meaning, Mr. Grey is responsible for the financial difficulties forced upon the women because he loses the small fortune he originally possesses. While this change in circumstance greatly impacts the women of the house, their priority is to ensure that life for Mr. Grey is comfortable and stress-free. For example, they are reduced to eating meals "simplified to an unprecedented degree," but their father's "favourite dishes" still remain.

Where before they had a small number of servants to help run the house, they are eventually reduced to one maid and required to attend to the majority of the domestic duties including gardening and cooking. They economize on coal and candles, when their father is away or ill in bed, instead "scraping the perishing embers together from time to time". Anne Brontë's emphasis on the sacrifices endured by Agnes and the other women of the Grey house "show[s] the ways that she defines herself as submissive," and "she relates this submissiveness to Agnes's sense of daughterly duty" (Frawley).

Further evidence of the hardships imposed on Agnes due to her gender is illustrated through the treatment she receives as a governess, particularly from males. While employed with the Bloomfields, Uncle Robson, a regular family visitor, treats Agnes as if she is invisible. She describes him as "the scorner of the female sex" because he ignores her "with a certain supercilious insolence of tone and manner" (Brontë 102). Even Tom, the male child of the Bloomfields and one of two children Agnes is supposed to supervise, dominates Agnes and bullies his sister. The only male in the schoolroom, Tom views his position as one of authority over the females, no matter that one is his teacher.

Later, while Agnes works for the Murrays, her invisibility returns when the rector, Mr. Hatfield, is so involved in fawning over Miss Murray that he often acts as if Agnes is not even present. At one point, he escorts the Murray ladies to their carriage and closes the door before Agnes can manage to get inside. According to Maria Frawley, this sense of invisibility and "voicelessness... enables Brontë to explore through her representation of Agnes... the unempowered position of middle-class women." Men of all social statuses, whether they are children, wealthy gentlemen, or a simple rector, exert their power over Agnes, who is forced into a submissive role due in part to the fact that she is woman—and a governess.

Now, I wish to return to questions raised by Virginia Woolf as to how and why this mixture of fiction and female rhetoric occurred. The voiceless, submissive, invisible female novelist is a primary subject of much of Woolf's work, especially in her book *A Room of One's Own* and her essay "Women and Fiction." As with most of her investigative rhetoric, Woolf begins with questions of "why," and as she picks up books off her shelf and wanders through the grounds of the Oxbridge men's college, she finds many answers to her questions. Why did it take so long to establish a female form of literature? Woolf begins searching for answers to this question by examining history as early as the fifteenth century. She soon realizes that just as Agnes Grey was invisible, history considered women "insignificant," and though "some of the most profound thoughts in literature fall from her lips," a woman "in real life... could hardly read, could scarcely spell, and was the property of her husband" (*A Room* 44).

Like Woolf, I wonder why, after taking so long for women to develop into authors, did so many choose the novel over other forms of writing? Woolf's examination provides a number of reasons beginning with the authors' limited spheres. Since women rarely left their homes, they did not have the same life experiences that were available to men. They wrote of what they knew, and this was often autobiographical. Furthermore, since their duties and lives revolved around domesticity, their employment never ended. It was their duty to provide familial services seven days a week, twenty-four hours a day. Novels could be picked up and put down when necessary (*A Room* 50).

But now it is time to attempt an answer to a question of my own: Given that so many female authors of the nineteenth century selected the genre of the novel, and it is evident that they interwove feminist notions throughout their writing, could it be possible that this was a conscious act? Or, perhaps a better question is: how could it not be? Elizabeth Bennet does marry a wealthy man, but she also refuses to be invisible or submissive. Agnes Grey finally finds her lover, Mr. Weston, as she strolls hopelessly along the beach; however, before she is allowed this happy ending, she must first submit to countless forms of injustice. Even Virginia Woolf would agree with me: "One of the motives that led them to write was the desire to expose their own suffering, to plead their own cause" ("Women and Fiction" 1259). So, I will let myself believe that Jane Austen and Emily, Charlotte, and Anne Brontë wrote about themselves but also wrote for their female audience. They crafted an entertaining narrative, and at the time, they couldn't help but let their feminist views slip into the story.

As they slid their manuscript under a desk blotter so they could help make dinner or amuse a guest at tea, they were thinking of the next event in their narrative and maybe how their story might empower another woman, a woman in their world of the nineteenth century and possibly a woman from the future who lives in a world they could only imagine. In preparation for filming the Ang Lee directed version of *Sense and Sensibility* in 1995, the film's cast had a letter-writing competition to see who could capture the spirit of Jane Austen's characters best.

Imogene Stubbs, who plays Lucy Steele, won the competition with a wonderfully simpering and satirical take on her character. A letter-writing contest seems a particularly good way to "get into" a character's inner thoughts, particularly in the case of Lucy, because in the novel the content of her letter to her jilted ex-fiancé Edward Ferrars is so exemplary of all the faults we have come to see in her. The novel provides us with the text of Lucy's letter to Edward so that we can laugh with Elinor and Edward at Lucy's insincerity and so that we can acknowledge her lack of consequence and education, revealed through the words on the page.

In Austen's novels, letters often serve this comic function of exposing the absurdities of the flawed men and women who send them—Mr. Collins's proposal letter is perhaps the best comic example; Lydia Bennet's letter announcing her ill-fated plan to elope with Mr. Wickham is perhaps the most shocking. Letters also provide confessional spaces for her novels' male characters: Austen gives Mr. Darcy, Frank Churchill, and Frederick Wentworth, for example, ample space to explain their feelings and behaviour. It seems surprising that, after Austen moves away from the epistolary form of "Lady Susan," her completed novels rarely provide us with the texts of heroines' letters. It seems doubly striking that such letters are absent, given the heroines' social context, in which, as Deirdre Le Faye explains, "[l]etter-writing was an essential part of social life". Although marriage plots are arguably always the focus of Austen's novels, the heroines' written expressions of feeling are rarely "safe" in the context of the marriage plot and they are almost always judged harshly by the narrative voices.

Thus, we begin this essay with some basic questions: Why are heroines' letters, in particular, almost entirely left out of Austen's novels? And, when heroines' letters do appear, in what form do they appear and what functions do they serve within their respective novels? To answer these questions, we examine the texts of letters written by Marianne Dashwood in *Sense and Sensibility* and Fanny Price in *Mansfield Park*.

Jane Austen's infallible narratorThe comparison of the traditional novelist to God has received many memorable formulations. While Flaubert and Joyce emphasize the author's ubiquity, invisibility, or silence, the quality usually adduced for comparison is omniscience, as in Sartre's complaint about Mauriac: like God, he "is omniscient about everything relating to his little world". For Sartre, of course, this is a bad thing: "God is not an artist. Neither is M. Mauriac". As Meir Sternberg has demonstrated, the god being compared in these formulations is specifically the God of the Old Testament: "Homer's gods," he notes, "like the corresponding Near Eastern pantheons, certainly have access to a wider range of information than the normal run of humanity; but their knowledge still falls well short of omniscience, concerning the past and present as well as the future". Sternberg explicitly includes Jane Austen's narratives within this biblical model: "Surely... one assumes that, like all novelists, she enjoys the privilege of omniscience denied to tellers ill everyday life. She invokes different rules, we say.

But if it is convention that renders Jane Austen immune from all charges of fallacy and falsity, it is convention that likewise puts the Bible's art of narrative beyond their reach. For the biblical narrator also appeals to the privilege of omniscience—so that he no more speaks in the writer's ordinary voice than Jane Austen does in hers, but exactly as a persona raised high above...". J. Hillis Miller explains how "This immanent omniscience is... like the knowledge traditionally ascribed to God. It is an authentic perfection of knowledge. The omniscient narrator is able to remember perfectly all the past, to foresee the future course of events, and to penetrate with irresistible insight the most secret crevice in the heart of each man. He can know the person better than the person knows himself...".

But in the twenty years since Sternberg's book—and in significant measure because of the interest sparked by his book—the premise that all heterodiegetic narrators exercise Godlike omniscience has been questioned. Sternberg argues that "omniscience is a qualitative and therefore indivisible privilege.... The superhuman privilege is constant and only its exercise variable". While this logic would doubtless be true of "real" omniscience, it does not seem compelling with regard to "pretend" omniscience, which might readily be imagined as divisible. The "demand for a God's Eye View or Nothing" (Putnam viii) may be a limiting dichotomy that prevents us from exploring alternative models.

Omniscience might instead be thought of as a toolbox, with different novelists using the different tools within it in distinctive ways. My own survey of discussions of omniscience identifies four primary tools in that box: omnipotence, omnitemporality, omnipresence, and telepathy. To get ahead of myself for a moment, I'll argue that Austen's narrators are more accurately described as "infallible" than "omniscient": at least on the basis of these four features, the infallible narrator as defined here is not a type of omniscient narrator. I take no position on the larger question of whether "omniscience" is always a misnomer; Austen's narrators, however, utilize so few of these standard tools so sparingly that the label is not useful for discussing her practice. Indeed, it seems to have hampered prior analyses of Austen's method. Austen's career, at least in her handling of point of view, has long been treated as the exemplification of Haeckel's Law that "ontogeny recapitulates phylogeny," as her novels rehearse in perfect sequence all of the evolutionary stages of the genre.

She begins with the early epistolary drafts, in which the novels have no omniscient narrators at all. Later, she revises them into third-person omniscient novels with engaging and judgmental narrators, effectively rendering extinct the earlier genre of the epistolary novel. During the course of writing these novels she gradually weans herself from what Marvin Mudrick calls her "early tendency to assert an arbitrary omniscience over the objects of her irony". Finally, in Emma and Persuasion, she evolves from the daughter of Dr. Johnson into the mother of Henry James, pioneering the novel with a central consciousness or filter and a more reticent narrator. In The Rhetoric of Fiction, Wayne Booth outlines the final stage of this progression: "In Emma there are many breaks in the point of view, because Emma's beclouded mind cannot do the whole job. In Persuasion, where the heroine's viewpoint is faulty only in her ignorance of Captain Wentworth's love, there are very few. Anne Elliott's consciousness is sufficient, as Emma's is not, for most of the needs of the novel which she dominates".

Just as a play has a certain number of speaking parts, so an Austen novel has a certain number of what we might call "thinking parts," characters whose consciousness the narrator reveals to us. Given the critical narrative outlined above, one might expect to see that number start out very large and narrow down to a single central consciousness. If one measures omniscience quantitatively, as Booth suggests, counting how many minds the narrator has access to, then Persuasion, in which the narrator reveals the consciousnesses of ten characters, is no different from Emma, in which she also reads the minds often characters.

But not only is there no progression from Emma to Persuasion in this regard, there is no pattern of progression at all in Austen's novels: Northanger Abbey has ten thinking parts, Sense and Sensibility twelve, and Mansfield Park thirteen. Only Pride and Prejudice, with nineteen thinking parts, stands out. Discussions of omniscience assign it a broad and variable range of characteristics, many of which have little to do with omniscience per se. Critics often apply the label to passages of exposition, but most of these, at least in Austen, communicate information about incomes or family ties that constitutes common knowledge in that world, known to the characters as well as the narrator. The narrator of Persuasion tells us that Anne and Captain Wentworth had fallen in love and separated seven years ago as a courtesy to us as newcomers to the neighborhood, but we learn nothing that Sir Walter, Elizabeth, and Lady Russell don't know.

In fact, we are assured that if Wentworth's brother and sister hadn't been out of the country and Anne's sister, Mary, away at school, they would have known all about it too, as would have anyone in the "Kellynch circle". Other critics conflate the idea of narrative reliability with omniscience, but as far as factual or mimetic matters go, virtually all narrators are reliable—lying narrators are very rare—and as far as narrative judgments go, Jonathan Culler seems right in his argument that the narrator's wisdom is "offered for our consideration and assent, in a mode of persuasion." When the narrator asserts, "It is a truth universally acknowledged, that a single man in possession of a good fortune, must be in want of a wife" (Pride and Prejudice 3), the reader is being asked to ponder the statement: to accept it literally (as does Mrs. Benner) or to dismiss it outright are both inadequate responses (the rich single men do turn out to need wives).

Many commentators of Jane Austen's fiction have expressed the view that she is particularly difficult to catch at her narrative game. Speaking of E, almost universally held to be the most complex and the most elusive of her novels, Virginia Woolf famously wrote that if you read it twelve times over, "at every fresh reading you feel anew that you never understood anything like the widening sum of its delights" (Southam 266). Lionel Trilling added that "the difficulty of Emma is never overcome. We never know where to have it. If we finish it at night and think we know what it is up to, we wake the next morning to believe it is up to something else; it has become a different book". More recently and more generally, Irvin Ehrenpreis has expressed the bafflement of all those who try to establish what Austen (or, her narrator) is "up to" in her novels:

So the explicitness of the novelist is sometimes only apparent, and at other times is a game played with the audience. By sounding blunt and outspoken in many of her judgments, Austen entices unwary readers into assuming that she is straightforward.... But it remains true that when Austen does plainly set forth her judgment, it is as I have said—quite reliable.

However, while certain commentators have put their fingers on Austen's invisibility (for a recent example, see

Miller's 2003 Jane Austen, or The Secret of Style), others have seen her novels as mirroring a definite world view—a world view which has been interpreted in diametrically opposing ways. A traditional reading of Austen as an upholder of the patriarchal values of her society has been challenged by "revolutionary" and/or feminist readings of the novels as subtle critiques of those same values. S&S has been interpreted as a satire on (excessive) sensibility, but some readers have observed that Marianne/sensibility is shown to be much more fascinating than Elinor/sense (Nardin 10). MP—the litmus test of Austen studies in this department—has been read as an evangelical plea for old gentrified England and as a covert manifesto against the moral and social strictness of Austen's time.

How can these positions be reconciled with Reginald Farter's (1917) image of the author as a joycean divinity, indifferently paring her fingernails elsewhere?... impersonality comes as the first ingredient in the specific for immortality. The self-revelation of the writer must be as severely implicit as it is universally pervasive; it must never be conscious or obtruded.... She is there all the time, indeed, but never in propria persona, except when she gaily smiles through the opener texture of "Northanger Abbey," or, with her consummate sense of art, mitigates for us the transition out of her paradises back into the grey light of ordinary life, by letting the word 'T' demurely peer forth at last, as the fantasmagoria in "Mansfield Park," "Emma" or "Northanger Abbey" begins to thin out to its final pages. It comes as no surprise, of course, that Austen's novels generate opposing interpretations: all great literature is supposed to do so, and conversely, the ability to instigate different readings has long been identified as a stigma of literary greatness.

What is at once interesting and baffling is that these opposing readings appear to be equally justified, that there is ample textual material in Austen's novels to support them both. At the same time, there seems to be uncertainty as to whether Jane Austen watches over her novels as a Victorian commentator or as a modernist detached observer. Is there a "point" to her depiction of English gentry between the eighteenth and the nineteenth centuries, or is there not? And if that "point" is there, what is it exactly? From our postmodern position in history, we might dismiss all the business of finding a "point" in Austen's fiction—in all fiction—as self-evidently irrelevant. Have we not been taught that novels are not pamphlets?

And is not the point of any narrative the telling of a story? On the most basic level, it most certainly is: novels are not pamphlets—and narrators, in written fiction, are not authors. Yet any story, besides telling itself, expresses, is "symptomatic of," a "world-view," in Roger Fowler's terms. And in Austen's case, this world-view seems to be, at one and the same time, contradictory and elusive. And while we might, once again, conclude that the "point" of (great) literature always eludes us, there may be a lesson to be learnt about how Austen's particular elusiveness is constructed—how readers are enticed into looking for a point which consistently evades their grasp. Before embarking on a linguistic investigation of how Austen's elusiveness is created, it may be useful to remind ourselves of two cultural facts.

The first one is contemporary: in our time, we have come to accept that the text does not contain its author—it contains a narrator, and can at most presuppose an "implied author" with whom all readers ideally wish to be acquainted. The second one is contemporary with Austen: in her time, it was customary to think of novels as ethical/ideological mirrors, and she would have expected at least certain categories of readers to deduce the author's opinions from her writings—to conflate narrator with author, implied author with "the real Jane Austen." In his seminal study on oral narratives told by young black Americans, Labov wrote that a story, in its simplest form, consists of two temporally ordered clauses. Besides this minimal definition, however, he also provided a more detailed pattern, in order to account for the higher degree of complexity to be found in some of the stories he analyzed.

Some of these parts or stages can be present or not, in written as well as in oral narratives. In written fiction, the "abstract" is usually provided by the title; the "orientation," if it is to be found at all, is most often found at the start (it is the "who, what, where, when," of the story); the "complicating action" unsettles the initial balance and prepares the "resolution;" the "coda," usually placed at the end of the narrative, is where things are rounded off—where the "(implied) author," or the "narrator," parts company with the "reader." "Evaluation," though it comes up fourth, is the most difficult "part" or "stage" to place, because though it tends to cluster in certain areas of a text (traditionally, at the beginning and end; but there is a lot of variation along the genre and period axes), it can be found anywhere, and evaluative elements are hard to identify with any certainty. "Evaluation," as Labov himself defined it, is the "point" of a story: it can be a moral, a religious, or a didactic point; more generally, it is what demonstrates that the story is worth telling?

In a novel, as well as in any other kind of story, evaluation is endemic, and no two readers will exactly agree as to which stretches of text are evaluative and which are not—though certain stretches are quite unequivocally evaluative. Evaluative elements can be found, to begin with, in dialogue as well as in narrative, in the characters' as well as in the narrator's discourse. Some of Jane Austen's novels (P&P, E, the unfinished TW) are mostly made up of dialogue, and when this is the case much of the evaluative work is as it were "embedded" in direct (or indirect) speech. In P&P, we learn something about Mr. and Mrs. Bennet before the narrator tells us "who and what they are:"

"My dear Mr. Bennet," said his lady to him one day, "have you heard that Netherfield is let at last?"

Mr. Bennet replied that he had not.

"But it is," returned she; "for Mrs. Long has just been here, and she told me all about it."

Mr. Bennet made no answer.

"Do not you want to know who has taken it?" cried his wife impatiently.

"You want to tell me, and I have no objection to hearing it."

The narrator, however, is always instinctively held to be

a more reliable evaluator than any single character. As Michael Toolan puts it, "narrators are typically trusted by their addressees... To narrate is to bid for a kind of power". Even first-person "homodiegetic" narrators, who take part in the story and can therefore be suspected of having a personal interest in directing audience reactions, are considered more "authoritative" than any other character, and can be confused with the "author" to a lesser or greater degree. Modernist writers such as Conrad and James, and latter-day followers like Ishiguro, have deliberately played with readers' expectations by exploiting this "authoritativeness." Third-person "heterodiegetic" narrators acquire an extra degree of authoritativeness by being impersonal (if that is the case) and situating themselves out of the action: within the space of their fictional world, they are like gods, and readers will tend to treat them as such—i.e., they will tend to believe all they say.

All of Austen's narrators are third-person heterodiegetic narrators, and as such command the reader's blind faith (or his/her gullibility, if we believe in the author mocking her audience). These narrators never take part in the action, and only rarely come out of hiding to speak in the first person. When I think about Jane Austen's *Emma,* and about what so affects me in this novel besides the sheer mental exuberance of its main character, I come to the plot. Jane Austen tells a great story. One reason I know that Austen was particularly fond of Emma, apart from her own explicit statement that "Emma is a character whom no one but myself will much like," is that she made Emma so much like herself. Emma Woodhouse and Jane Austen are both imaginists, both storytellers about other people's lives.

Moreover, Austen certainly did not write a story in which Emma was required to give up her creativity, to see her clouds of glory, in Wordsworth's phrase, fade into the light of common day. Near the end of the story Emma can still claim persuasively that she always deserves the best treatment because she never puts up with any other. The resolution to Austen's plot does offer her beloved creation and fellow creator only the best treatment, which does not include having to give up her imagination. The real difference between the author and her flawed but fabulous heroine is that Austen tells a better story than Emma. And part of what's better is Austen's more inventive, and less conventional, vision of romance.

It is one of the great triumphs of *Emma,* the novel, that it is a love story about a young woman and the man who has lived next door to her for all of her life, in which for most of the narrative, and certainly for all the years that they have been neighbors before the story opens, neither of them even notice that they have any such feeling for each other. She's a spoiled girl, he's been a fond but critical family friend. The families have been close, her sister even married his brother. My daughter, who is 12, has yet to have the pleasure of reading Austen's novels. You can see this lack in the oh-so-skeptical reply she offered a few days ago to a new friend of hers who asked her if she thought a certain boy was really cool. "Did you know, he wouldn't take off his snow boots for all of the second grade." Mr. Knightley and Emma would have known all about each other's habits in snowboots. And they still fell in love.

Austen holds our attention for most of the story with Emma's love plots, her speculations and machinations for other people. And we are riveted by it all. Then, near the end, Austen suddenly waltzes the romance between Mr. Knightley and his lively young neighbour onto her narrative stage, effectively upstaging the little dramas Emma has spun. And almost as suddenly, we realise that we are looking at a far superior style of matchmaking to any of Emma's inventions, that this is a much better kind of love story after all. The plot of this novel is a tribute to everyday life, to the extraordinary richness of the world that is to be found in our very own neighborhoods, to the enormous potential for happiness that can be fulfilled by going no farther than right next door. I think one reason so many of us love this novel is that it celebrates the high possibilities, the real thrills, the enthusiastic creativity and even the "perfect happiness" to be found in the small worlds of ordinary life in which almost all of us live.

What I want to talk about today is what the novel does

not celebrate: a commitment to, a belief in, the superiority, both moral and aesthetic, of remaining in our small worlds, of choosing the sedentary and the circumscribed–whether that choice is based on fear or on ego. We need to be wary of our own tendencies, as readers and imaginists ourselves, to romanticize, to look at Hartfield and Highbury as some sort of charming portrait of an idyllic rural life. I want to look at *Emma* and its relations to Austen are other novels from what I am calling the perspective of geography. By that I simply mean where Austen's heroines are located and the range of their locations, how much they move around.

On even the most literal level, readers of Austen's novels know that her heroines usually do not stay in that "country village" Austen spoke of to Fanny, and often do not spend much time there at all. Let me just remind you of their mobility. *Northanger Abbey,* probably the earliest written of Austen's published novels, which actually came out posthumously together with *Persuasion,* sports a heroine who is on the road for almost the entire novel. Catherine Morland is introduced to us in Chapter One, and the narrator moves quickly from her infancy through age ten to seventeen. So much for her home life. She leaves home on the very first page of Chapter Two, and is delighted to do so. As I am sure you all remember, the rest of the novel is Catherine in the public world of Bath and then as a houseguest at Northanger Abbey. Finally, in Chapter Twenty-Nine, eleven weeks after her departure and with just three chapters left in her story, Catherine quite reluctantly comes home.

Of Austen's five other completed novels, three also begin with the heroine leaving home. At ten years old, Fanny Price is sent away from a nuclear family with too many children and too little money, to live with her relatives at Mansfield Park. She will never come home again, though she does return to Portsmouth for a visit when she is grown. *Sense and Sensibility* and *Persuasion* open with the heroines being literally forced out of their homes by the financial carelessness of their fathers, the Dashwood sisters when their father dies without leaving them any savings and their half-brother inherits their home, and Anne Elliot when the Elliot family must move to rented lodgings in order to pay their bills.

In other words, four out of six of Austen's completed novels offer, as the opening move of their plots, the heroine leaving home. In the earliest, and I would say the simplest, plot of the four, seventeen-year-old Catherine Morland goes cheerfully off to begin her adventures at being an adult, and returns home briefly at the end of the book. The next three versions are darker and more complex. They open with acute financial problems which result in the heroine regretfully leaving home. All three stories introduce a heroine forced out of the familiar and into the greater world. Nor do they simply move to another place and stay there, though Fanny Price comes closest to this. The Dashwood sisters, driven off by the heirs to their estate, will stay in their rented Devonshire cottage for only a part of the narrative. They soon travel to London and later to yet another country estate, Cleveland, before returning at the end of the book to their cottage.

While Anne Elliot is given a brief visit back to Kellynch Hall, most of her story takes place in other houses and villages and towns, at Uppercross and Lyme and Bath. And even in *Northanger Abbey,* though the narrator explicitly states at the outset that the Morlands were not "poor," the heroine must leave her family behind and travel with a neighbour, in part because the largeness of her family makes it too expensive to make their own trip to Bath. Fanny Price may move around the least, but on the other hand her very entrance into the novel is as a child out of place, an exhausted "little girl [who] performed her long journey in safety."

My point is that all this changing around hardly adds up to a stable, in the sense of settled and static, domestic universe as the geographic setting of Austen's work. We can see clearly how Austen's own reluctant move from Steventon to Bath after her father retired, and then, after he died, her years of social wandering with her mother, her sister Cassandra, and her friend Martha Lloyd before settling at Chawton, were the biographical basis for the mobile openings of Austen's plots.

But biographical explanations are not enough. If we are

intent upon claiming that Austen's fiction offers representations of the narrow domestic sphere of upper class country females in regency England, we need to be very precise about where to locate that domestic sphere. In four of the six completed novels it is quite literally not to be found in the heroines' homes. Instead, I would say that what interests Austen, the moment at which the lives of young women become interesting to her, is precisely the moment when they, whether by choice or by economic force, leave the protection, the safety, and the sheltering innocence of their homes. When they move, and thus become changeable, their stories can begin. And for three out of four (the exception being Fanny Price), the traveling will continue, as the novels, along with their heroines, shift from place to place. Their geography is the geography of England.

It is time for us to acknowledge how vexed Austen's notion of home really is. And it is time for us to recognize just how often Austen's heroines move around, how frequently they seem detached from any particular one spot that can be called home, how many places in England they visit, how very itinerant they can be. One major component of the domestic lives Austen creates for her heroines is their lack of domesticity, their wandering feet, the way they are drawn outward, however often reluctantly at first, away from their private and insufficient homes and toward a beckoning larger social world.

The extent to which Austen's novels are infused with the social issues and public debates of Regency England, the myriad ways the novels take place in a public rather than in a private and domestic sphere, is not a new insight. Many readers of Austen's work have studied the ways in which her novels examine such topical issues as the economics of marriage and the rights of women, the aesthetic movement and the improvement of estates, theaters and amateur theatricals in the Regency period, and the role of the Royal Navy in British imperial enterprise.

One of the most useful recent books to place Austen's work within the frame of the topics and issues which pervaded the public spaces of her age is *Jane Austen and Representations of Regency England* by Roger Sales. I found particularly exciting his discussion of the Regency obsession with invalidism, its links to ideas of leisure and consumption, and to the pervasive role of watering places in Regency society and in Austen's work. Mobility was certainly commonplace for country gentry in Austen's time. And the reasons for traveling are not hard to see. Given both the financial pressures to marry and the fashionable obsession with illness that Sales delineates, it was a kind of tourism which was virtually required of the men and women of Austen's class.

But Austen does not always tell her stories through the convention of departures. *Pride and Prejudice* is one of two Austen novels in which the heroine does not begin her story by leaving home. Elizabeth Bennet spends a great deal of the narrative ensconced in the family estate at Longbourn. I make just two quick points about this. First, I am hardly claiming that Austen's novels all have or should have the same pattern, but simply that a geographic range covering many locales around England is a central motif in Austen's novels. My second point has probably already occurred to all of you.

Elizabeth may live at Longbourn with her family for most of her story, but she does, of course, leave home during the novel, taking two crucially significant journeys. In the first, the visit to the parsonage at Hunsford, she receives Darcy's marriage proposal and in the second, touring Derbyshire with the Gardiners, she sees Darcy on his home ground. Both trips are centrally important, operating as key moments in Elizabeth's process of changing the ways she has looked at and evaluated the world around her. The insights gained on those journeys are high points of the education in perception which will lead to Elizabeth's final journey: the move to marriage and to life at Pemberley.

Emma

And then there is Emma, the exception—as she would probably be pleased to hear—to all these patterns. It is hard to overstate the extent to which Emma does not move around, the narrowness of her physical sphere. She simply never goes anywhere. From the first page of her story to the last, Emma spends all her nights, and virtually all her days, comfortably in her own home. She does stroll the village and have dinner at the Westons. She attends a party at the Coles and a dance at the Crown, visits the estate adjoining Hartfield for the first time in many years, and even goes as far as Box Hill, for the first time in her life. That's about it. Geographically speaking, Emma remains solidly in the neighborhood of her own home.

What are we to make of this relentless immobility? Well, not only did Austen repeatedly use plot patterns of moving away from home as ways of educating her heroines in her other novels, I would say that she also did so in *Emma*. Emma's story, too, offers claims for the value of wider experience, of literal as well as perceptual movement out from the confines of self into the larger world. After all, this strikingly exceptional heroine is wrong for most of the novel, wrong in the personal and class snobbery that keeps her so geographically limited and wrong in the melodramatic conventionality of the romance stories she invents. The narrative point, surely, is that such stases, and such certainty, are not particularly desirable.

Emma should have left home, imaginatively if not literally, should have moved beyond the blindnesses attendant on her overly confined-life. She and her sister have been shaped by a father who is committed to being an invalid, committed, that is, to sustaining the degree of power and control made possible through refusing ever to move outward from the small boundaries of the world you personally rule. Mr. Woodhouse, that gentle tyrant, has taught Emma well, has assured her of her superiority in the little world they dominate and has, through his very inaction, encouraged her in the belief that the only way always to be first is never to leave home.

Emma can be read, then, as a novel about geography, an extended debate between the forces for stasis and the forces for movement out to the regions stretching beyond our domestic sphere, each side struggling to persuade the young woman with "the power of having rather too much her own way, and a disposition to think a little too well of herself" to join their point of view.

The novel, after all, is full of movement, of repeated instances of traveling. With the exception of the Woodhouses and the Bates, no one seems to stand still. Since, through the narrative technique, we stand with Emma, we can only get reports about all the trips the other characters take. But those reports are almost continuous. Recollect that Frank Churchill seems to travel so much as to appear virtually adrift. As Mr. Knightley, suffering from stabs of jealousy, so sharply puts it, "'He cannot want money—he cannot want leisure. We know, on the contrary, that he has so much of both, that he is glad to get rid of them at some of the idlest haunts in the kingdom. We hear of him for ever at some watering-place or other'".

Frank's conduct, in spite of Mr. Knightley's rather sniping account of it, reminds us that covering a lot of territory is not really the point, that one can move around with no more purpose than self entertainment—a goal the sedentary Emma is herself far too familiar with. On the other hand, it was on one of those trips to a watering-place, Weymouth that Frank was so blessed as to get to know Jane Fairfax well enough to become engaged to her, clearly the best thing that could have happened to him. Thinking about Frank suggests that whatever an active geographical sense may mean in one of Austen's novels, that meaning is complex.

Yet not to move out to the world beyond Highbury is clearly a mistake, and probably an egotistical position to take. I want to emphasize how pervasive movement is in this story, how virtually everybody is doing it. Mr. Weston had traveled all over before settling at Randalls, both as a Captain in the militia and as a businessman. Jane Fairfax, of course, was orphaned as an infant, and in her third family before the age of nine. She has grown up traveling around with the Campbells, and her very presence in the story is as a temporary visitor whose next destination is unknown. Emma's sister, Isabella Knightley, for all she shares her father's fondness for the privileges and controls made possible by sickness and invalidism, does her share of traveling, not only living in London and visiting Highbury but even taking a vacation trip to the seaside. Mr. Knightley takes a sudden trip to London to avoid watching Emma flirt with Frank, a motive for travel in no way superior to Frank's popping into London to buy a piano for Jane.

Even Harriet can make a significant journey, accomplishing in London what she did not in Highbury: seeing the dentist and accepting the hand of farmer Martin. And surely one sign of the ways Emma has moved out from the self-centered vision which distorted her better understanding for so much of the novel is that her plan at the end is precisely to travel a little, for she and Mr. Knightley to take as their honeymoon "a fortnight's absence in a tour to the sea-side". Clearly, then, leaving home, seeing something of a world beyond the neighborhood, is a major part of all of Austen's novels, including even *Emma*. It was, after all, a major part of Austen's own life.

Geographic range, whether it took the form of trips to London, to Bath or Weymouth or Brighton, or to other family's estates, was typical behaviour for the leisured gentry of Austen's time. One implication of this historical point is that one cannot define the domestic sphere, either in or out of Austen's novels, as somehow isolated or retired or set apart from public life. In fact, the line between private and public life, unless we mean by public those activities which were explicitly restricted to men, such as serving in Parliament or being in the militia or the navy or riding in horse races, becomes harder and harder to draw.

If the domestic sphere, or private life, takes place not only in girls' bedrooms or sitting rooms in their homes or in the back rooms of their dressmaker's shop, but also in the drawing room and at dinner parties at a whole range of houses in various counties of England, and also at the theater or in shops and carriages or on the street or in public rooms, perhaps in London or Bath or Lyme or Portsmouth; then that sphere is surely the sphere where everyone lives, men as well as women, and not some separate women's world. Austen's novels are certainly focused on young women who come from the rural gentry, but even in her limited number of narratives these young women go almost everywhere. Her novels are not set so much in domestic spaces as in social spaces: all the places where men and women, whether relatives, friends, acquaintances or strangers, meet and make connections and live their lives.

Emma's stasis, her geographic narrowness, is finally not sustainable either in the England in which Austen lived or in the England which she created. In terms of the plot, where the other characters often travel is precisely to Emma's enclosed little sphere. The movement of the action is like wave after wave of increasingly less manageable invasions of what Emma had considered her own turf. Mr. Elton and Harriet are more or less locals, it is true. Then along come Jane and Frank, locals but surely from the larger world. And then Mrs. Elton, clamoring, often successfully, to take over Emma's position as first. There is no place, not even Hartfield, protected from the claims, and the possibilities, of the larger world.

Most of us would agree that Austen's visions of personal lives carry a political meaning. That meaning is usually discussed in terms of contemporary debates about women's rights. Roger Sales has argued that "the detail about the travel arrangements in *Emma*, together with the way in which much of it highlights relationships between mobility and power, needs to be seen as an important part of a political argument about the positioning of women". He suggests that mobility is a kind of opportunity not open to women as it is to men. I would also suggest, somewhat differently, that mobility can as easily represent lack of power. Jane Fairfax has mobility because she travels with a Colonel and his family, not because she has the economic right to control her own location.

Without money, Jane must move around as others dictate, while her equally impoverished relatives, Miss and Mrs. Bates, can't go anywhere. The narrative point is not that men have mobility and women don't but that both settling down and moving around involve money, and the social independence that economic independence can bring. But money is not the only issue here. The politics of *Emma* are concerned in many ways with the position of women, with their economic and their social constrictions and, most eloquently, with their future possibilities. Both the constrictions and the possibilities are presented in generational terms, in Austen's insight that daughters are inheritors, and they may inherit a great many things besides an income. What they inherit adds a national dimension to Austen's debate about the future of her heroines.

The question of what young women can and should become, cast in terms of what the past has to offer them, turns out to include a perspective on England's inheritances and possibilities as well. A telling moment in *Emma* is when we are introduced to Jane's "inheritance." She is the daughter of a Lieutenant Fairfax who had died "in action abroad", most plausibly in the Napoleonic Wars, her mother dying soon after and Jane left without financial or personal support. Jane's parents, the fighting lieutenant and the widow dead of grief, represent the values and sacrifices of an England caught up for more than two decades in the Napoleonic Wars. Jane is one of the multitudes of casualties from those Wars.

By 1814, the year Austen wrote *Emma,* the Wars had been defining national values for years in terms of active aggression and suffering. Paralleling this military view the novel also offers a civilian version, a sketch of those who watched the wars from home, represented by Emma's father. Mr. Woodhouse is as militant as any soldier in an invalidism which provides him with the victories possible through a policy of isolation. War without and a defensive isolationism based on fear, particularly fears of French invasion, within were the twin poles of British politics during the Napoleonic Wars. These are the two stances which the new generation received as a legacy of those wars. But in 1814, with Napoleon defeated and banished to Elba, peace looked possible at last. Fighting and isolationism looked like an inadequate inheritance, to shape a young woman or a nation.

The daughters who have inherited these legacies, Jane and Emma, must put them aside. Instead, they must forge a new form of relating to the larger public sphere, one which, I would say, can combine Jane's mobility with Emma's power to be creative. Jane, who has long since moved extensively in the larger world, will have restored, in extravagant measure, the one element the war had taken from her: the financial security to make her own decisions. And Emma will relinquish the false control inherent in living a confined life and join with Mr. Knightley to take a little trip out into the greater world. She will never become as far-ranging a traveller as Jane. Nor need she. For these new young women, and the new England they will help to make, all the chance for a future requires is the optimism to move outward and that right to make that choice themselves.

The joy of future peace which so animates this novel is seen in its hopes for young women's new choices and its hopes for a new national identity. Emma's personal move away from isolation without losing personal power also carries a possibility for England. The nation too needs to abandon attitudes of self-defensiveness, entrenched opinions and conservative identities, both about itself and about other nations. The novel argues for a personal politics of openness and expanding relationships. It argues for the possibilities, political as well as personal, international as well as domestic, in throwing off the protective insularity of the war years and engaging sympathetically with the ever interesting, ever expanding, wide wide world. That is the kind of geographic promise which Austen offers Emma, and which her novels are still offering to her readers.

And yet, and yet..., there remains something still to be said. Emma's story is hardly a simple hymn to the charms as well as the virtues of engaging with the larger peacetime world of Regency England. In terms of the love story, it is hard to see any significant reason for leaving home if what home can offer is Mr. George Knightley cheerfully dropping by. That is surely part of Austen's point. Home is a wonderful place to be. But that was true at the very beginning of the novel, when Emma reigned at Hartfield, Mrs. Weston had just left to be married, and Mr. Knightley stopped by, bringing with him the affection of long years. Yet all this is not enough to bring Emma and Mr. Knightley together, for affection to be ignited into passion, or there would be no book to write.

Both become aware of their love through jealousy,

through thinking another might gain the heart of the person whom they had not even been aware they loved. They need Frank Churchill dashing around looking like such an appropriate beau, and Harriet finding romantic Mr. Knightley's kindness in asking her to dance, then speaking her admiration for him. Austen's radical argument is that for Emma and Mr. Knightley to find their happiness rural retirement is not enough.

They need the help of the rest of the world. Once a definition of home and of nation includes the imaginative geography required for women to acknowledge and then to participate in shaping a larger community, the way is cleared in *Emma* for the happy ending. This larger definition of home helps to explain the narrative function of one of the odder characters in this novel: the other brother, the doppelganger Knightley, John. George and John are presented as notably alike, but with a fundamental difference. John argues, without the gentleness of Mr. Woodhouse (with whom he has more in common than he knows), for the old ways.

He represents a domestic tyranny which reads only as "folly"—"people's not staying comfortably at home when they can" and announces with discomforting isolationist certainty that "'I never dine with any body.'" John, of course, has chosen control, with the larger world as a threat and home as a safety zone. And part of what makes home so safe is the presence of a dependent woman. Isabella, his wife, is appropriately the sister whose conversations can be ignored and whose decisions can be made for her.

The difference between the two brothers is that George Knightley has long since learned the charms of "not staying comfortably at home when [he] can." And thus he has come to love a far different kind of woman, a woman never loath to be first, a heroine who will never put up with being ignored and will never understand domesticity as keeping life cozy for a man. Mr. Knightley and Emma both, though he perhaps a little earlier than she, have come to appreciate not only themselves but also the life that lies outside their imaginations and their knowledge. And because they have, the two are capable of that beautifully liberated social and geographic solution to the problem of their romance: that as Emma's husband, Mr. Knightley will leave his home, and move into hers. All those who have studied Austen texts carefully soon realise that she develops her stories through a careful sequencing of time. Scenes, pictorial narratives, meditations are all placed in a rhythm which imitates diurnal time as all people communally experience it.

This sequencing is the framework within which she will suddenly slow down a narrative and devote chapters to a single experience which psychological or individual time remembers as having occurred over a long while. To achieve the on-going rhythm of two kinds of verisimilitude she used the almanacs of her day as the structuring underpinnings of her books. There have been numerous articles by Austen scholars arguing that a particular novel is set in a particular year and what we may infer from this. What I have done is read all these and through a close reading of Austen's works drawn a probable calendar out for each. The visitor to my site is invited to look at each of the calendars in order to discover the ways in which each novel is put together. When you discover this, you can see the different goals Austen had for each novel, and geologize into the early history of the revisions, and the ways in which she uses omniscient, epistolary, and psychological narrative. Or the reader can use these calendars to understand the novel that is in front of them more clearly simply to enrichen reading of the novel, to see what is literally there and the fineness of Austen's art.

The calendars are also intended to help people writing about and teaching Austen who want to reach her text in the most fundamental way. In each of the sections I have included a bibliography for further research for each novel. For general information on almanacs in the period, the reader is referred to Bernard Capp's *English Almanacs, 1500-1800: Astrology and the Popular Press* (Ithaca: Cornell University Press, 1979), For persuasive arguments that Austen was more or less continually at work on her novels from the initial writing of the first drafts beginning in 1793-94 of *Susan* (later *Northanger Abbey*); *Elinor and Marianne* (later *Sense and Sensibility*); and *First Impressions* (later *Pride and Prejudice*; to the rough first draft gotten down in 1817 of the fragment of a novel Chapman entitled *Sanditon* (perhaps called by Austen *The Brothers*); see Q. D. Leavis, "A Critical Theory of Jane Austen's Writings", *Scrutiny*, 10 (1941-42), pp. 114-142, 272-294; 12 (1944-45), pp. 104-119, Brian Southam's *Jane Austen's Literary Manuscripts: A Study of the Novelist's development through the surviving papers* (Oxford: Clarendon Press, 1964) and Yasmine Gooneratne's *Jane Austen* (Cambridge: At the University Press, 1970).

My work on Anne Finch came into this project too: in Heneage Finch's later years (after Anne died), he kept his diary on the back pages of an almanac; he also recorded one of her poems which does not appear in any edition printed yet on the back page of one of these sheets. Having studied his almanac very thoroughly, I had a good understanding of what such books were which Austen kept beside her as she wrote. They include such things as interest in astrology which makes the place of the moon, planets and stars significant. Austen will use the position of the sun in the sky at a given time, on a given day in a specific year as part of her setting.

I present the calendars in the order in which I think the texts were written. I have not yet drawn the calendar from the very early epistolary fragment "Lesley Castle" (from *Volume the second*) but list the fragment and hope to include an abstract of the calendar eventually.

- "Lesley Castle" from *Volume the Second*
- *Lady Susan*
- *The Watsons*
- *Sense and Sensibility*
- *Pride and Prejudice*
- *Mansfield Park*
- *Emma*
- *Northanger Abbey*
- *Persuasion*
- *Sanditon*

Using these calendars and my study of all the primary documents and much secondary literature on Austen of all kinds, I have written a chronology of Austen's writing life. These calendars also reveal a startling pattern built into the novels by Austen. Excepting only *Northanger Abbey,* Austen makes sure a certain kind of pivotal event in her longer finished novels occurs on a Tuesday. This pivotal event is a snubbing or humiliation of the heroine or hero (or anti-hero or co-heroine), some sort of mortification or unpleasant awakening which climaxes, or provides important turning points in Austen's narrative. This "bad Tuesday" occurs as early as the *Juvenilia* (in "A Collection of Letters" in the fourth letter the unhappy Miss Grenville arrived in Essex on Tuesday). For most of these dramatic moments one does not even have to work out that the day is Tuesday. Austen will cite the day as Tuesday at least once, in some cases a couple of times — apparently determined to make Tuesday a significant day.

AESTHETICS AND ETHICS

In a memorable scene in Joseph Andrews, Henry Fielding likens Lady Booby, sexually rebuffed by her virtuous servant, to "the statue of surprize" spoken of by poets. Presumably, he invokes an old metaphor of astonished or fearful people as petrified, but the ambiguity of his phrase raises the possibility of a sculpture fashioned to represent an allegorical figure named "Surprize." If such a deity did not exist, it would be necessary to invent it as the presiding spirit of the eighteenth-century novel, an emergent genre that signally promised to exceed the reader's expectations, as well as the equally new discourse of aesthetics, which adopted surprise as a key term in the emotional lexicon of artistic experience.

The full title of Robinson Crusoe's narrative, to cite only one example, advertises the wayward sailor's Life and Strange Surprizing Adventures, the adjective of the new modifying an old signifier of romance. Defoe's title indicates both the strangeness and veracity of the narrator's experiences: real rather than fantastical, and thus all the more surprising; or, in Michael McKeon's formula for the epistemology of seventeenth-century news-ballads and early novels, "strange, therefore true". What the adjective "surprising" adds to "strange" is affect—the emotional response activated by the extraordinary, the foreign, or the inexplicable. It also encompasses a wider range of experience, since not everything that is surprising is necessarily strange; the mundane, too, can be arresting. In its participial ambiguity, the word aptly suggests the intersection of characters and readers in the eighteenth-century novel: both are meant to be jolted out of ordinary patterns of perception and thought; both will be seized by an experience of the new.

As an adventure-narrative, Crusoe promises an aesthetic form of surprise (delight in the new); and as a spiritual autobiography of self-correction, it delivers a salubrious moral surprise (the experience of being jolted from inattention into awareness). Jane Austen's Northanger Abbey, famous as a novel about novel-reading, crystallizes many salient features of the eighteenth-century discourse of surprise. Its young heroine Catherine Morland, who temporarily leaves the provincial routine of Fullerton for the social intrigues of Bath, is perpetually startled by the books she reads and the people she meets, even as Austen's narrator archly registers the presumably jaded reader's familiarity with novelistic conventions and the ways of the world. The emotion of surprise is important to all of Austen's novels, but it appears with particular intensity and frequency in this one. Even more than in Sense and Sensibility or Persuasion, the heroine's courtship is mediated by eighteenth-century aesthetic discourse.

Discussing the plots and merits of novels, acquiring the language of the picturesque, parsing the lexical nuances of words for the sublime ("shocking") and the beautiful ("nice"), learning to love a rose—all are alibis (and stimuli) for the growing erotic interest between Catherine Morland and Henry Tilney. These things are, like Henry himself, novelties to Catherine, and it is partly for this reason that surprise figures so prominently in the narrative. In reading Northanger Abbey through this lens, I wish to challenge critical accounts that either dismiss surprise as a symptom of the young heroine's naivete or overlook it in favour of its stronger relative, alarm; and thus to identify in the novel a powerful eighteenth-century idea and narrative device.

Stuart Tave, the first critic to comment on the prevalence of the word in the novel, offers this gloss: "Surprise is a foolish thing, as it offers itself in, for example, the indeterminateness of what is 'odd' as it creates the emotion of an undefined 'alarm,' it is dissolved; in its stead is a process of understanding by means of 'observation' of what is and a determination of 'probability'". In what is essentially a novel of education, Catherine Morland must abandon her gothic suspicion that her host at the abbey, General Tilney, has murdered his wife, and yield to a clear-eyed reckoning of the probable. Critics have since revised Tave's premise by retrieving "alarm" from the realm of the naive and feeble-minded to assert genuine, lingering concerns that the novel cannot resolve or contain. As Tony Tanner phrases it, borrowing Austen's own terms, "'Common life' has proved to be capable of producing surprising uncommonness; anxiety may be a form of controlled alarm".

The patriarchal tyranny of General Tilney, who summarily banishes Catherine from the abbey after discovering that she is not the wealthy catch for his son that he had imagined, is momentarily softened rather than decisively cured; and in Tanner's punning observation, the ghostly traces of "anger"—snobbery, cynicism, emotional coldness, patriarchal irritability—still linger. Similarly borrowing Austen's own terms, Claudia Johnson observes that Northanger Abbey is "an alarming novel to the extent that it, in its own unassuming and matter-of-fact way, domesticates the gothic and brings its apparent excesses into the drawing rooms of 'the midland countries of England'". Echoing D.A. Miller's argument about the novel and its anticlosural discontents, Johnson suggests that Austen draws our attention to the fact that "the convention of the happy ending conceals our all-too-legitimate cause for alarm".

The real cause, in Johnson's reading, lies in the arbitrary power of paternal figures like General Tilney, a domesticated

English version of Radcliffe's villainous Montoni. There is no more incisive commentator on this dynamic than Austen herself, who summarizes Catherine's enlightened disenchantment at the end of the novel as a change of genre, feeling, and linguistic register: "The anxieties of common life began soon to succeed to the alarms of romance". It is not at all surprising that Austen's affective language would be so readily imported into late twentieth-century critical rubrics of anxiety, subversion, interrogation and critique; and Tanner's and Johnson's readings tell a fundamental truth about the novel's dialectic.

These accounts, as well as Tave's, use the gothic as a reference-point: for Tave, a foil to the domestic and ordinary, for Tanner and Johnson, an amplification of issues of gender and power. But Austen's parodic staging of gothic sensations appears late in the novel, and by the time Catherine reaches the abbey, she has already experienced plenty of jolts, none of them tinged with the horror of Radcliffe or Lewis. I would agree with Tanner and Johnson that Austen asserts genuine causes for alarm in the novel, but I also wish to emphasize the importance of an often-overlooked emotional correlate. The difference between alarm and surprise is, in part, a function of time: the former is a state of sustained fear or anxiety; the latter is a briefer flare of feeling, a passage to some other emotional or cognitive state, and an experience that can be a source of either discomfort or pleasure, or both.

Many readers have noticed the novel's stylistic unevenness, the awkward fit between the parody of romantic fiction and the Burneyesque narration of a young woman's entrance into the world; and by focusing on surprise, I wish to identify an emotional current that runs through both parts. I will make several arguments about the function of surprise in Northanger Abbey. First, it is a feature of the narrative itself, which is concerned with the reader's experience of the novel as both familiar and new; it is not only a state to transcend through rational judgment but also a figure of delight. Catherine's susceptibility to surprise serves not merely as a sign of naivete or ignorance but also as a moral register of other characters' foibles; like Candide's perpetual astonishment, it is an instrument of satirical commentary.

Rather than merely mocking Catherine's susceptibility, Austen places it in dialogic relation with other ways of being in the world: the novel is peopled with characters who adopt defenses against shock, and these attitudes are as much a subject of comedy as Catherine's episodes of bewilderment. Such defenses come in several forms, often inflected by elements of masculine control: the assertion of special knowledge or omniscience, the attitude of stoic confrontation, the claim of intuitive or predictive powers. Surprise in Northanger Abbey might be called the emotional corollary to the novel's often-noticed preoccupation with the probable - the ordinary or normal, the statistically typical, the logically inferred, the devoutly wished-for. Finally, as we shall see, it is a reflection of Austen's conspicuous concern with her readers' response to the novel—their familiarity with conventions, their literate resistance to surprise.

PHYSICAL ATTACKS AND COGNITIVE JOLTS

In its earliest sense, the word "surprise" meant the military strategy of attacking without warning, from the French surprendre (to seize or, more literally, to overtake); but that meaning quickly migrated into the cognitive realm. The flux between these senses is memorably registered throughout Paradise Lost, in its Christian revisions of epic battles and sneak-attacks. When the tutelary angel Raphael advises Adam to "govern well thy appetite, lest Sin / Surprise thee, and her black attendant Death", he invokes both senses of "surprise": Sin is an external foe that attacks in a moment of weakness, and in the immediate aftermath, the sinner is astonished—too late—by what he has done. Traces of the earlier etymology persist in eighteenth-century usage.

Applied to women's experience, for instance, the word "surprise" often had a sexual connotation. Richardson's Pamela, to use an emblematic example, often registers the surprise of Mr. B's unwanted advances—a mixture of physical assault and emotional disturbance. As a cognitive phenomenon, meanwhile, surprise became an important component of eighteenth-century aesthetics: in Joseph Addison's terms, it is the emotion associated with Novelty, one of the three primary pleasures of the imagination. In this spectrum of feeling, surprise stands between the astonishment of Greatness and the "secret Satisfaction and Complacency" of Beauty. "Every thing that is new or uncommon raises a Pleasure in the Imagination," Addison says, "because it fills the Soul with an agreeable Surprise, gratifies its Curiosity, and gives it an Idea of which it was not before possest". We are so vulnerable to habit and boredom that this emotion "serves us for a Kind of Refreshment, and takes off from that Satiety we are apt to complain of in our usual Entertainments".

Edmund Burke, in simplifying Addison's triad into the binary of Sublime and Beautiful, passed over surprise to focus on the more powerful feeling of astonishment, noting that the word comes from the French participle etonne, "thunderstruck"; the word thus names an experience of terror in the face of forces beyond our control. Surprise, on the other hand, is milder than this—an "inferior" affect, along with admiration, reverence, and respect. By implication, whereas astonishment involves a solitary and utterly terrifying experience, surprise belongs to the realm of social existence.

Adam Smith makes precisely this point in the Theory of Moral Sentiments: "The amiable virtues consist in that degree of sensibility which surprises us by its exquisite and unexpected delicacy and tenderness. The awful and respectable, in that degree of self-command which astonishes by its amazing superiority". Along similar lines, Hugh Blair discriminates among a cluster of affective terms sometimes used in interchangeable ways: "I am surprised with what is new and unexpected; I am astonished, at what is vast of great; I am amazed with what is incomprehensible; I am confounded, by what is shocking or terrible". Sucia points would not be lost on the pedantic Henry Tilney, in whose presence female companions are threatened with being "overpowered by Johnson and Blair".

In *Northanger Abbey* John Thorpe tells Catherine Morland

that she can forget her scheduled walk with the Tilneys because he saw them leaving town a half-hour ago; he then gets Catherine into his gig, only to pass the Tilneys walking on the sidewalk coming to meet her. She calls to him to stop, but he refuses. In spite of her repeated pleas for him to stop the carriage and let her out, he merely whips the horse into a faster pace, laughing as he goes.

This scene perfectly illustrates a familiar scenario in Jane Austen: that of someone riding roughshod over someone else's rights. If the obvious, surface plot of her novels is courtship, there is, I suggest, a less obvious but equally intense plot at work in the Austen novels, a plot that provides a sort of metaphorical context within which the courtship story unfolds. This backgrounded plot is the struggle between aggressors and their victims. To explain what I mean, I will borrow a distinction made by the popular books on "assertiveness training" that have appeared in the last few years, teaching shy folk that they should stop letting people walk all over them, should learn to say "no" when they have taken on all that they can handle, should express their preferences more readily, and so on.

These books (of which *Your Perfect Right*, by Alberti and Emmons, is perhaps the most intellectually respectable, being written by two bona fide academic researchers) usually make a distinction between "assertive" and "aggressive" behaviour, a distinction that will be useful in discussing Jane Austen:

"Assertive" behaviour is any behaviour toward another person that directly, firmly and honestly expresses one's feelings, wishes, needs, or legitimate rights – but which at the same time respects the feelings, needs and rights of the other person.

"Aggressive" behaviour, by contrast, is any behaviour that *blatantly disregards* the needs or rights of other people in the blind, juggernaut pursuit of the aggressor's own goals.

A third type of interpersonal behaviour implicit in this analysis is non-assertive or passive behaviour – the total failure to take *any* definite action on one's own behalf at all. The want of resolution thus exemplified leaves the person highly vulnerable to the machinations of bolder, more aggressive types. Turning to Jane Austen, I contend that in an Austen novel the courtship plot is only the surface plot. The real plot is the incessant struggle of decent, well-behaved, considerate people to hold their own against self-seeking, aggressive types who disregard the restraints of etiquette or ethics and ruin the plans of any who stand in their way. This other plot is not exactly a sub-plot, in the sense that in *Pride and Prejudice* the courtship of Jane and Bingley is a sub-plot to the main plot of Elizabeth and Darcy.

Rather it is a "constant" in the social scheme, operating somewhat as static on a radio does: the action of the courting couple always proceeds in spite of it, and they are always at least half-aware that it may break forth in their own relationship. Before looking at this phenomenon in *Pride and Prejudice*, let me offer brief examples from the other novels:

Northanger Abbey: Isabella Thorpe consistently lavishes the most insincere nonsense upon Catherine Morland, proclaiming deep and lasting friendship, only to further her designs upon Catherine's brother, James. Naïve Catherine has developed no defences against aggression and takes a long while to become wise to it. John Thorpe shows his own brand of aggressive behaviour toward her, as we have already seen. For some time the naïve and well-bred Catherine meekly and non-assertively goes along with Thorpe's behaviour. However, the day finally comes when she does assert herself: when he runs to the Tilneys and makes her excuses for her, Catherine at last rebels. She races to the Tilneys (not only against his protest, but against that of Isabella and James as well) and rights the wrong. She is learning her first lesson in getting tough with aggressors.

Sense and Sensibility: the name Fanny Dashwood will call to mind a stupifyingly insensitive action: "No sooner was [Henry Dashwood's] funeral over than Mrs. John Dashwood, without sending any notice of her intention to her mother-in-law, arrived with her child and their attendants." She comes to occupy Norland, with her mother-in-law barely home from the funeral! – a perfect example of the *territorial* aggression mentioned earlier. The next chapter contains the famous scene in which Fanny persuades her husband to give no money to Mrs. Dashwood at all, in spite of Henry Dashwood's specific instructions to his son. Here is double aggression, for not only are the Dashwood women being cheated of their inheritance, but John Dashwood himself is being manipulated to a fare-thee-well.

But these are early scenes, and we can tick off many other instances of aggression in the novel:

Lucy Steele pre-empts Edward from Elinor; Willoughby uses Marianne for his summer pleasure; Mrs. Ferrars treats Edward like a welcome mat; Fanny chooses to have the Steele sisters come to stay at their London house instead of Elinor and Marianne; Robert Ferrars filches Lucy from Edward (not that Edward minds); and so on. People are victimized by aggression from start to finish. *Mansfield Park*: the entire novel chronicles the career of aggression versus non-assertion, as Fanny Price, the meek, non-assertive heroine, attempts to survive the blatant onslaughts of Mrs. Norris and the subtler but equally damaging harassments of Sir Thomas, Henry Crawford, Mary Crawford, Maria Bertram, and even Edmund Bertram, her sometime champion and confidant.

Space will not permit detailed examination, but perhaps one example in each case will suffice to indicate the extent of Fanny's besiegement:

Mrs. Norris, who first thought of having Fanny come live at Mansfield, tries to deny Fanny everything: a fire in her room, a horse, a trip to Sotherton, the use of a carriage to go to a dinner engagement, and so on. Maria Bertram delights to remind Fanny daily of her place as a non-Bertram and a nobody. Sir Thomas causes Fanny excruciating pain when he tries to force her to marry Henry Crawford and makes her feel ungrateful and selfish when she refuses. Henry Crawford blatantly announces to his sister that he plans to make Fanny fall in love with him, as an amusement for himself on his non-hunting days. Mary Crawford pretends to be a friend but abets Henry's egotistic pursuit by manipulating Fanny into accepting the necklace. Even Edmund exploits Fanny by using their confidential relationship for his own selfish end, that of harping forever on his infatuation with Mary Crawford and asking Fanny's advice as to how he should proceed. Fanny outlives this aggression; she never confronts it.

Emma: Emma herself is a major aggressor: consider her manoeuvring of Harriet into rejecting Robert Martin's proposal. She believes she is doing it for Harriet's good, but we see that it is an action of pure ego on Emma's part: she believes she knows what is best for everybody, and she is in a position to force her infallibility on poor Harriet. Harriet's submission to Emma in this matter is *non-assertion* at its worst: she does not say, as a more assertive person might, "Miss Woodhouse, I love Robert Martin and want to marry him. I am going to accept his proposal. I'm sorry if I have to lose your friendship in the bargain, but that is a sacrifice I'll have to make." She has a perfect right to say that, but she just doesn't have the assertiveness to do it.

Knightley's reaction, on the other hand, is characteristically assertive: "You saw her answer! You wrote her answer too. Emma, this is your doing," and so forth. Knightley's schooling of Emma is nearly always a matter of assertiveness confronting aggression. Other aggressors show their colours in *Emma*: Mrs. Elton's mode of behaviour from the very first moment of her arrival in Highbury is aggressive; she sets up as the superior woman in the society, advertising herself with slogans and logos, à la Madison Avenue (Maple Grove, Selina, my caro sposo, etc.). She is a junior-grade Lady Catherine, without the money or the style. Frank Churchill is another aggressor: his behaviour toward Jane Fairfax, the repeated occasions of flirting with Emma in his fiancée's presence, is inexcusable; we cannot pardon him any more than we can pardon Maria Bertram's flagrant behaviour with Henry Crawford in front of Mr. Rushworth.

As in the other novels, the surface plot of *Emma* is courtship: but the subtler and more pervasive plot is the damage, potential and actual, inflicted by these three primary aggressors upon other characters who are either too unassertive to defend themselves (Harriet, Miss Bates) or are simply not in a position to do so (Jane Fairfax). Mr. Knightley provides the assertive norm: he does not hesitate to upbraid Emma for her mistreatment of people; he sees through Frank Churchill's shallowness and refuses to join in Highbury's general adulation of him; he thwarts Mrs. Elton's designs several times (he dances with Harriet when Elton refuses her and joins his wife in smirking; he insists on making out his own guest-list for the strawberry party, when Augusta proclaims she will do it for him).

Persuasion: Anne Elliot suffers daily slights and insults to her maturity and intelligence at the hands of her father and her sister Elizabeth. A typical example is found in Elizabeth's notion of a good way to save money for the sake of the family finances: it consists of not bringing Anne a present from London! In fact she slights Anne on all occasions, out of an abiding need to be the first lady of the family. Sir Walter acts almost as though Anne did not exist, for the very good reason that she does not flatter his ego as Elizabeth does. Her sister Mary also uses Anne for her own selfish needs. Thus is she exploited by the whole family. As in the case of Fanny Price and Harriet Smith, we see Anne taking no really assertive action in response to the aggression: we overhear her private thoughts as she regrets the tactless, snobbish behaviour of her father and sister, but she never speaks her mind to them.

We understand why, of course: she would be wasting her time remonstrating with fools. Still, the author who created Elizabeth Bennet and Mr. Knightley, if she had chosen to do so, could have found a way to let Anne put Sir Walter and Elizabeth in their place. One would have enjoyed an exchange in which Anne might have caused them to see what ego-ridden fools they really are. These hasty suggestions of the workings of aggression in the other novels provide a context within which we may look at the presence of that phenomenon in *Pride and Prejudice,* and at the way that it is (for once in the six major novels) triumphantly thwarted. As an early example is the scene in which the Bingley sisters slash at Elizabeth after she has left the room to attend to Jane: "I hope you saw her petticoat, six inches deep in mud," and so on. Bingley's response is mildly assertive: "Your picture may be very exact,

Louisa, but this was all lost upon me. I thought Miss Elizabeth Bennet looked remarkably well when she came into the room this morning. Her dirty petticoat quite escaped my notice."

The growing hostility of Caroline Bingley toward Elizabeth, born of her all-too-obvious determination to have Darcy for herself, creates the prickly atmosphere that prevails throughout the Bennet sisters' stay at Netherfield. The dramatic high point of this part of the novel is reached when Caroline acidly comments on Elizabeth's "paltry device" of recommending herself to the opposite sex by undervaluing her own. Darcy, answering aggression with cool assertion, says: "Undoubtedly, there is meanness in *all* the arts which ladies sometimes condescend to employ for captivation. Whatever bears affinity to cunning is despicable." The narrator slyly remarks, "Miss Bingley was not so entirely satisfied with this reply as to continue the subject." In fact – though she holds her own very well – Elizabeth is plagued by a succession of aggressors. Caroline Bingley's jealous, catty aggression is followed very soon by Mr. Collins's pompous, stupid, territorial aggression: smacking his lips in anticipation of taking over Longbourn itself, he comes to gobble up one of Longbourn's daughters.

Next comes the sexually exploitative aggression of Mr. Wickham, an evil spirit who charms Eliza into believing the worst of Mr. Darcy and thus largely predetermines her vehement rejection of Darcy's first proposal. And finally, there comes Lady Catherine. Lady Catherine's brand of aggression is tyrannical, self-opinionated; she belongs with Mrs. Norris among those rare humans blessed with infallibility yet condemned to share the earth with their inferiors. At the end of the party, says the narrator, they "gathered round the fire to hear Lady Catherine determine what weather they were to have on the morrow," suggesting that Mother Nature herself hesitates to be assertive with Lady Catherine. (Ironically, Lady Catherine's own daughter provides a perfect example of the scared, non-assertive personality.) However, Lady Catherine's insufferable behaviour sets the stage for the one thoroughly satisfying example, in all of the Austen novels, of aggression being perfectly answered and defeated by a determined application of assertiveness. I refer, of course, to the magnificent confrontation between Lady Catherine and Elizabeth Bennet, when Lady Catherine comes to Longbourn.

The interesting thing for our purposes is that, although Lady Catherine makes one inexcusably aggressive assault after another, Elizabeth never once steps beyond the line of legitimate assertiveness in answering her. She does not give way to abusive language, to name-calling, to insults – in fact, she hardly even becomes heated. Instead, she counters every offensive remark from her assailant with cool, polite logic. The scene is too familiar to require much quoting, but three exchanges will illustrate the point:

- Lady Catherine: Miss Bennet, I insist on being satisfied. Has he, has my nephew, made you an offer of marriage?

Elizabeth: Your ladyship has declared it to be impossible.

- Lady C: You will be censured, slighted, and despised, by every one connected with him. Your alliance will be a disgrace; your name will never even be mentioned by any of us.

E: These are heavy misfortunes. But the wife of Mr. Darcy must have such extraordinary sources of happiness necessarily attached to her situation, that she could, upon the whole, have no cause to repine.

- Lady C.: You are then resolved to have him?

E: I have said no such thing. I am only resolved to act in that manner, which will, in my own opinion, constitute my happiness, without reference to *you*, or to any person so wholly unconnected with me.

The first of these rejoinders includes nothing that an unbiased observer could call offensive, but it stoutly refuses compliance with the demand. The second speech politely undercuts the effect of Lady Catherine's threat and leaves her high and dry. The third could almost stand as the very definition of assertiveness, as Eliza deftly defines what her inalienable human right is: the right to pursue her own happiness without being inhibited by a self-centred aggressor.

But now a question arises: why is it that such a triumphant rout of aggression by assertion occurs so seldom in the Austen novels? It happens occasionally, to be sure. We rejoice when Sir Thomas does eventually quash Mrs. Norris: it happens when he enters the room and says, "Fanny, at what time would you have the carriage come round?"

"My dear Sir Thomas!" cried Mrs. Norris, red with anger, *"Fanny can walk."*

"Walk!" repeated Sir Thomas, in a tone of most unanswerable dignity, and coming farther into the room. – *"My niece walk to a dinner engagement at this time of the year! Fanny, will twenty minutes after four suit you?"*

Ah, we feel, this is more like it; this is what we'd like more often. We feel the same way when Mr. Knightley squelches Mrs. Elton upon her announcing that she will make out the guest-list for his strawberry-party at Donwell Abbey. *"I hope you will bring Elton," said he, "but I will not trouble you to give any other invitations."*

She presses him: "Leave it all to me. I will invite your guests."

"No," he calmly replied, "there is but one married woman in the world whom I can ever allow to invite what guests she pleases to Donwell, and that one is – "

"Mrs. Weston, I suppose," interrupted Mrs. Elton, rather mortified.

"No – Mrs. Knightley; and till she is in being, I will manage such matters myself."

Take *that,* Augusta! These are delicious moments, but how few they are. Most of the time the aggressor is allowed to get away with his/her bullying; other characters on most occasions suppress their true feelings or mutter them privately to a confidante, but do not speak up to the offender. Why does Emma never say anything to Mrs. Elton, whose conduct deserves at least one reprimand per conversation? Emma is neither shy nor weak. Why does she not deliver Mrs. Elton some sort of rebuff? Again, we would like to see Catherine Morland tell Isabella Thorpe that her everlasting insincerity is not only comical but downright harmful, and she ought to stop it. We would like John and Fanny Dashwood to receive a thumping from somebody, preferably Elinor or Marianne, or perhaps Colonel Brandon. Having shown how triumphantly she could do it with Elizabeth and Lady Catherine, why does Jane Austen not give us these scenes? I would offer the following speculations:

- Jane Austen's women have been nurtured on the food of "proper feminine conduct." As Claudia Johnson says, women of Jane Austen's time were required "to be amiably weak, retiring, and docile so as to assure the authority, the chivalry, even the identity of men". Now, in fact, the premise that women and men are made from the same stuff, and that neither sex as a whole is inferior to the other as a whole (though certain individual men may be inferior to individual women, and vice verse) – this premise underlies the action of every Jane Austen novel. The admirable women command the same respect as the admirable men; the unadmired characters of both sexes stand on an equal footing. Nevertheless, Jane Austen could not be unfaithful to what she saw around her every day. In real life an Elinor Dashwood, intelligent, mature, and well-spoken, would not say anything to anyone that could be regarded as "uppity" or "abrasive" ("bitchy" would be the modern term). More accurately, she would probably not have the nerve to do so. She would be letting herself in for shame and disgrace. Some of Byron's society-women could brazen it out (Lady Caroline Lamb, for example), but they accepted the notoriety that went with the careless behaviour. Elinor could not and would not do that, nor would Fanny Price or Anne Elliot.

Thus Jane Austen was probably indulging a fantasy in allowing Eliza Bennet to get away with as much frank expression as she uses; young women of her time would in all likelihood not have survived socially with that degree of outspokenness. The author's remark about *Pride and Prejudice* being altogether too "light and bright and sparkling" may reflect a feeling that she had fudged on reality a little in making Eliza freer than most women were actually able to be, just as she had done in allowing Eliza to be as idealistic about marriage as she was; Charlotte Lucas's views come closer to the sad truth of female necessity in her time. Hence, there would have been a reluctance on Jane Austen's part to get quite that far from actuality again. So, in her next novel she chose to depict a young woman repressed by everyone in her household. Fanny's literal repression by everyone at Mansfield, if taken figuratively, signals the general repression of women by the entire society.

- Paradoxically, the very desire to *subvert* this entrenched notion of woman's place may have led her to muzzle her heroines in order to make the injustice more keenly felt. Feeling the daily and hourly frustration of the intelligent woman unable to speak her mind for fear of censure, how was she to drive home the wrongness of it except to make the reader *feel* the same frustration that she and every other intelligent woman of her time (Mary Wollstonecraft and Mary Godwin Shelley, to name two) must have felt under the prevailing edicts of the conduct books, parental training, dull sermonizing, and general socialization that emphasized to young women the necessity of demureness, sweetness, modesty, and acceptance of inferiority? As Mary Poovey has said, in writing of *Persuasion*,

For, given the liabilities of both individualism and paternalistic values, Austen's ideal solution was to use one system of values to correct the abuses of the other. But in doing so, Austen inadvertently exposed tensions inherent in both ideologies, and even in her symbolic resolution of these tensions, she laid bare the ideological configuration that was finally most damaging to women. Thus it is easy for us to say, for example, that Elinor Dashwood's mother *should* have said to Fanny Dashwood, "Fanny, you may be legally entitled to occupy this house; but to move into it the moment my husband's funeral was over is the most unfeeling and improper behaviour I have ever witnessed by any human being." It is, I say, easy for us to write such speeches and smugly announce that that is what *we* would have said if *we* had been Mrs. Dashwood.

But it was *not at all* that easy for a woman of that time to say such things in a public, social situation. The rarity of assertive confrontations with aggressors in these novels is not incompatible with an authorial decision to let the terrifying frustration of women's entrapment in social repression be felt to the point that the reader *would* cry out in exasperation for the heroine to tell somebody off. Having driven the reader to the wall, the author can smile and say, "Aha, my friend! I perceive that you begin to see how it feels." But when all is said and done, there is a retribution for aggression in the novels. We tend to overlook – because it never comes up in the novels – Jane Austen's private devotion to Christianity. Consider her prayer for humility:

Incline us oh God! to think humbly of ourselves, to be severe only in the examination of our own conduct, to consider our fellow-creatures with kindness, and to judge of all they say and do with that charity which we would desire from them ourselves.

Transgressions of this humble approach to human relationships abound in her novels, and the non-assertive heroines alone seem to carry it out (Anne Elliot perhaps most serenely). The prayer says a great deal about the impression a John Thorpe, a John or Fanny Dashwood, a Lady Catherine, a Mrs. Norris, or a Sir Walter Elliot (to name a few) must have made upon her when she encountered their human counterparts in a social situation. On the surface the prayer may seem to underwrite the notion of accepting one's inferior station, but it is not written for a woman any more than for a man; it counsels Christian humility, regardless of sex. And Christian humility is precisely what the Fanny Dashwoods, Lady Catherines and Sir Walter Elliots do *not* evince.

The Lady Catherines of the world will not "be severe only in the examination of their own conduct"; they will not examine their conduct at all. Instead they will assign a living to a toady like Collins so as never to face any unpleasant truths about themselves, except on those revolting occasions when they run afoul of an Elizabeth Bennet or a Mr. Knightley. Thus, keeping her heroines from assertive rejoinders is not inconsistent with a decision to leave final judgements and punishments to Providence. We sense the subtle workings of psychological revenge upon those without the intelligence and the Christian humility to change their perceptions and their behaviour. Increasingly cut off from the warmth and love felt by the more open-hearted, generous, decent members of society, these self-seeking, hurtful aggressors will live in wretched isolation – wealthy, perhaps, but emotionally impoverished, the ironic victims of their own aggression. Mrs. Norris and Maria Bertram will live out their days with none but each other for company. So will Sir Walter and Elizabeth Elliot, and John and Fanny Dashwood, and all the other insensitive, self-focused, static personalities of the novels. Incapable of emotional and intellectual growth, they will smolder all their days in a hell of their own devising.

SCHEMES OF SISTERLY HAPPINESS

"An Englishman's home is his castle." By the end of the first quarter of the nineteenth century this castle-home becomes the axiological sign standing for an entire system of social and personal values, which, when mapped out, look conspicuously like the blueprint of a middle-class house and simultaneously like a feudal system of fortifications. The vulnerable core and inner sanctum of that hard and inviolable edifice is the sister's chamber. The family romances of the period depict the sister figure as the most pure, selfless, innocent and vulnerable—and therefore, most valuable—member of the English family. It is she who is the true angel in the house, as only she remains sexually untouched and neutral, and therefore only her dedicated service to the family (and particularly to her siblings) endures uncompromised.

Sororal love is self-evident and requires no explanation; it rationalizes all other acts and emotions, and its rejection demands recrimination and retribution. In other words, its abuse provides the motive for plots. The family is organized around the sister's innocence as a defensive system and its protection justifies the family, just as much as the rest of society—including its bellicose commercial, imperial and colonial practices—is justified by virtue of its function as protector of the family. Yet, a close scrutiny of the representation of siblings in nineteenth-century British literature discloses a dialectic of sororal desire which—like all dialectics—involves as much destructive power as it does creative force, as the pressure placed upon the sister figure in the form of moral demands, surveillance, constriction, mediation and channeling of desire reveals that the inner sanctum of the castle, the sister's chamber, is also its dungeon. It thus becomes a site of rebellion, subversion and sororal rage.

This action manifests itself in a system of metonymical links, displacement of emotions and identities, and dissolutions of familial and social boundaries which record on the part of author and audience alike a distinct fascination with and dread of the destructive possibilities of unleashed sororal desire. If Florence Dombey's sweetness, innocence and selfless devotion maps out all the dimensions of English familial ideology, Edith Skewton, Florence's figurative sister (as she is clearly so designated by Dickens) is an angel of destruction, threatening all familial and social values. If George Eliot never questions the inexplicable intensity of Maggie Tulliver's sororal love, its internal logic must necessarily lead to an incestuous necrophilia. If passion in Wilkie Collins's No Name is deepest, most dedicated and most altruistic in the sororal love between Madeleine and Nora Vance, no force is more destructive.

If no love is as all-encompassing as Catherine Earnshaw's for her new brother, none is ultimately so corrosive. This Victorian dialectic of sororal desire may be partially an aftereffect of a somewhat cruder novelistic formula employed in the eighteenth century using pairs of sisters—one good and one bad—to explore feminine identity. But the first sophisticated use of the dialectical ideology that would dominate in the nineteenth century is already evident in Richardson's Clarissa, where we see the disastrous effects of a family's failure to appreciate and protect sororal love, and where we also see that same love initiate a series of discursive and epistolary performative acts whose ultimate effect is the erasure of all familial lines of identity. If such a continuity exists between Richardson in the eighteenth century and nineteenth-century writers like Mary Shelley, Emily Bronte, Harriet Martineau, George Eliot, Charles Dickens, Wilkie Collins, and even Edgar Allan Poe, it should surely appear in the works of Jane Austen, for no great novelist is more famous for her depictions of sororal relations than she.

Indeed, the most well-known and perhaps most beloved of all sisters in English fiction are her creations. Yet, such is not the case: Austen neither engages in the nineteenth-century self-indicting cultural mystification of sisterly love, nor does she display either indignation or rage over the encasement of sororal desire. She reflects neither the formulaic patterns of mid-eighteenth-century sororal typology nor does she act as a bridge between it and the nineteenth century's contradictory sororal perfection and potential subversions. But she certainly had something to say about sisters. Mansfield Park, Sense and Sensibility, Pride and Prejudice, and Persuasion all contain sisters as central figures. And, even though neither Northanger Abbey nor Emma can be called sibling novels, their stories are told with constant allusions to and contexts determined by relations between brothers and sisters.

Michael Cohen has written of Pride and Prejudice that it "insists that all its women are sisters." Commenting on Austen's metaphorization of the sister figure, Cohen writes: "Austen has embraced the idea of using sisters so enthusiastically that she will not stop with the five daughters in the Bennet household but will construct relationships that imitate those of sisters among all women in the book." The novel, he says, "finally... asserts universal sisterhood". But the problem with universal sisterhood is that, if all women are sisters, no woman is a sister. If all similarities, differences, loves, hates, agreements and disagreements are sisterly in nature, then, like the zeroes on both sides of an equation which cancel each other out, sisterhood has lost its explanatory force. Moreover, we seem suddenly to be doing scant justice to Austen's uncanny psychological perspicacity.

Austen indeed peoples her novels with sisters, but of so many shades, hues, intensities, complexities and moral qualities that sisterhood often seems to become mere sisterhood—i.e., only one category among many. Cohen might have seen this for himself. Summarizing the moral of Pride and Prejudice, he says:

We are left with marriages that seem to occur as they must. with as little (Lydia-Wickham) or as much (Jane-Bingley) expectation for happiness as the world ever offers, and a marriage (Elizabeth-Darcy) that shows us not that prudent choices lead to happiness but that the prudent are happy choosing prudently. If there is moral judgment in the book, it has come before any plot events, in rating the capacity of each character for happiness.

In startling contrast to so many of the novels which follow later in the century, and even that of Richardson's Clarissa, in Austen's world the capacity for happiness is not generated by sisterhood, nor is it ultimately limited by it. Austen's novels all have at their centre one or two principal young female figures—where there are two, they are sisters, as in Sense and Sensibility and Pride and Prejudice—and their eventual love objects, who, though usually flawed are ultimately perceptive, reasonable, clever, considerate, dutiful and capable of self-sacrifice. These principal figures are surrounded by a swarm of characters that are either shallow and indifferent, or foolish, egotistical, manipulative, self-seeking, deceitful, obtuse, and spiteful, taking joy in the misfortunes of their competitors. These, the great majority of characters in Austen's fictional world, are intentionally conceived as maddeningly stupid and pretentious-prying, gossipy, preening individuals of both sexes and of varying ages.

Toward the latter, Austen's narrators exhibit a scathing contempt, usually expressed in humorous, ironic tropes, but sometimes in vicious cynicism (as in the account of the death of "poor Richard" Musgrove in Persuasion). A similar dichotomy can be drawn concerning the sibling relationships in Austen's novels. The few that are "true" are flawed and open to development—a development that will eventually bring them close to the formula for sibling love that will dominate much of the literature of the nineteenth century. But unlike so much of that literature, Austen's use of that formula (involving absolute devotion, service to the point of servitude, self-sacrifice and open transparency) is sparingly applied only to those few siblings who, through natural talent and struggle, prove themselves meritorious of the high honour that the designation of "sister" or "brother" automatically bestows elsewhere.

These elect are surrounded by a gaggle of dull, indifferent sibling groups, or stupid, insipid, nasty, opportunistic brothers and sisters who far outnumber the worthy sibling characters and their worthy (sibling-like) lovers. A principal formula in the logic of English domestic ideology involves the selfless sister dedicated to her brother's service. Although Austen wrote no sister-brother novels as such, brothers of varying significance and character do abound in her works. (Of the major novels, only Persuasion contains no sister-brother relationships.) The two books in which sister-brother bonds are most significant are Northanger Abbey and Mansfield Park. In Northanger Abbey, Austen's earliest novel, family ties are visible but not overwrought. We are told almost nothing about eight of the heroine's ten siblings. The bulk of the story takes place in Bath, to which Catherine Morland has been dispatched with a send-off so lackadaisical that the narrator says that it suggests "unpromising auspices."

Following suit, the relation between Catherine and her older brother James, though important in the plot, rarely reaches an intense pitch. Only after he has tried to intimidate her into participating, against her better judgment, in a foolhardy scheme that might further his romance with the dreadful Isabella Thorpe, and only after Isabella has broken his heart, does he write to his sister, "You are my only friend; your love do I build upon." There are two other sister-brother groupings in the novel. The dashing but villainous Captain Tilney and the charming but problematic Henry Tilney (Elizabeth's love object and eventual husband) are siblings of Eleanor Tilney (Catherine's friend and eventual sister-in-law). Eleanor's brothers are "very affectionate" when they are at home, but unfortunately they are usually away. She is particularly pained by Henry's absence; but, when he is home, Henry is "a great comfort to [his] sister".

There are hints here of the kind of sibling ideal that will come to dominate later in the century, but none of this achieves the moral status that is demanded in the Frankenstein family, or in the village of Deerbrook, or at Wuthering Heights, or in the Dombey and Nickleby households, or at the Tulliver hearth—where it is so intense that its betrayal is always diabolically punished. The most interesting sister-brother relationship in the novel is that depicted in the small sub-plot revolving around the Thorpe family. John Thorpe, Catherine Morland's grating, obnoxious, lying, self-serving suitor, insults first his mother ("where did you get that quiz of a hat, it makes you like an old witch"), and then proceeds to insult his sisters. "On his two younger sisters he then bestowed an equal portion of his fraternal tenderness, for he asked each of them how they did, and observed that they both looked very ugly".

Twice he refuses to allow his sisters into his carriage: "I did not come to Bath to drive my sisters about". But the manipulative, social-climbing Isabella stays "loyal" to her brother, seeing in his marriage to Catherine a definite advantage to herself. She tries to convince Catherine that, in urging her to attend to John's protestations of love, she is not thinking of her brother's happiness, but of Catherine's—"What I say is, why should a brother's happiness be dearer to me than a friend's" when in fact it is only her own happiness that is dear to her. No one, certainly not a brother, will stand in the way of that. In Mansfield Park (the plot of which, incidentally, is motivated from the first moment by the bitterness of the three squabbling Ward sisters) we come the closest to finding anything like the "formulaic" sibling relationship in Austen's works.

The curious and much-debated heroine Fanny Price, has five siblings, though the novel only develops in any detail her relationship with her brother William and her younger sister, Susan. Even Susan is a late arrival in the story. She is not mentioned by name until the last fifth of the novel, when Fanny is sent away from Mansfield Park and returns to the chaos of her childhood home in Portsmouth. There, after years of absence, she reunites with Susan. Fanny's emotions move from initial shock at Susan's brazenness, to respect and admiration for her fearlessness and independence of thought.

Chapter 6

Jane Austen and Theatricality in English Novel

"Our society," Michel Foucault argued famously, "is one not of spectacle but of surveillance." This book takes as its point of departure that rather stark representation of "our society," which, in Foucault's account, is also the society of the nineteenth century. That is, the readings offered here presuppose the *overtly* nontheatrical, even antitheatrical, character of the culture inhabited—indeed, to a certain extent, constructed—by the novels under analysis. Yet if these readings depart from that assumption in the sense of proceeding from it, they would also depart from it in the sense of leaving it behind—or would at least challenge it insistently and inventively enough so that a richer understanding of social interaction, both in the nineteenth century proper and in its lengthy, ongoing sequel, might begin to emerge in its place. One of my primary concerns, accordingly, is to show how the novelistic tradition examined here unsettles the distinction between a society of spectacle and a society of surveillance. Of course, if *spectacle* is taken to imply extravagance and ostentation, then *spectacular* is probably not the first word one would apply to the works of Jane Austen, Charlotte Brontë, George Eliot, or even Henry James.

On the contrary, just as this tradition marks the triumphant climax of the well-known rise of the novel, so it has been shown less to record than to help institutionalize what has been dubbed, almost as memorably, the fall of public man—a fall from the theatricality of eighteenth-century culture into the world of domesticity, subjectivity, and psychology, whose intimate, personalized scale, far from providing refuge from surveillance, installs it, with remarkable hospitality, in an apparently infinite number of snug little homes, where it can go about its business under cover of an endlessly idealizing misrecognition.

Thus, while recent studies of eighteenth-century English fiction deploy explicitly theatrical paradigms, it might seem anachronistic or merely wishful to look for theatricality in novels of the privatizing and privatized nineteenth century.[] But I will demonstrate that, though such texts may be less showy than their eighteenth-century predecessors, their very implication in a widespread social network of vigilance and visibility—of looking and of being looked at—renders them inherently, if covertly, theatrical.

After all, Foucault himself has to describe the cells of Bentham's Panopticon, the model of modern discipline, as "so many cages, so many small theatres, in which each actor is alone, perfectly individualised and constantly visible."[] Foucault is obviously not promoting this displaced theatricality as compensation or consolation for the oppressiveness of the regime that contains it, nor is it my intention to celebrate the generalization of the carceral scene in nineteenth-century novels and their culture. The point, rather, is that, instead of simply precluding or negating spectacle, a society of surveillance entails certain rigorous spectacular practices of its own.

Observing those practices at work in and around a series of nineteenth-century texts, the present study repeatedly emphasizes the *normalization* of theatricality, its subtle diffusion throughout the culture that would appear to have repudiated it. However cagey, then, however deficient in the Bakhtinian "carnivalesque" exuberance or (as rehearsed in the opening pages of *Discipline and Punish*) in the sheer Grand Guignol excess that one might associate with earlier manifestations of theatricality, the spectacles of surveillance pervade nineteenth-century fiction.

Yet, another major concern of this book is to make clear

that they thereby account not only for the peculiar efficacy of that fiction as an instrument of social regulation, as Foucauldian literary critics have argued, but also for its unpredictability, for its tendency *not* to accomplish—or not to accomplish quite as faithfully as might have been expected—the cultural task assigned to it. If this book therefore maintains a certain distance from the Foucauldian interpretations to which it is nonetheless indebted, it also differs from, even as it intersects, another recently influential approach to nineteenth-century fiction. I am referring to a group of studies—focused somewhat more on American than on British novels, and somewhat more on the later than on the earlier or the middle nineteenth century—that link nineteenth-century fiction with precisely a "society of the spectacle," reading it as a commentary on, or as an accomplice of, the seductive new hegemony of advertising and of a necessarily *conspicuous* consumption.

Although some of the distinctive preoccupations of critics working in this mode—the marketplace, the commodification of the self—figure significantly here, I hope ultimately to project a more affirmative sense of "spectacle" than that which seems to inform their often scrupulously opaque, even deadpan, accounts. I intend no more to play up any "subversive" potential of consumerist theatricality than to glamorize the theatricality of surveillance. My aim, however, is to show how, if theatrical structures and techniques underlie or enable various coercive cultural mechanisms, the same structures and techniques can threaten those mechanisms' smooth functioning. In the process, I seek not to reclaim some primordial, anarchic essence of theatricality, but to reveal its pragmatic overdetermination, its perverse capacity for doing more than just serving the interests of whatever political ideologies or cultural dispensations happen to have appropriated it.

Indeed, theatricality, as I develop it here, signifies not a single, unitary style or content, but a set of shifting, contradictory energies. Unlike "theater," which may denote a fixed place, institution, or art form, "theatricality" resists such circumscription, owing its value as a critical term to this very open-endedness. Nevertheless, the term is meant to have a specific force and to achieve specific effects in the readings that follow: it is directed not only against the coherent, stable subjectivity that the nineteenth-century novel supposedly secures for both its protagonists and its readers, but also against the domestic, domesticating closure—or, in the case of Henry James, against the aestheticization of that closure as the "house of fiction"—in which that subjectivity supposedly discovers its "natural" habitat. This double function may explain why this book is about "theatricality," rather than about, say, "textuality," in the nineteenth-century novel.

For though the latter term would have (in fact, in the work of other critics, already has) lent itself admirably to the project of deconstructing subjectivity, the trope of "theatricality" enables us both to unpack subjectivity as performance and to denaturalize—to read as a *scene*—the whole encompassing space in which that subjectivity gets constituted: the intricate web of "romantic" bonds and family ties apparently consolidated by the novels in question.[] In other words, if the self is treated here as not just a text but a contingent cluster of theatrical roles, then it becomes possible to make a spectacle of the imperious domestic, sexual, and aesthetic ideologies for which, and in which, it is bound.

And that spectacle, I hope to show, often generates a number of spin-offs, unruly sideshows liable to cause further embarrassment for those forces in the novels (whether characters, author-effects, or other ideological emissaries) that would seem to uphold traditional family values. One consequence of this interpretation of theatricality, then, is that considerable attention is paid in the pages ahead not only to the ways in which theatrical energies are absorbed into what one might imagine, somewhat too organically, as a narrative's flow, but also to the ways in which such energies break or complicate that kind of natural-seeming teleology. Although I by no means see theatricality as necessarily opposed to narrative—indeed, it often allows the latter to enfold it without any trouble whatsoever—at several crucial points here I invoke a distinction, most productively mobilized by feminist film theory, between the patriarchal, heterosexualizing pressure of narrative linearity, on the one hand, and the antilinear counterpressure of a feminist or gay spectacle or masquerade, on the other.

The differences between nineteenth-century theatrical and twentieth-century cinematic categories should not, of course, be elided, but neither, as others have argued, should their continuities be denied, nor should we overlook the mediating role played by the nineteenth-century novel in the process of transmission. This question of method bears not so incidentally on that of the book's scope. As a glance at the table of contents will confirm, I do not undertake a comprehensive study of theatricality in the nineteenth-century English novel. A novelist like Thackeray, who might have seemed an obvious candidate for inclusion here, makes no appearance, and though I devote considerable space to the even more obvious Dickens, he has to share that space with those presumably lesser figures, the "sensation" novelists.

What mainly impels my reading of Dickens, in fact, is my conviction that the most interesting theatricality in nineteenth-century English fiction is not necessarily the most "ebulliently" and most immediately recognizable. I focus more extensively on four other canonical novelists, who are at once more representative of their culture's overt, dominant antitheatricality and more plausibly motivated to rebel against it. For what these four more or less "psychological" novelists have in common, beyond their apparent willingness to produce (in their own distinctive ways, of course) the patriarchal, heterosexualizing narratives for which their culture has so insatiable a demand, is membership in groups (women and gay men, to be precise) that this culture, operating in no small part *through* such narratives, oppresses and marginalizes. This book attempts to determine how the resulting conflicts of interest play themselves out—or fail to play themselves out—in these four authors' works.

Thus, it suggests that when theatricality surfaces in the novels of Austen and Brontë, what gets performed is a complex disruption of the patriarchal narrative enterprise in which those authors are otherwise engaged, and that when James or one of his characters "makes a scene," what we observe is a gaily provocative acting up within and against the policing, pathologizing case histories that he simultaneously inscribes. Eliot would seem to stand out as the anomaly here, refusing the excesses of theatricality in favour of a "poetic" or theoretical metacommentary that would master them. Yet, as we will see, James turns out to have his own investment in dissevering the link between theory and theatricality, and in promoting the former as a defence against the latter.[] Situating the gay male author at the end of a heterosexual female novelistic tradition, this book reads the Jamesian text as a stage on which that tradition's definitive resistances and compliances get recapitulated and reinterpreted in an especially condensed and telling way.

It demonstrates that, though James's sexual and historical positioning may make him unusually anxious about inheriting a repertoire of female and feminist theatrical strategies, accounting for his apparent wish at times to transport himself into the magisterial, ostensibly disembodied realm of aesthetic theory, the same positioning may explain his powerful identification with a certain figure of "the actress" and with the peculiar "commotion" she repeatedly causes. Though it is easy, when writing about texts from an earlier century, to frame such ambivalences in terms of a tension between conscious complicity and unconscious subversiveness, as if the less official-looking aspects of an older text somehow had to exceed authorial awareness, I try not to draw too heavily on this particular implication of the return-of-the-repressed model. Not only does it aggrandize the critic at the expense of the author, but it prejudges and probably misrepresents a wide range of hermeneutic and historical issues, deluding us into thinking that we know what we mean when we talk about such things as authorship, agency, consciousness, and unconsciousness.

In short, I prefer not to create the impression that Austen, Brontë, Eliot, and James enact their *coups de théâtre* in spite of themselves; I try (not always successfully, I am sure) to give them credit for being as politically sophisticated and as rhetorically adroit as, for instance, late-twentieth-century academic critics. Admittedly, the book's title might lead readers to expect that, if I do not set out to uncover what the authors *cannot* know, I have invested in the even more authoritarian fantasy of surprising them in their performance of what they would not want *us* to know.

While I have no doubt occasionally given in, here again, to the all but irresistible interpretative temptations of voyeurism and sadism, it is important to note that I take my title from a passage in James's autobiography where, as we will see, he writes about catching *himself* in the act.

If my critical gaze sometimes seems to recall the fascinated hyper-watchfulness of a certain style of pedagogue from the previous century, it should still be apparent that I aim not so much to expose or to embarrass the authors whom I "catch" as to show them in the process of catching and embarrassing *themselves,* of calling attention parodically or hyperbolically to their own agitated entanglement in the social scripts that determine them, and thus perhaps of agitating or rewriting those scripts from within.

If acting is a kind of interpretation, the reverse is equally true. Organized around the identification of figures in the novels and in their cultural milieu who function as precursors of contemporary reading practices, the book's main subtext is indeed about the theatricality of interpretation; and while the elaboration of this subtext means that, with varying degrees of sympathy, I (get to) catch other critics in the act, I make a point of catching myself as well.

Depending upon the individual reader's tastes, these episodes of "self-consciousness" may embarrass her or him more or less than they embarrass me. In any case, the risk of appearing "self-important" or "pretentious" (terms the mere thought of which terrifies—which is to say, forms—the middle-class subject, not least the middle-class academic subject) seems worth running, for, despite the recent proliferation in literary and cultural studies of work on theatricality, vital questions about the performative effects of criticism itself—most basically, about *what* contemporary critics are performing, and about what or whom they are performing *for*—are only beginning to be posed. If, as Foucault argued, "our society" is an extension of that of the nineteenth century, then we may learn some useful lessons from the acts of interpretation on view in some of that century's most surprisingly and acutely histrionic novels. While one of the most sobering of those lessons would doubtless be how readily almost any would-be oppositional theatrics can be neutralized (if not sponsored from the outset) by the hegemonic culture, the following chapters evince a reluctance to stop with that paradoxically comforting critical trope.

To be sure, as anyone who has ever read an article on contemporary literary-critical discourse in, say, the *New York Times* can attest, it would be a mistake to underestimate the counterparodic genius of cultural orthodoxy. Perhaps the reading that persists in looking for—What should one call them?—transgressive openings in a text will always seem more naïve than the reading that eventuates in an ironic recognition of the capacity of Power to contain subversion; such a consideration may in fact explain the tentativeness with which some of my more optimistic formulations are proffered. At the same time, however, these readings proceed from the assumption that, by strategically reenacting certain scenes inscribed in the novels of Austen, Brontë, Eliot, and James, one may identify and release unsuspected energies of feminist and antihomophobic critique and revision, whose play our culture's theaters of oppression may not, for all their supervisory machinery, be able to keep within bounds.

THEATRICALS AND THEATRICALITY

Though *Mansfield Park* seems the least inclusive or dialectical of Jane Austen's novels, it has failed to produce the critical unanimity that so unambiguous a work ought to permit. Despite repeated attempts to lay the groundwork for scholarly consensus, this ostensibly nonironic novel continues to elicit incompatible commentaries. Paradoxically, its very dogmatism is what makes for disagreement: the question of why Austen, in championing the priggish Fanny Price, should appear to dishonour her own artistic verve, may be answered, it seems, in more than one way. Recent critics are divided between those for whom *Mansfield Park* is an emphatically anti-Jacobin, staunchly Christian work, and those who find in it a disguised yet all the more potent version of the feminist or anti-authoritarian message that other Austen novels develop less obliquely.

From this discord, one is tempted to conclude that the novel's dogma is somehow shakier than it ought to be. This chapter seeks not to determine once and for all whether the presiding genius of *Mansfield Park* is Edmund Burke or Mary Wollstonecraft, but to examine the central instability within the novel itself, the instability that renders such determination impossible. I will argue that the novel is neither unequivocally conservative nor unequivocally progressive, but rather that it is governed by a conservatism so riddled with internal contradictions as to trouble the authoritarian temperament more radically than would the dialectical leniency of, say, *Pride and Prejudice* or *Emma*.

To argue as much, however, will also mean showing the tenacity of that conservatism, qualifying any interpretation too eager to claim *Mansfield Park* as a document of humanistic amplitude. One recent call for a synthesis in Austen criticism asks us to imagine a "structure large enough to accommodate an affirmative text with a subversive subtext." *Mansfield Park* reveals how precarious such a structure must, by definition, be. In a novel that abounds in talk of structures—of their erection, their improvement, and their dismantlement—the most problematic structure is the makeshift "theater" set up in the billiard-room of Mansfield Park. This structure literalizes a somewhat more abstract "structure"—the episode of the theatricals, the textual locus on which so much critical attention has centered. As Jonas Barish has pointed out, "the theatricals come charged with a mysterious iniquity that challenges explanation."

The "crux of the book," the theatrical episode disturbs

us because we cannot see why *Austen* should have been so disturbed by an art form whose energies seem so similar to her own. Yet one might also say that it disturbs us even more insistently precisely because it *is* the crux of the book—because, that is, it has the power to become more than just a local structure, to spread perplexingly throughout the novel, just as the "theater" at Mansfield Park soon extends from the billiard-room, encompassing, of all places, Sir Thomas's study. The episode, which occupies the last third of the first volume, is abruptly terminated by his return from Antigua: he wastes no time in eradicating all traces of the theatricals, not only ordering the sets to be torn down but going so far as to burn every copy of *Lover's Vows,* the play chosen for private performance. Despite this aggressive attempt at effacement, however, and despite the destruction of the theater as place, theatricality as topic turns out to pervade the novel.

In this movement from a literal structure to a more metaphorical one, we witness a process of refinement, of increasingly subtle infiltration. After describing Sir Thomas's swift campaign of destruction, Austen informs us, slyly, that at least *one* remnant of the episode has escaped his ravages: Mrs. Norris has appropriated the curtain, surreptitiously removing it to her cottage, "where she happened to be particularly in want of green baize." This appropriation and transformation might stand for that adaptability which allows the theater to survive and flourish in a less conspicuous form, reaching into the most unlikely recesses of the text. Yet if this shift from theater to theatricality suggests the triumphant expansion of a "subversive subtext," we need to specify just what theatricality entails. As we will see, the political implications of theatricality in *Mansfield Park* are ineluctably ambiguous.

Critics have tended to associate it with the most attractively self-dramatizing characters in the novel, Mary and Henry Crawford, thereby construing it in terms of metropolitan glamor and decadence. Theatricality has a less glittering side, however, and this variant turns out to be surprisingly consistent with the authoritarianism represented, in different ways, by Sir Thomas, Mrs. Norris, Fanny, and Edmund. Wavering between affirmative and subversive poles, the generalized, ubiquitous structure of theatricality begins to expose their relationship as one not of opposition but of almost systematic interdependence. An all-embracing theatricality would seem to threaten the very foundations of a novel whose heroine epitomizes what Tony Tanner calls "immobility," yet theatricality is in fact capable of such wide diffusion only because it has certain features that not merely conform to but even enable the novel's overriding conservatism.

The question, in other words, is not so much "What motivated Austen's anti-theatricalism?" as "What motivated her to create the *impression* of anti-theatricalism?" Alien enough to give her pause yet not so alien as to resist the uses to which Austen puts it, theatricality in *Mansfield Park* affords the spectacle of a distinct overdetermination.

But what in the nature of theatricality allows supposedly rival ideologies to converge upon it? When Fanny Price and Henry Crawford offer their respective descriptions of the theatricals, we note the similarity of their language as much as the difference between their tones. Here is Fanny's view of the rehearsals:

So far from being all satisfied and all enjoying, she found every body requiring something they had not, and giving occasion of discontent to the others.—Every body had a part either too long or too short;—nobody would attend as they ought, nobody would remember on which side they were to come in—nobody but the complainer would observe any directions.

Henry Recalls the same Experience with Nostalgic relish

"It is as a dream, a pleasant dream!" he exclaimed, breaking forth again after a few minutes musing. "I shall always look back on our theatricals with exquisite pleasure. There was such an interest, such an animation, such a spirit diffused! Every body felt it. We were all alive. There was enjoyment, hope, solicitude, bustle, for every hour of the day. Always some little

objection, some little doubt, some little anxiety to be got over. I never was happier."

Though one response suggests the bemused omniscience of detachment while the other evokes the giddiness of absolute involvement, both Fanny and Henry characterize the theatricals in terms of "discontent" or "anxiety." As Ruth Bernard Yeazell has written, theatricality provokes an "anxiety of boundary-confusion" that "is everywhere felt" in *Mansfield Park*. Yet for Fanny and Henry the theater is not just an *object* of anxiety but the very *site* of anxiety, a site that crosses its own boundaries to figure the anxiety of the novel as a whole. For *Mansfield Park*, however much it may favour repose, is, as Yeazell notes, certainly one of the most anxious novels ever written.

Anxiety may be the condition of all narratives, but here, in its generality as "a spirit diffused," it seems especially acute. Indeed, Fanny's composure is merely superficial, a defensive fiction: Austen tells us that, during the rehearsals, "her mind had never been farther from peace", that she is agitated by "many uncomfortable, anxious, apprehensive feelings", that she observes the preparations in a baffled state of "longing and dreading". Fanny is anxious about the theater precisely because she knows that it is less a structure toward which one can locate a safely external position than the fluctuating space in which all positions find their tenuous footing. A Henry Crawford may thrive within this milieu while a Fanny Price may inhabit it more unhappily, but neither the libertine nor the evangelical moralist can choose to function outside of it. In *Mansfield Park*, the theater, or the theatricality by virtue of which it disperses itself and colonizes the rest of the novel, becomes virtually synonymous with the inescapable context of all social existence and all political postures.

Resembling Henry Crawford in abhorring "any thing like a permanence of abode", theatricality turns up where one least expects it—even in the innermost meditations of the self-effacing Fanny. Discussions of the theatricals have not stressed sufficiently their *privateness: Mansfield Park* is about the incursion of public values upon private experience, about the theatricality of everyday life, in which to say, with Fanny, "No, indeed, I cannot act", is already to perform, whether one wants to or not. Like Fanny's anti-theatricalism, then, Austen's begins to emerge as a futile protest against the theatrical imperative—futile in large part because it is disingenuous, given the extent to which the political order of *Mansfield Park* depends upon a certain theatricality. Actual theaters may be circumscribed places that one can have demolished, but in its most generalized form theatricality, like Flaubert's divine artist, is present everywhere though visible nowhere.

If this invisibility induces paranoia in the Tory mind, it also makes possible a more efficient policing of the social practices by which authority sustains itself. Austen, moreover, is not alone in recording this ambiguity. *Mansfield Park,* which was published in 1814, figures in a broader cultural discourse about theatricality, a discourse shaped by authors whose differences appear even more irreconcilable than those between Fanny Price and Henry Crawford.

Like Fanny and Henry, however, these real-life conservatives and progressives exhibit a striking kinship when they engage the problem of theatricality, which seems to inspire not only a number of tellingly recurrent images but also a certain rhetorical oscillation in writings otherwise divided along lines of political allegiance. By looking briefly at a few of these writings, we may arrive at a more precise sense of what theatricality meant in late-eighteenth- and early-nineteenth-century England, of how it tended to comprehend those who would comprehend it, and of how Austen's novel both reproduces and illuminates this predicament. Our first two authors are evangelical ideologues whose wariness vis-à-vis the theater almost goes without saying. But here, as in *Mansfield Park,* the concern is less with the theater as an institution than with the possibility that the theater might have overstepped its institutional limits and invaded private life, establishing in private theatricals the symbol of an irreversible contamination.

Indeed, in its recourse to metaphors of infection, Thomas Gisborne's *Enquiry into the Duties of the Female Sex* (1797) anticipates Austen's insight into the theater's refusal to stay within bounds. Gisborne identifies the ills of the modern stage, warning, "He knows little of human nature, who thinks that the youthful mind will be secured from the infecting influence of a vicious character, adorned with polished manners, wit, fortitude, and generosity, by a frigid moral, delivered at the conclusion, or to be deduced from the events of the drama." Gisborne's slightly disorienting syntax already indicates an uncertainty characteristic of contemporary discussions of theatricality, for it is not at first clear whether the vicious character will infect the youthful mind *because* such a mind is adorned with polished manners and the like, or whether it will infect that mind *even though* it is so adorned.

On closer inspection, it turns out that Gisborne intends the former; in theatrical discourse as a whole, the polish that would serve as an antidote to poison often becomes indistinguishable from the poison itself. Metaphors of infection lead almost irresistibly to metaphors of seduction. As Tom Bertram, trying to justify the theatrical scheme to his father, says, the "infection" of acting "spread as those things always spread you know". But Gisborne's language, somewhat less vague than Tom's, suggests that "those things always spread" because the poison may beguile us into mistaking it for the cure. Austen, after all, refers to acting not only as an "infection" but also as a "charm", and what "spreads" is nothing other than a play *about* seduction.

Gisborne uncovers the logic of this mixed metaphor when he explains why young women are particularly susceptible to the enchantments of playacting:

A propensity to imitation is natural to the human mind, and is attended with various effects highly favourable to human happiness. This propensity shows itself with especial strength in the female sex. Providence, designing from the beginning that the manner of life to be adopted by women should in many respects ultimately depend, not so much on their own deliberate choice, as on the interest and convenience of the parent, of the husband, or of some other connection, has implanted in them a remarkable tendency to conform to the wishes and examples of those for whom they feel a warmth of regard, and even of all those with whom they are in familiar habits of intercourse....As the mind, in obeying the impulse of this principle, no less than in following any other of its native or acquired tendencies, is capable of being ensnared into errors and excesses; the season of youth, the season when the principle itself is in its greatest strength, and when it has yet derived few lessons from reflection and experience, is the time when error and excesses are most to be apprehended.

Young women are even more liable to corruption than young men, since the very thing that keeps them healthy—their unusually strong "propensity to imitation"—can easily make them ill. Acting, whose essence is imitation, seduces by diminishing the distance between negative and positive terms—between poison and cure, sickness and health. Properly controlled, of course, the latent theatricality of the female sex, "implanted" in women by "Providence," can have a salutary effect, ensuring that they will "conform to the wishes and examples" of their (male) superiors. Yet at what point does the very act of "obeying" turn into its opposite, with the result that these no longer merely latent actresses are "ensnared into errors and excesses"? What is required, obviously, is a vigilant patrolling of the border between "good" acting and "bad" acting.

Acting, however, in addition to blurring the lines between sickness and health, or between poison and cure, frustrates the attempt to define—let alone to patrol—the border between the safely domestic and the menacingly foreign, between the private and the public, between the inside and the outside. For no sooner has Gisborne asserted that Providence has implanted the "principle" of imitation in the female sex than he appears unsure whether this principle is "native or acquired." It may seem uncharitable to read vacillation into what is perhaps nothing more than a pseudophilosophical aside, yet these minor rhetorical fluttering hints at the boundary-confusion that becomes a leitmotif of the literature on theatricality. We encounter this theme again in another tract directed at saving young women from themselves.

In *Strictures on the Modern System of Female Education* (1799), Hannah More animadverts more harshly than Gisborne on the theatricalization of private life. Where Gisborne sees theatricality as a merely potential danger—as the aggravation of otherwise healthy "tendencies"—More describes it as a disease in its advanced stages, at least "among women of rank and fortune": "If the life of a young lady, formerly, too much resembled the life of a confectioner, it now too much resembles that of an actress; the morning is all rehearsal, and the evening is all performance." More blames this vitiating penetration of the public into the private on a more specific form of crosscultural trespass: the "modern apostles of infidelity and immorality," among whom she must number Elizabeth Inchbald, the translator and adapter of August von Kotzebue's *L3overs' Vows,* have strengthened their attacks on female virtue by enlisting the subversive services of German literature.

Yet what might strike others as grounds for clemency invites More's sharpest censure: "In many of these translations, certain stronger passages, which, though well received in Germany, would have excited disgust in England, are wholly omitted, in order that the mind may be more certainly, though more slowly, prepared for the full effect of the same poison to be administered in a stronger degree at another period." In the preface to her translation of *Lovers' Vows,* Inchbald defends her omissions and modifications by appealing to her own theatrical savvy, to her sense of what will play in Germany but not in England. According to More, however, such changes are designed precisely to undermine rather than recognize the differences between the two nationalities. As in so much right-wing literature of the period, the poison of theatricality is inseparable from the poison of foreignness—specifically, of the revolutionary doctrines threatening to spread to England from the continent.

Theatricality destroys the body politic by destroying that body's immune system, which, like all such systems, consists in the ability to distinguish between the native and the foreign, between self and other. The most insidious translation is that which seems so reassuringly familiar as to prevent us from identifying and repelling the alien substance. Here, the poison owes its seductive power not to its polished exterior but to its deceptive folksiness: the *Unheimliche,* or unsettling, masquerades as the *Heimliche,* or cozy. Interestingly, one of the ways in which Jane Austen signals the gravity of the theatrical infection is by having Edmund say of the Grants, through whom Mary and Henry Crawford were introduced into the Bertram family circle, "They seem to belong to us—they seem to be part of ourselves".

If even the normally watchful Edmund has trouble distinguishing between insiders and outsiders, then the immune system of Mansfield Park has clearly broken down. Against such calamities, more counsels a renewed alertness. But if her tone seems particularly melodramatic—apparent improvements in the translation serve in fact to poison the mind "more certainly, though more slowly"—then some of this straining to equate less with more and better with worse may indicate that she herself has become a victim of what she would contain. For her rhetoric of suspicion rests upon a logic of paradox, whereby quantitative differences disappear and everything ends up as its opposite. Is not this inability to differentiate one of the primary symptoms of the theatrical disease?

Indeed, even as More rails against the tendency of upper-class young women to resemble actresses, her own prose draws heavily on theatrical metaphors, referring repeatedly, for example, to the duties that a young Christian woman must "perform." It is worth noting that, earlier in her career, More had been a playwright, a friend and ardent admirer of Garrick, and a member in good standing of the London theatrical community; regardless of her present sympathies, her writing bears the marks of this past. Yet where Gisborne might distinguish between moral and immoral performance, More's new militancy excludes this possibility, as if to cover the traces of its own infection.

Once again, the attempt to situate oneself outside the anxious world of playacting merely produces more anxiety, more evidence of one's inextricable implication in that world.

Gisborne seems more inclined to acknowledge what More prefers to repress—namely, that all social experience presupposes some degree of theatricality. But, as we have seen, to acknowledge the contagion is not to escape its effects: in its own, admittedly milder, discrepancies, Gisborne's language joins More's in illustrating the plight of an authoritarianism compelled to come into contact with forces it would rather regulate or pronounce upon from a distance. The awkward position of these two evangelical conduct-book writers recalls that of Edmund Bertram, who, in order to halt the spread of the theatricals, has to plunge into their midst, playing the highly compromising role of Mary Crawford's lover in the Mansfield production of Kotzebue's play.

Yet if Gisborne and More exemplify the difficulties of a certain conservatism in coping with theatricality, we would expect a liberal and more sophisticated writer to approach the subject with something like urbane equanimity. This attitude does in fact characterize William Hazlitt's essay, "On Actors and Acting" (1817), a shrewd and lively rejoinder to the enemies of the stage. Oddly enough, though, Hazlitt's defence shows some of the same instabilities that we have noticed in the language of the detractors. Where Gisborne and More accuse the theater—or at least the theater in its present form—of encouraging immorality, Hazlitt recommends it as the "best teacher of morals" because the "truest and most intelligible picture of life."

Matters become more complicated, however, when he proceeds to explain how theatrical mimesis effects this moral education: "It points out the selfish and depraved to our detestation; the amiable and generous to our admiration; and if it clothes the more seductive vices with the borrowed graces of wit and fancy, even these graces operate as a diversion to the coarser poison of experience and bad example, and often prevent or carry off the infection by inoculating the mind with a certain taste and elegance."[] As in the previous texts, seduction and infection seem to invoke each other almost automatically, but here their relationship is more intricate. If, for Hazlitt, polish is not the poison but indeed the antidote, these "borrowed graces of wit and fancy" participate in what looks like a homeopathic programme. For, as Gisborne and More would remind us, wit and fancy, or the "taste and elegance" with which they "inoculate" the mind, may *become* seductive vices in their own right. Hazlitt appears to share this view, insofar as he contrasts the theatrical graces with the "*coarser* poison" of vices not wearing this borrowed "clothing."

Yet the mixed metaphor itself may signal a deeper trouble. Though Hazlitt began by affirming the morally instructive properties of mimesis, the process he is now describing has to do neither with mimesis nor with instruction, but with a kind of seduction of the mind itself. Adorning rather than imitating reality, wit and fancy "prevent or carry off the infection" of the mind by seductive vices by seducing it toward other, less coarse ones. Not only is the mind seduced: it is also reduced, demoted to the role of a passive object that can only submit to being "diverted" toward the lesser of two evils. By way of arguing for the salutary influence of the theater, Hazlitt resorts to the somewhat disconcerting image of the playgoer as patient, and in so doing comes surprisingly close to Gisborne's ideology of social control, with its notion of latent theatricality as the basis of female "conformity."

Of course Hazlitt's politics permit him to speak in less sinister terms: when he says of actors, "The height of their ambition is to be *beside themselves*," he celebrates the freedom of the "improvised self," the Protean exuberance of a Henry Crawford. Alongside this overall humanism, however, Hazlitt's apparent endorsement of theatricality as a means of manipulation becomes all the more significant, for it testifies to the readiness with which theatrical forms lend themselves to disciplinary purposes. Perhaps the congestion of Hazlitt's language symptomatizes uneasiness in the face of inconsistency, or perhaps the clutter was designed as a "diversion," at once an alternative to and a distraction from this inconsistency. In either case, though, Hazlitt's unstable rhetoric reveals yet another peculiarity of the theatrical discourse to which *Mansfield Park* contributes. Where Gisborne and More worried that the theater might encroach upon everyday life, Hazlitt's tergiversations point to the difficulty of keeping everyday life from encroaching upon the theater.

It is not that Hazlitt rejects representation: as we have seen, he bases—or tries to base—his defence of the theater on a plea for its mimetic value. Yet in order to sustain one's view of the theater as an "epitome, a bettered likeness of the world," one has to bar from this idealized enclosure the more cynical calculations that too often prevail in everyday life; such cynicism may accord with pragmatic schemes of social regulation, but it hardly becomes a large-spirited humanism. The theater can be a bettered likeness of the world only by remaining free from ideological complicities *with* that world, complicities that would jeopardize its ability to imitate and to instruct. In explaining how the theater operates as a guardian against *moral* infection, however, Hazlitt opens it to just this kind of *ideological* infection. Moreover, if the theater starts to look a little more likes the world, the world starts to look a little more like the theater; as the different poisons play upon the mind, it becomes hard to tell where reality ends and art begins.

Together, Gisborne, More, and Hazlitt delineate the landscape of dis-ease in which *Mansfield Park* takes place. To situate the novel in this context, though, is not necessarily to arrive at a clearer understanding of what Jane Austen really thought about the theater. Much of the criticism of *Mansfield Park* tries to solve the mystery of the author's intention, but the point of the preceding survey is that theatricality wreaks havoc on intentions. Whether they stand on the left or on the right, authors who set out to elucidate the problem soon find themselves baffled by unexpected complexities. Hazlitt undertakes to offer a liberal paean to actors and acting, and yet cannot help being pulled in the direction of authoritarianism. Contrary to our assumptions about the lawlessness of theatricality, the subject seems to impose an almost inexorable rightward drift.

Yet, contrary to what we might assume about drifts to the right, the texts of our evangelical authors betray a remarkable restlessness. Calling for an attentive monitoring of the theatrical impulse, Gisborne succeeds in showing why such monitoring may be impracticable. More, for her part, continues the sermon against theatricality as the enemy within, unwittingly providing evidence of the lengths to which a discourse will go in concealing the signs of its own occupation. As a novel about theatricality, *Mansfield Park* dramatizes both the conservative appropriation of theatrical forms and the way these forms endanger the very interests that appropriate them, threatening to turn the captors into captives. Just how does conservatism appropriate theatricality? Following Hazlitt, we might see a certain homeopathic logic at work in the novel.

The patriarchal authority who "keeps every body in their places", Sir Thomas embodies a cunningly manipulative authority, one that will not hesitate, for example, to exile Fanny to Portsmouth in the name of a "medicinal project upon [her] understanding, which he must consider as at present diseased". Though the theatrical scheme suggests a flouting of his authority, since it is conceived and begun during his absence and in spite of the likelihood of his disapproval, the theatricals may function quite differently, as a kind of medicinal project upon Mansfield Park itself, which a conscientious authority must also consider as diseased. For even before the Crawfords arrive, Mansfield Park suffers from an overdose of theatricality. Indeed, the regime in question seems more like a parody of authority than like authority in the strict sense. Sir Thomas has delegated too much power to the officious Mrs. Norris, who, with her "love of directing", views the household as a showcase for her own talents of management and domestic economy.

Small wonder that she becomes such an energetic sponsor and supervisor of the theatricals. She has already assisted in the education, or miseducation, of Sir Thomas's daughters, Maria and Julia, who typify the sort of "accomplished" young women about whom Hannah More complains:

The Miss Bertrams were now fully established among the belles of the neighbourhood; and as they joined to beauty and brilliant acquirements, a manner naturally easy, and carefully formed to general civility and obligingness, they possessed its favour as well as its admiration. Their vanity was in such good order, that they seemed to be quite free from it, and gave themselves no airs; while the praises attending such behaviour, secured, and brought round by their aunt, served to strengthen them in believing they had no faults. Actresses in everything but the title, Maria and Julia manifest their illness by concealing it. Just as, for Mrs. More, the poison of sub versive ideas works most effectively when introduced under a familiar disguise, so the height of vanity is to "seem quite free from it," and the perfection of theatrical artifice is an apparent artlessness.

Given this state of affairs, why not attempt to cure like with like, "treating" theatricality itself with doses of more theatricality? Obviously, Sir Thomas has nothing to do with the theatrical scheme. I am not intimating that he masterminds and controls it in some implausibly subterranean way. Yet, as the major authority *within* the book, he may well represent the authority *behind* the book—namely, Jane Austen herself. As he states at the outset, it is his duty to "authorize" various practices and relationships at Mansfield Park, and this responsibility echoes a more fundamental author-izing. Perhaps Austen not only authors but also authorizes the theatrical episode, working out in terms of narrative structure a medicinal project or experiment upon the diseased body politic of Mansfield Park and, by extension, of the English gentry as a whole.

The injection of the Crawfords—and, to a lesser extent, of Mr. Yates—would serve to shock the system of Mansfield Park into protecting itself against such intruders. The infection that they bring would have the theatricals as its most alarming symptom, but this attack would culminate in a return to health. Indeed, the episode does seem to have some of the desired effect, for it ends with the banishment of Yates, the retreat of the Crawfords, and the departure of Maria and Julia, and initiates both the rise of Fanny and the fall of Mrs. Norris. The only trouble with this scheme is that it scants the considerable distance between the end of the theatrical episode and the end of the novel itself: two whole volumes stand between the ostensible purgation and the complete recovery of Mansfield Park from the evils that have plagued it. However daring the homeopathic experiment, the disease lingers.

For the Crawfords are only temporarily repelled by Sir Thomas's displeasure; their exclusion, in fact, lasts for a mere two chapters. Moreover, it is immediately after this drastic attempt at cleansing that Edmund makes his remark about how the Grants, half-sister and half-brother-in-law of the Crawfords, "seem to be part of ourselves."▯ And instead of taking steps to resolve this familial identity crisis, Sir Thomas actually exacerbates it, trying to maneuver Fanny into marrying Henry Crawford. Sir Thomas does not seem to recognize the Crawfords as the real "daemon[s] of the piece", as the chief perpetrators of the "bustle and confusion of acting". Like Maria and Julia, whose vanity is so advanced that it conceals itself, Mary and Henry are such adroit actors that they know how to dissemble their theatrical busy-ness.

As a result, they are soon readmitted, while the less skillful Mr. Yates, who "bustles" more discernibly, is cast out. Of course, Yates is not merely a scapegoat, since it was he, after all, who carried the infection of acting from Ecclesford to Mansfield in the first place. But this very sanctioning of a covert theatricality at the expense of an overt one inheres in the deeper logic of the narrative: the theatricals serve not as a homeopathic cure—although Austen might want us to view them as one—but as a "diversion," as Hazlitt would say, from the subtler and more comprehensive theatricality that persists long after Sir Thomas has reclaimed his study. Jane Austen diverts our attention from this theatricality so that we may not notice how indispensable a role it plays in the rehabilitation of Mansfield Park.

The reason that the Crawfords, who, through metonymic slippage, "seem to belong to us," and the bustling Mrs. Norris, who "seemed a part of" Sir Thomas, are not expelled until the end of the novel is not that it takes so long to eliminate theatricality, but that theatricality requires this much time to, as it were, take effect. By the end of the novel, these characters have done their work so well—have "implanted" theatricality so firmly—that they themselves no longer need to remain at Mansfield: they have not so much overstayed their welcome as outlived their usefulness.

A sort of sideshow, the homeopathic experiment fails because it was never intended to succeed. Theatricality inhabits Mansfield Park before, during, and after the theatrical episode. Are there differences, though, between the theatricality of the Miss Bertrams and the theatricality of the Crawfords, or between the theatricality of the Crawfords and the theatricality of Fanny? We may begin to answer this question by suggesting that, where Fanny's cousins embody a dangerously centrifugal sociability, Fanny installs a steadfast and almost inaccessible inwardness at the other end of the narrative continuum. Mary and Henry Crawford do not so much stand between these two extremes as upset the very dichotomy on which this model is predicated.

Mary, for example, is the subject of numerous tortured conversations between Fanny and Edmund, in which they struggle to decide whether her apparent irreverence indicates some profound flaw in her nature or merely the unfortunate effect of the company she keeps.

We can understand Fanny and Edmund's perplexity: on the one hand, Mary displays what looks like genuine warmth and affection for others; on the other hand, Austen often emphasizes the enormous amount of technique that underlies this display, as when, at Fanny's coming-out party, Mary takes great pains to tell everyone what (she thinks) he or she wants to hear. In her artful artlessness, she puts even Maria and Julia to shame, seducing not only Edmund but many a suspicious, if not cantankerous, critic as well. Yet her brother is an even better actor, in whom play and seriousness are inseparably intertwined. Thus Fanny, whose mind tolerates only either/or distinctions, is at a loss to interpret his amorous behaviour toward her:

How could *she* have excited serious attachment in a man, who had seen so many, and been admired by so many, and flirted with so many, infinitely her superiors—who seemed so little open to serious impressions, even where pains had been taken to please him—who thought so slightly, so carelessly, so unfeelingly on all such points—who was every thing to every body, and seemed to find no one essential to him?...Every thing might be possible rather than serious attachment or serious approbation of it toward her. She had quite convinced herself of this before Sir Thomas and Mr. Crawford joined them. The difficulty was in maintaining the conviction quite so absolutely after Mr. Crawford was in the room; for once or twice a look seemed forced on her which she did not know how to class among the common meaning; in any other man at least, she would have said that it meant something very earnest, very pointed. But she still tried to believe it no more than what he might often have expressed towards her cousins or fifty other women.

An inveterate player of roles—a man who is "every thing to every body"—Henry seems incapable of meaning what he says. How could such semiotic promiscuity coexist with the "seriousness" that Fanny keeps invoking? And yet Crawford presents the anomaly of one who not only combines role-playing with sincerity but reveals sincerity as an *effect* of role-playing. Fanny is bewildered by Crawford because she assumes that, if one is not serious, then one must be acting, manipulating conventions rather than speaking from the heart.[] Austen's *style indirect libre*, however, discloses more than Fanny's consciousness can contain: words and deeds that one can "class among the common meaning" or insert into a conventional slot are not those that *lack* sincerity but those that convey it. Though he seems to personify an illicit deviation from the norm of seriousness into the no-man's-land of artifice and conventionality, Henry in fact exposes seriousness as a product of artifice and conventionality. He is the exception that infects the rule.

What is infectious in Henry, moreover, is not the unmanageable indeterminacy that Fanny sees in him, but something surprisingly close to the ideals of hierarchy and propriety that we associate with a character like Sir Thomas. For although Henry enters the novel trailing clouds of undecidability—as befits one whom Leo Bersani calls an "ontological floater"—the aim of the authoritarian appropriation of theatricality is to demystify it, to shift its focus from glamorous excess to a more pedestrian trading in certain codified procedures. Where before there was the prospect of reckless, infinite self-invention, now we find an almost mechanical shuffling and reshuffling of a limited repertory of tricks of the trade.

Once the more or less spectacular attack of the theatricals has subsided, the novel can address itself to the task of domesticating the theatrical Crawfords—not, as More would have it, in order more certainly, though more slowly, to subvert Mansfield Park, but in order to rob them of their subversive power. By the end of the novel, potentially subversive impulses—which Austen groups under the heading of the "itch for acting" —will have been converted into props of authority.

The conquest of the Crawfords is a crucial intermediate phase in the ideological conflict enacted in the novel. For if Mary and Henry emblematize at first the anarchy of the unbounded self, they magnify the objectionable theatricality of Maria and Julia, who, as Sir Thomas finally admits, "had never been properly taught to govern their inclinations and tempers". The triumph of Fanny at the end of the novel symbolizes the triumph of governance over a selfhood run wild, but the demystification of Mary and Henry marks the turning point in that war. And though Fanny is appalled by the way the Crawfords reduce sincerity to a convention, she herself represents the consummation of that process. Of course, we have identified artful artlessness as the most distinctive trait of the Bertram sisters, yet their theatricality is too dispersive, too outer-directed, to comply with the novel's centripetal ethos.

The burden of the middle section of the novel is to stage the theatricalization of the self in such a way that theatricality virtually disappears into that inner space, submerged in the form of rigorously inculcated habits of mind and modes of response. *Mansfield Park,* that is, attempts to move backward from Gisborne's theatrical young women, "ensnared into errors and excesses," to the latent actresses whose "propensity to imitation," carefully shaped and supervised, becomes the very guarantee of their virtuous "conformity." Lending themselves to a demonstration of how the theatrical self may be redefined, the Crawfords enable this corrective movement from the theatrically extroverted Maria and Julia to the theatrically introverted Fanny. When Henry reads aloud from Shakespeare, for example, Fanny's involuntary absorption in the performance signifies more than just the transitory power of actor over spectator. An important lesson is being impressed upon her mind:

In Mr. Crawford's reading there was a variety of excellence beyond what she had ever met with. The King, the Queen; Buckingham, Wolsey, Cromwell, all were given in turn; for with the happiest knack, the happiest power of jumping and guessing, he could always light, at will, on the best scene, or the best speeches of each; and whether it were dignity or pride, or tenderness or remorse, or whatever were to be expressed, he could do it with equal beauty.—It was truly dramatic.—His acting had first taught Fanny what pleasure a play might give, and his reading brought all his acting before her again; nay, perhaps with greater enjoyment, for it came unexpectedly, and with no such drawback as she had been used to suffer in seeing him on stage with Miss Bertram. Up until now, reading, for Fanny, has represented an escape from the public exposure implicit in acting. Whenever the eroticism of the rehearsals impinges too painfully upon her claustral sensibility, Fanny withdraws into the chill of her fireless room, where her books offer the solace of silent and purely spiritual intercourse.

It is not surprising that at her greatest crisis during the theatrical episode—the point at which she nearly capitulates to the company's request that she read the part of the Cottager's wife—Fanny can think only of returning to her room. She has, of course, been helping the others learn their lines by reading opposite them, but what is disturbing about this request is that it makes reading look all too much like a form of acting. It is one thing to rehearse with individual actors, quite another to read aloud as a member, however temporary, of the entire cast. Reading aloud points to an infection of reading proper by the very values it ought to exclude. Fanny's desire to maintain a polarity between reading and acting manifests itself throughout the novel, since any kind of heightened attention in the rooms below—any compulsion to look at and to be looked at—merely reinstates the theatrical threat on a less obvious level.

Yet Henry's reading aloud once again undermines her cherished opposition: as Lady Bertram says, "It was really like being at a play". "His reading [brings] all his acting before [Fanny] again," revealing the didactic purposiveness of both pursuits. For where, before, her retreats to the converted schoolroom that is her own apartment were a way of "shrinking again into herself", as if in flight from the free play of wandering libido, now she realizes that Henry's "acting taught...what pleasure a play might give." His acting teaches her a more essential lesson as well—that the act of shrinking into oneself, of cultivating inwardness, has certain inevitable histrionic implications. All along, in eschewing acting, Fanny has in fact been playing a role, albeit "sincerely." As Sandra M. Gilbert and Susan Gubar point out, "Fanny silently plays the role of the angel by refusing to play." From Henry's performance, she learns not the necessity of acting but the impossibility of *not* acting.

Many critics have cited Henry's remarks about the inability of most preachers to deliver an impressive sermon as a sure sign of his moral turpitude: he is actually a "bad reader" (and thus a bad person), the argument runs, because he is "not concerned with belief, only with applause or admiration." This sort of reasoning, however, may tell us more about the conduciveness of Austen's novels to moral position-taking than about the ideological ironies that generate their moralism. For Henry's preoccupation with the "rules and trick" of preaching merely foregrounds the obsessive and omnipresent conventionality upon which the moral system of the entire novel depends.

Whatever taint we may detect in Henry's tendency to see

theatricality in everything—even in the religious vocation that is the novel's purported theme—turns out to colour the authoritarian vision of *Mansfield Park* as a whole, especially as that vision is entrusted to Sir Thomas. Indeed, if Henry's cynicism—or, what is even worse, his conflation of cynicism and conviction—offends our moral good taste, Sir Thomas's medicinal projects should strike us as equally exploitive. If they do not, it is only because the novel has succeeded in concealing its indebtedness to what it pretends to disown. One almost senses a collusion between Henry and Sir Thomas, for while the former would seduce Fanny into marriage, the latter expends considerable energy in encouraging this seduction. Any difference between the two male characters lies in Austen's presentation of their strategies. In the case of Henry, she chooses to italicize, literally, his conscious use of rhetorical convention.

When, for example, he tells Fanny that he has had William promoted to second lieutenant, he "used such strong expressions, was so abounding in the *deepest interest*, in *twofold motives*, in *views and wishes more than could be told*, that Fanny could not have remained insensible of his drift". In the case of Sir Thomas, Austen adopts a coy tone in order to cast a somewhat more benign light on the same manipulativeness. At the end of Fanny's party, when Sir Thomas orders her, in the presence of Crawford, to go to bed—" 'Advise' was his word, but it was the advice of absolute power"—Austen comments tellingly on the devices whereby patriarchal authority perpetuates itself: "In thus sending her away, Sir Thomas perhaps might not be thinking merely of her health. It might occur to him, that Mr. Crawford had been sitting by her long enough, or he might mean to recommend her as a wife by shewing her persuadableness". Readers of Austen's last complete novel know what an ominous ring the word "persuasion" can acquire.

In "shewing her persuadableness," Sir Thomas puts Fanny on stage, exhibiting her just as Henry exhibits himself, deploying theatrical technique as craftily as his younger collaborator. In fact, he may be even shrewder, since he is manipulating both actress (Fanny) and audience (Henry). Displaying Fanny in the role of the obedient young woman, Sir Thomas in effect concocts, for Henry's benefit, a preview of and invitation to the marriage he seeks to bring about. With his keen sense of timing—he judges that "Mr. Crawford had been sitting by [Fanny] long enough"—and his eye for the symbolically resonant detail, Sir Thomas is the novel's preeminent juggler of theatrical conventions. Fanny's dramatic exit is merely the finale to an entire evening of skillfully directed moves, one that began with her "practising her steps about the drawing-room", looking perhaps more like one of Hannah More's amateur actresses than like one of Gisborne's demure mimics.

The ball in her honour, conceived and staged by her uncle, constitutes her official entrance into society, the moment at which the ugly duckling steps into the spotlight to discover herself a swan. It is thus a thoroughly theatrical event, but instead of receiving the stigma that one might think it merits, it functions both as a pivotal point in the heroine's development and as a validation of the "absolute power" by which that development has been supervised: Sir Thomas "was pleased with himself for having supplied every thing else [but Fanny's beauty];—education and manners she owed to him". Fanny, however, does not seem fully to appreciate the extent of her debt to Sir Thomas, for she of course rebels against his plan for her to marry Crawford, leading many commentators to propose that she is perhaps not so docile after all.

Admittedly, her secret yet unwavering devotion to her cousin Edmund, in spite of her suitor's relentless blandishments and her uncle's merciless charge of *ingratitude,* seems to adumbrate a rejection of theatrical management and a brave defence of the inviolate self. But we would do well to consider the long-range effects, as well as the immediate consequences, of this recalcitrance. Fanny's insubordination precipitates the medicinal project according to which Sir Thomas dispatches her to the petit bourgeois chaos of Portsmouth, where she learns to esteem rather than disdain the theatricality of the Mansfield Park regime.

After only a week amid the filth and anarchy of the parental abode, where "Nobody was in their right place, nothing was done as it ought to be", she longs for the scrupulous decorum of her uncle's home, where his insistently watchful authority "keeps every body in their place." If Fanny showed a regrettable tendency to disobey theatrically organized power, her exile serves as a valuable reminder of the virtues of such theatricality.

Sir Thomas's project upon her diseased understanding is a success, not because Fanny relinquishes her claim to an unassailable self, but because she realizes that that very integrity is possible only on the intensely supervised stage of Mansfield Park. Ultimately, that is, she acknowledges her debt to Sir Thomas, and to the elegant conventionality for which, and by which, he stands:

Her eagerness, her impatience, her longings to be with them, were such as to bring a line or two of Cowper's Tirocinium for ever before her. "With what intense desire she wants her home," was continually on her tongue, as the truest description of a yearning which she could not suppose any school-boy's bosom to feel more keenly.

The citational mode of Fanny's yearning is itself a token of the experiment's success. It demonstrates that Austen's most inward heroine is also, as many readers have observed, her most bookishly formulaic. Whenever she feels the urge to dive deep into her innermost self, Fanny comes up with a handy touchstone, usually borrowed from Cowper. She is most herself when she is quoting someone else.

It might be objected that theatricality is not the same thing as conventionality, that, although Fanny may think in clichés, she does not therefore acquiesce to the theatrical imperative. Yet the contention of this chapter is that, in the case of *Mansfield Park,* theatricality is in fact identified with conventionality to such a degree that the two terms eventually become synonymous.

That theatricality-as-conventionality replaces theatricality-as-subversion reveals itself most vividly in the shift from metaphors of infection and of seduction to metaphors of debt and repayment. By the end of the novel, an omniscient authority has placed this world sufficiently under its control so that it may be said to own its subjects just as a conventional utterance or gesture owns a fixed and stable meaning.

In marrying Edmund instead of Henry Crawford, Fanny indeed helps Sir Thomas to consolidate his empire and to protect his property from dispersion at the hands of outsiders. In keeping the family circle closed, she affirms repetition over difference, and legitimates Sir Thomas's patriarchal programme: "Sir Thomas saw repeated, and for ever repeated reason to rejoice in what he had done for them all". At last, after the disappointments arising from the "grievous mismanagement" of his own daughters, he sees in Fanny a handsome return on his investment: "Fanny was indeed the daughter that he wanted. His charitable kindness had been rearing a prime comfort for himself. His liberality had a rich repayment". "Prizing" in Fanny "more and more the sterling good of principle", Sir Thomas prizes as well the sterling good of principal.

Indeed, in the final chapter of the novel one has the impression that its protagonist is less Fanny than Sir Thomas himself, or the "governing body" that he represents.[] Fanny and Edmund live happily ever after, but they do so in order to repay the authority that created them.

As we have said, Sir Thomas may be viewed as an agent of Jane Austen, insofar as both appear to endorse the fortification of a conservative social order. Just here, however, where this order seems to have prevailed over the forces of subversion, authority starts to look oddly vulnerable. We would not be the first to notice a rather mechanical quality to this last chapter, which Austen begins with a perfunctory remark about her "impatience to restore every body...to tolerable comfort", and which she punctuates with other disquieting glimpses of the novelist ostentatiously in a hurry to tie up loose ends.

When did Edmund transfer his love from Mary Crawford to Fanny?: "exactly at the time when it was quite natural that it should be so, and not a week earlier". What became of the prodigal older son, Tom?: "He became what he ought to be".

Austen takes greater trouble to describe the fates of Maria and Julia, the Crawfords, and Mrs. Norris, but her own somewhat noisy interventions are all too reminiscent of this last character's theatrical bustle.

No sooner has Sir Thomas expelled his demonic counterpart—whose "anxiety for every body's comfort" mocks his own need to keep everybody in "their place"—than Mrs. Norris returns in the form of the anxious, "impatient," comfort-oriented author herself. Not only does Mrs. Norris parody the authority of Sir Thomas; as Gilbert and Gubar have written, she is a "parodic surrogate for the author, a suitable double whose manipulations match those of Aunt Jane." In the embarrassing moment when the ordinarily discreet Jane Austen advances to the proscenium to ring down the curtain on the final scene of her drama, we witness something like a return of the repressed.

The lesson of *Mansfield Park,* it seems, is that subversive theatricality can *only* be repressed, temporarily neutralized by a concerted effort of demystification. This process can occur, however, precisely because theatricality is not a single, unitary phenomenon but an already self-divided set of practices capable of serving both reactionary and subversive causes. If it can serve both, it can betray both, offering at best a precarious purchase on whatever interpretation of reality it has been recruited to promote.

Mansfield Park has been praised as a psychological study that uncovers the impurity of even the most admirable motives, yet it also performs a political analysis, yielding insight into the necessary inconsistency of any ideological position that appropriates theatricality for its own purposes. A final reference should illustrate this point. When Edmund decides that duty compels him to give up his censorious stance and join in the theatricals, he tries to persuade Fanny, and himself, that this about-face produces only the "*appearance* of...inconsistency".

He explains that, if he does not play the romantic lead

opposite Mary Crawford, someone from outside the immediate circle will. Thus he must act so that he "can be the means of restraining the publicity of the business, of limiting the exhibition, of concentrating our folly". And, of course, his folly *is* concentrated, not only in the sense of being circumscribed but also in the sense of being intensified. For in becoming an accomplice to the theatrical scheme, Edmund loses some of his status as moral paragon, incurring the disapproval of both Fanny and his father.

He may genuinely wish to "limit the exhibition," but he may also wish to exhibit his desire for and to Mary Crawford. Acting (the word itself is suggestive) in what he imagines is his father's interest, he manages at the same time to accommodate certain designs of his own, designs that may be at odds with the preservation of law and order. In Edmund's inconsistent behaviour, authority nearly subverts itself. Faced with this emergency, Jane Austen summons Sir Thomas back to Mansfield Park—so that authority may attempt, yet again, to include what could disrupt it.

Why do you like Miss Austen so very much? I am puzzled on that point. What induced you to say that you would have rather written *Pride and Prejudice* or *Tom Jones,* than any of the Waverley Novels? I had not seen *Pride and Prejudice* till I read that sentence of yours, and then I got the book. And what did I find? An accurate daguerreotyped portrait of a commonplace face; a carefully fenced, highly cultivated garden, with neat borders and delicate flowers; but no glance of a bright, vivid physiognomy, no open country, no fresh air, no blue hill, no bonny beck. I should hardly like to live with her ladies and gentlemen, in their elegant but confined houses. These observations will probably irritate you, but I shall run the risk.

"Elegant but confined": Brontë's formula epitomizes a certain way of dismissing Jane Austen's work. Had Brontë read *Mansfield Park* rather than *Pride and Prejudice,* moreover, her assessment might have been even less charitable, for while "elegance" serves in *Pride and Prejudice* as a kind of atmospheric *compensation* for confinement, the demystifying narrative of *Mansfield Park* makes "elegance" the very *mode* of

confinement. As we saw in the last chapter, the demystification enacted in that novel requires a distinctly inhospitable domestication, whereby the glamor or subversive éclat of a free-wheeling, insouciant theatricality is replaced by an "elegance" or decorum that, far from softening the disciplinary standard upheld by the forbidding Fanny Price, efficiently enforces it, "keep[ing] every body in their place."

So dampening is the effect of this demystification that we are grateful when, at the end of the novel, the narrator uncannily impersonates the bustling Mrs. Norris, permitting an almost grotesque officiousness to unsettle the smooth surface of her prose.

Once we could enjoy the rakish seductions of Mary and Henry Crawford; now that a rigorous "elegance" is the order of the day, we find ourselves oddly cheered by mere intimations of comic meddlesomeness. Yet this vulgar travesty of the powers that be is more than just a consolation prize: it reminds us forcibly of the energies that had to be repressed or contained in order for the reign of decorum to be secured, and it thereby compels us to recognize the shakiness of this dispensation. As the curtain descends on the happy household of Edmund and Fanny Bertram, we are allowed to glimpse the outlines of a sequel that begs to be written, in which, say, The Return of Mary Crawford overtakes the scrupulous disenchantments effected by Part One.

Although Charlotte Brontë is clearly impatient with Austenian confinement, it would seem rather inappropriate to characterize any of her novels as a "carnivalesque" rewriting of Austen such as that described above. In differing from Austen, Brontë hardly seems interested in taking her cue from the ways in which Austen differs from herself.

A powerful polemicist, Brontë instead establishes the terms not only for a certain confinement of Austen herself but also, as a result, for her own liberating entry into the history of the novel. Asserting the superiority of "open country" and "fresh air" (fresh *Eyre?*) to her predecessor's "carefully fenced, highly cultivated gardens," Brontë prescribes the distinction that would take hold in more or less canonical accounts of the development of the English novel.

Raymond Williams, for example, though by no means a canonical critic, seems to endorse Brontë's version of literary history when he writes:

A certain worldliness, readily understandable in earlier periods (though never, I think, as persuasive as is made out), made for the qualification of love; found its value as social exchange and respect, as most coolly in Jane Austen.... What was directly expressed in Blake and in Keats and in different ways in Shelley and Byron seems to have gone underground, before the 1840s, in fiction and even in drama; indeed is literally underground in the dark images of the Gothic and in the produced straining extravagances of melodrama. The achievement of the Brontë sisters, before we say anything else, is that in different ways they remade the novel so that this kind of passion could be directly communicated.

Williams articulates a widespread, commonsensical understanding of what happens to the English novel around the time of, indeed through the intervention of, Charlotte Brontë and her sisters: their novels breathe "passion" and "love" into what has seemed a rather "coolly" restrictive tradition of "worldliness."

Yet it is not hard to see how Williams complicates his account by tracing the latent or "underground" Romantic impulses liberated by the Brontës not only to the "dark images of the Gothic" but also to the "produced straining extravagances of melodrama."

In other words, although it is tempting to honour Brontë by describing her difference from Austen as an escape from the constricting elegance associated with the tyranny of "manners"—from the various forms of "social exchange" and compulsory indirection that come under the heading of "theatricality"—her "remaking" of the novel involves the rehabilitation of elements that have themselves had, as it were, a theatrical career, and that may continue, even after their recovery, to bear the marks of that history.

Indeed, one of the charges Brontë had to answer in her

defence of *Jane Eyre* (1847) was that of being too "melodramatic."

Admittedly, the "produced straining extravagances of melodrama" represent a different theatricality from either Mary and Henry Crawford's libertine glamor, the ultimate elegance of the Bertrams' cool (not to say chilly) regime, or even Mrs. Norris's noisy managerial style. Moreover, we should not simply assimilate the theatrical implications of Brontë's first-person narratives to those of Austen's third-person narrative. I want to argue, however, that the expressive openness and "directness" of Brontë's novels is significantly bound up, after all, not only with melodramatic extravagance but also with the other embarrassing kinds of theatricality she and many of her critics discern in Austen. Brontë's "achievement" owes at least as much to these forces of "qualification" as to its sources in Blake, Shelley, Keats, and Byron.

Theatricality and its subsidiary metaphors have enjoyed considerable prominence in a number of recent, skeptically driven critical projects. Derrida's delineation of "the scene of writing" and Foucault's work on the (ostensibly nonspectacular) stagecraft of modern power are perhaps the most obvious examples of and models for the deployment of "theatricality" as a trope of demystification, whereby the apparently immediate and unproblematic can be resisted or preemptively framed on the grounds of its factitiousness or its unsuspected ideological complicity. In proposing to read Brontë's fiction in the light of theatricality, I am not, however, merely seeking to add yet another supposedly invulnerable repository of truth and presence to the ever-growing list of compromised masterpieces.

Not *merely*, since, if one hopes to do more than just repeat a by now familiar and even respectable critical gesture, one cannot simply dispense with it, as though supplementation equaled transcendence. If *Jane Eyre* and *Villette* are in some sense founding texts in the tradition of the novel, this is not for the reasons Williams and others adduce, but because they embody so graphically two apparently antithetical yet interdependent functions of the novel in modern culture: on the one hand, they represent a potent identification of novel-writing and novel-reading with the creation, consolidation, and safeguarding of an autonomous subjectivity; on the other hand, they situate that subjectivity in an inescapable, ever-menacing context of surveillance, suspicion, circumvention, and unmasking.

That is, they dramatize the inevitability—for the author, for the protagonist, and, perhaps less saliently but no less crucially, for the critic—of a certain will to demystify: demystification is not what happens *to* the novel (although the critic may feel as if he or she were exercising that prerogative) but what happens *in* and *through* the novel. In her preface to the second edition of *Jane Eyre,* for example, Brontë admits that one of her aims has been "to pluck the mask from the face of the Pharisee," "to scrutinize and expose, to raise the gilding and show base metal under it." And if it still seems somewhat surprising that she should have seen Thackeray, of all contemporary novelists, as a kindred spirit (signaling her admiration by dedicating this edition to him), this improbable affinity points up the central imperative of truth-telling, satirical or otherwise, in Brontë's fiction.

More powerfully than Thackeray's works, however, or than the somewhat later instances of the sensation novel and the detective novel, Brontë's texts epitomize the contagious dialectic of *evasion* and *exposure* that will henceforth loom large in the novel, even (or especially) when it is less overtly "psychological" or "Romantic." For where the narrative of sensation or detection typically enacts a linear movement toward transparency and closure, the plots of Brontë's novels notoriously refuse the comforts of linearity, intensifying the demand for demystification precisely by frustrating it. For all their vaunted commitment to direct communication, and despite their author's reputation as one who "pours forth her feelings...without premeditation," these novels virtually institutionalize the *obstacles* to unmediated and unpremeditated expression and understanding. If they stand out as emblematic demonstrations of the will to unveil, they do so because they install opacity as a permanent fixture of the novelistic world.

In the veritable theater of self-fashioning that they constitute, theatricality-as-display and theatricality-as-deception articulate the conflictual masquerade of the modern novel, which seems, in its cult of interiority, to have left its theatrical prehistory far behind. Brontë's novels stand as memorials to the process whereby the novel as cultural production absorbs and covers over the traces of its historically and politically *supplementary* relation to the theater, of its genealogy as repetition-in-difference. "The inscription of theatricality" denotes the ambiguity of this process: to inscribe theatricality is at once to replicate it and to displace it, incorporating this generic other and at the same time disguising it. In the nineteenth century, the novel becomes a crypt in which theatricality lies concealed, but only half-concealed, since this very encrypting bespeaks an intrinsically theatrical subterfuge.

But though one cannot, therefore, choose *not* to reenact the ritual of demystification, there is another, more interesting reason why I hope "not merely" to deconstruct Brontëan subjectivity. *Mansfield Park* shows that demystification, far from being a neutral cognitive process, in fact serves a highly coercive ideological purpose, however unpredictably or unreliably.

For their part, Brontë's novels extend this insight, by unfolding a multiplicity of dramas in which demystification turns out to have a specific, though often overdetermined, political and erotic agenda of its own. It is important to point out that this discovery does not necessarily discredit the diverse acts of unveiling at work in—or in response to—the text. What it does is to open up a range of performative possibilites behind a series of cognitive scenes, to present them *as scenes,* rather than as so many disinterested projects of reception taking place passively and invisibly out, as it were, in the audience.

Though the question of theatricality figures importantly in all of Brontë's novels, I will be concerned here with only two—the most famous and the one most deadeningly pasteurized and homogenized for absorption into the collective unconscious, *Jane Eyre,* and the last and the one most bristlingly "textual" and "complex," *Villette* (1853). Of these two, the latter would appear to be the logical place to begin showing how theatricality, as in *Mansfield Park,* spreads from the assigned locus of the literal stage to encompass not only spectators but participants in transactions—for example, reading, writing, teaching, lovemaking—supposedly untainted by theatrical obliquity.

Villette, after all, thematizes theatrical issues overtly and recurrently, and, with its cosmopolitan, or at least Continental, setting, seems more likely than *Jane Eyre* to illustrate a suitably corrosive confrontation between the domestic, the private, and the inward—the world, in short, of "the governess"—and the foreign, the public, and the centrifugal—the world, in short, of "the actress."

But I want to discuss *Jane Eyre* first, not only in deference to chronology but also because this less obviously theatrical text has concomitantly more power to illustrate the ways in which theatricality gets camouflaged, in which the novelistic space denies its theatrical structure by internalizing it. In *Villette,* as we will see, the governess—a role that Brontë herself had of course played in real life—in fact turns into an actress; and if that progression, from one Victorian female paradigm to its apparent opposite, is not quite as definitive or as thematically coherent as it is in, say, *Vanity Fair,* its greater conspicuousness in relation to the economy of roles in *Jane Eyre* suggests that we may have more to learn, at least initially, from the governess whose acting is never even momentarily literal, but always furtively and disingenuously figurative—that is, highly characteristic of theatricality in the nineteenth-century novel.

Brontë may have disliked Austen—and she may not even have begun to read her until after *Jane Eyre* was published—but in one sense her novels seem oddly reminiscent of *Mansfield Park:* Fanny Price might well be seen as the precursor of Brontë's "undelightful" heroines.

Where Fanny insists, "No, indeed, I cannot act," Jane Eyre rebuffs Rochester's attempt to objectify her by warning him, "I will not be your English Céline Varens". Céline Varens, of course, is the French opera dancer with whom Rochester had the liaison that, to the dismay of many Victorian readers, he has recounted to Jane, and that, his rather half-hearted denials notwithstanding, has apparently resulted in the birth of little Adèle, Jane's pupil at Thornfield Hall. And as in *Mansfield Park,* the use of theatrical themes and imagery in *Jane Eyre* seems mainly homeopathic.

For, though Rochester's theatrical escapade plays a paradoxically crucial role in the narrative insofar as it motivates Jane's presence at Thornfield, and though one could argue that, as the "miniature" of her mother, Adèle introduces the "French" disease of theatricality into the domestic interior of the novel, Rochester provides more reassuring terms for the metaphorical recuperation of theatricality: "I…took the poor thing out of the slime and mud of Paris, and transplanted it here, to grow up clean in the wholesome soil of an English country garden".

As everyone knows, the climate of the house itself can hardly be called "wholesome"; but the force of passages such as this one is to suggest that whatever dangers are lurking nearby have nothing to do with the French connection: it is rather the much more fiery Spanish or Creole presence of Bertha Mason that should give us pause.

This transplant or graft provides an exemplary graph of how a certain potentially hazardous foreign substance may be subsumed safely within a domestic order. Most references to theatricality in the novel have a similarly diminishing effect, as in the "miniaturization" of Adèle whereby we are invited to dismiss her, as Blanche Ingram does when she greets her with the exclamation, "Oh, what a little puppet!". Unlike *Mansfield Park,* however, where the reduction of theatricality to convention becomes the normative, if covert, gesture of the novel itself, here the novel defines itself over and against that reduction.

At the beginning of the novel, for example, when Mrs.

Reed refuses to release Jane from the red-room, the heroine explains, "I was a precocious actress in her eyes"; the implication is that Jane's oppressor is too brutishly enslaved by commonplace assumptions about artifice and sincerity to understand her.

Or when, in a more metacritical register, the narrator writes that "a new chapter in a novel is something like a new scene in a play", the perfunctory, merely approximate character of that "something like" effectively empties the analogy of any disruptive potential. Indeed, the subsequent stage directions that tell us what to imagine in this "scene" underscore not the distractions of decor but the prevailing intimacy that obtains in the relationship between narrator and reader.

The rhetorical parallel becomes a hygienic bar separating the novelistic from the theatrical. Thus, if a certain theatrical infection *does* take hold in *Mansfield Park, Jane Eyre* would appear to inoculate itself more consequentially: a conventionalizing rhetoric would render the text immune from that very conventionality, making this novelistic world safe for authenticity, freedom, and direct communication. That a legitimate domain has been secured for the founding of a unitary, autonomous self is the enabling assumption of the most influential feminist reading of *Jane Eyre*.

In the chapter that serves as the iconic centerpiece of *The Madwoman in the Attic,* Sandra M. Gilbert and Susan Gubar rechristen the narrative as "Plain Jane's Progress," as a "pilgrimage toward selfhood," culminating in Jane's exorcism of her "truest and darkest double," the demonic Bertha Mason. But while the animalistic Bertha figures so centrally in this psychoanalytic allegory, any minatory allure that might attach to such culpably *social* female characters as Céline, Adèle, and Blanche gets minimized here: functioning merely as so many "important negative 'role-models' for Jane," these characters "suggest problems she must overcome before she can reach the independent maturity which is the goal of her pilgrimage". The teleology of this interpretation privileges Jane's "unseduceable independence in a world of self-marketing

Célines and Blanches". Whatever their importance as "negative 'role-models,' " these sexually commodified women never exceed the thematic determination of problems-to-be-overcome, and therefore never loom much larger than the puppet-like Adèle.

Characterizing the latter, along with her mother and Blanche, as "denizen[s] of Vanity Fair", Gilbert and Gubar ask, "May not Adèle, the daughter of a 'fallen woman,' be the model female in a world of prostitutes?", but they see little likelihood of Jane's taking this model seriously. If, on the one hand, these characters—to whose numbers we may add Jane's frivolous, "stylish" cousin Georgiana, who is at one point compared to "waxwork"; the hypocritically fashionable Brocklehurst women; and even the "coquettish" Rosamond Oliver—typify a certain proverbial construction of female sexuality in terms of both acting and prostitution, on the other, heavier hand, the very brittleness or blankness (Blanche-ness?) of the stereotype guarantees, as in the novel itself, that the woman who "sings and dances for her supper" will never turn into anything more subversive than "a clockwork temptress invented by E. T. A. Hoffmann".

Insofar as Jane's developmental drama is seen to centre on her confrontation with the Madwoman in the Attic, not with the Dancer in the Boudoir or the Coquette in the Parlor, there is little reason to doubt her when she says, "I will not be your English Céline Varens."

Not only will Jane Eyre never turn into Becky Sharp, something of a "clockwork temptress" herself; more important, she is saved from the contemptible world of "social exchange" in which Jane Austen's "elegant but confined" female characters are doomed to circulate. But Brontë's novel betrays a remarkable fascination with the very world and worldliness that she would soon patronize in Austen. Admittedly, Brontë seems to set up the "lady" merely to have Jane unmask her as already disreputably masked—to have Jane debunk her, that is, as her ostensible opposite, the "prostitute."

Yet if, in "plucking the mask," Jane reveals not naked truth but *another mask*, however "base," then the project of debunking—of "scrutinizing" and "exposing"—cannot be described as simply antitheatrical: it may in fact be impelled surreptitiously by something like a desire for theatricality.

Precisely by encouraging us, for instance, to concur with Jane in her decision that Blanche Ingram is "beneath jealousy" because, though "very showy," she is "not genuine", the narrative also compels us to join Jane in emulating the "ceaseless surveillance" to which Rochester subjects Blanche; and, as we discover, the act of surveillance seems almost inevitably to precipitate the would-be demystifier into a volatile state of both "ceaseless excitation and ruthless restraint".

Just as Fanny Price's refusal to participate in the theatricals at Mansfield Park fails to exempt her from the theatrical disease of mingled "longing and dreading," so too does Jane discover the instability of the binary opposition between spectator and spectacle. Jane's longish dramatization of her surveillance is all the more worth quoting because of its appropriately turbid logic. "Why can she not influence [Rochester] more, when she is privileged to draw so near him?" I asked myself. "Surely she cannot truly like him, or not like him with true affection! If she did, she need not coin her smiles so lavishly, flash her glances so unremittingly, manufacture airs so elaborate, graces so multitudinous.

It seems to me that she might, by merely sitting quietly at his side saying little and looking less, get nigher his heart. I have seen in his face a far different expression from that which hardens it now while she is so vivaciously accosting him; but then it came of itself: it was not elicited by meretricious arts and calculated manoeuvres; and one had but to accept it—to answer what he asked without pretension, to address him when needful without grimace—and it increased and grew kinder and more genial, and warmed one like a fostering sunbeam.

How will she manage to please him when they are married? I do not think they will manage it; and yet it might be managed; and his wife might, I verily believe, be the very happiest woman the sun shines on."

If it is not "jealousy" that troubles Jane, neither is it exactly altruistic sorrow on behalf of Rochester, destined though he appears to be for a loveless marriage. Instead, one gathers that Jane's anxiety stems from the fact that only she seems to have recognized the disparity between her own superior "genuineness" on the one hand and Blanche's "meretricious arts and calculated manoeuvres" on the other.

But though she knows that Blanche would do better by "merely sitting quietly at his side," Jane is soon agitating herself by imagining how she might "manage" as Rochester's wife. Indeed, the previous paragraph shows Jane vacillating between visions of out-Blancheing Blanche and of adopting an even subtler, more "pacifistic" strategy:

When she failed, I saw how she might have succeeded. Arrows that continually glanced off from Mr. Rochester's breast and fell harmless at his feet, might, I knew, if shot by a surer hand, have quivered keen in his proud heart—have called love into his stern eye, and softness into his sardonic face; or, better still, without weapons a silent conquest might have been won.

These passages suggest that it is not enough merely to write Blanche off as a bad or insufficiently inspired actress, although—more accurately, *because*—the spectacle of her failure is gratifying indeed.

As she keeps missing her target here, she exemplifies better than she knows the novel's insistent formulation of theatricality as an endless, dizzying dialectic of power and subservience, whereby to act is to be simultaneously empowered and vulnerable. Commanding Rochester to sing for her, she adds, "If you don't please me, I will shame you by showing you how such things *should* be done". Or again: "Both her words and her air seemed intended to excite not only the admiration, but the amazement of her auditors: she was evidently bent on *striking* them as something very dashing and daring indeed".

Blanche's performance, of course, "excites" something other than "admiration" and "amazement": its (unintended) effect is precisely the drama of "ceaseless excitation" traversing

Jane Eyre, which excitation, merged with "ruthless restraint," constitutes both an internalization and an intensification of the agonistic theatricality already demonstrated by Blanche. As we can see from the long passages in which Jane criticizes Blanche's histrionic technique, Blanche's punitive, self-aggrandizing, but also oddly self-abasing agenda in fact gets appropriated and enacted in the consciousness of her silent observer, the governess hiding "behind the window-curtain". Blanche boasts of how, as a child, she "took care to turn the tables" on such "nuisance[s]", but here it is rather Jane Eyre who turns the tables on her, for the ruthlessness of Jane's self-restraint enables the ruthlessness of her rhetorical triumph over the hapless Blanche.

Indeed, the "ceaseless excitation and ruthless restraint" that Blanche's egregiously miscalculated assault on Rochester triggers in Jane represents a complicated, "striking" play not only of self-pity and envy (if not "jealousy") but also of self-congratulation, disdain, and a vindictiveness whose voyeuristic pleasure is only barely moralized. Satirical demystification—the adversarial uncovering of Blanche's inept theatrical "calculations" as such—emerges here as an ardent vicariousness that does not so much undermine as upstage it. The novel offers many such scenes of overdetermined spectatorship on Jane's part, scenes that, far from constituting mere detours in her "pilgrimage toward selfhood," both articulate that trajectory and provide the measure for the weight, volume, and density that define the "selfhood" in question.

If the product of this narrative—the elaborated subjectivity named "Jane Eyre"—is in fact ultimately theatrical, that theatricality entails far more than the protagonist's arriving at a proper stance toward the various "role models" placed in her way. To be sure, Jane Eyre's selfhood *is* formed against the relatively flat backdrop composed by more conventionally theatrical characters like Blanche, Céline, and Adèle.

This does not mean, however, that Jane is the "opposite" of those characters; rather, they serve as pretexts or contexts, enticingly pregnant blanks, in relation to which her "surveillance" manifests itself as a self-charging ("exciting"), at once sadistically and masochistically "ruthless," performance in its own right.

Nor does this performance occur only when Blanche, Céline, Adèle, or any other "merely" stylish woman is on stage. That, before her marriage to Rochester, Bertha Mason was "a fine woman, in the style of Blanche Ingram", should point to an important link between Jane's "truest and darkest double" and those blanched or whitened female characters whose worldly falseness and vacuity come laden with a paradoxical power to induce in the heroine extravagant spectacles of self-construction.

The latter may be puppets, but, like their counterparts in *Vanity Fair*, they are all "magnified puppets", as Jane describes two other characters, and therefore "provoking puppet[s]" as well, as Rochester provokingly calls Jane herself. In appreciating Brontë's impressive revision of the novel as a genre, we should not underestimate the role played in that revision by a vigorously magnified and repeatedly projected meretriciousness, saliently but not exclusively embodied in non-English women, and invested with a provocative (i.e., at once energizing and irritating) glamor and even pathos by virtue of its very contemptibility.

The worse the acting—and, in *Jane Eyre*, almost all acting promises to be delectably "bad"—the better the show. Nothing succeeds (for Jane) like failure (on the part of her showy, worldly Others).

Much as we should acknowledge the extent to which Jane is constructed in and by these complicated power-plays, we must also take into account the considerable rhetorical effort involved in occluding this entire process.

In other words, if I have been emphasizing thus far the "excitation" and even the empowerment that attends Jane's surveillance, I want now to focus on the "restraint" that turns that ex-citation back *in* upon itself, that makes expansiveness look like inwardness, so that Brontëan exteriority (the outdoorsiness of "open country," "fresh air," etc.) becomes indistinguishable from Brontëan interiority. It is as though

Brontë were fending off Austen even before having read her: where mere *intro*version might recall Austen at her most oppressively "confined," unchecked *extro*version might suggest Austen at her most culpably social. Brontë avoids both of these pitfalls by means of a certain invagination. In a brilliant recent study of repression in Victorian fiction, John Kucich has written:

> The most striking thing about expressions of passion in Brontë's fiction is that they are most often histrionic—the performance of a mask that conceals, rather than reveals, an interior condition of desire. For Charlotte Brontë, passion implies the existence of an aroused, hypersensitive self that it simultaneously withholds.
>
> In her Byronically passionate male characters—and also in her female protagonists, though in more ephemeral ways—passion is a means of distancing others in order to preserve a desirable state of inward tension. By marking an inward instability, an eccentricity of the self to itself, passionate expression actually defeats any knowledge of its nature by others, and marks itself in opposition to them, rather than as a fusional impulse. Passionate expression is a mark of estrangement and distance, of self-elaboration in isolation, which brings it very close to the Brontëan repression we usually think of as its adversary.

Kucich's account of the virtual interchangeability of "passion" and "repression" in Brontë's fiction as a whole confirms my own sense of the inextricable entanglement of "excitation" and "restraint" in Jane Eyre's many acts of surveillance: as Kucich would suggest, the "inward tension" that defines Jane's spectatorship arises not from a war of polar opposites but rather from the repeated collapsing of an opposition.

Yet my argument differs from Kucich's in two respects. First, I want to claim that, although the complicity of "excitation" or "passion" and "restraint" or "repression" seems to establish the solipsistic isolation that Kucich identifies as Brontë's most distinctive effect, the "inward instability" of Jane Eyre at any rate is more social and more political than Kucich will allow, not so much an escape from Foucauldian relations of power as a heightened reinscription of them.

Second, while I obviously agree that Brontëan passion is mainly histrionic, I want to look at the ways in which the histrionic, which Kucich rightly associates with the "mask that conceals," is itself masked by Brontë. These two points may seem to contradict each other, the one claiming greater sociality in Brontë, the other arguing for greater reticence. But in fact I will also argue that Brontë is most responsive to social pressures precisely when she herself restrains and dissembles the dramas that her heroine at the same time rehearses so excitedly. The persistence of a certain critical tradition begun by Brontë herself would indeed persuade us that the ruthless restraint that is an integral component of Brontëan theatricality functions instead as a guarantee *against* theatricality, that the dropping of a curtain in front of these dramas succeeds nonetheless in not looking like a theatrical effect at all: it seems instead to consecrate "the depth" or the "visionary hollow" that the cagey heroine first sights during her imprisonment in the red-room, and whose mapping and furnishing will be the programme of the ensuing narrative.

Protestations of antitheatricality thus proliferate unsurprisingly throughout the book, although they reach a kind of crescendo during the period immediately before the aborted wedding, when Jane is at pains to keep rejecting the "stage-trappings" of courtship. (And when, soon after that non-ceremony, Jane famously leaves Thornfield, she does so to avoid the implicitly theatricalizing fate of becoming the latest in Rochester's series of mistresses.) Perhaps the oddest of all Jane's deflections is her impatient observation that Rochester, who wants to deck her out in prenuptial finery, "would yet see me glittering like a parterre". While the immediate reference seems to be to the sense of "parterre" as an ornamental (or "Austenian") arrangement of flower beds, one cannot help noticing, in this context of disavowal, the more specifically theatrical reference as well.

Though prepared, even eager, to cast herself as the spectator par excellence—Mrs. Reed, for example, could never tolerate her niece's "continual, unnatural watchings of one's movements"—the heroine would evade any interpretation of her spectatorship as a spectacle in itself, meticulously effacing (or covering up) any hints of "glitter" in her ceaselessly vigilant prose.[]

Accordingly, the narrative must obey a stringent logic of decor—and of decorum—in converting the shining plane of the red-room mirror, or the showy plain of an ostentatious audience, into a semimatte surface that will reflect only the visionary recessiveness (and "depth") of an unimpeachably plain Jane. The lineaments, as well as the risks, of this logic may be glimpsed in a letter Brontë wrote describing how, during a rare trip to London, she and her sister Anne visited the opera in the company of their publishers:

We attired ourselves in the plain, high-made country garments we possessed, and went with [George Smith and his sisters] to their carriage, where we found Mr. Williams. They must have thought us queer, quizzical-looking beings, especially me with my spectacles. I smiled inwardly at the contrast, which must have been apparent, between me and Mr. Smith as I walked with him up the crimson-carpeted staircase of the Opera House and stood amongst a brilliant throng at the box door, which was not yet open. Fine ladies and gentlemen glanced at us with a slight, graceful superciliousness quite warranted by the circumstances. Still, I felt pleasantly excited in spite of headache and sickness and conscious clownishness, and I saw Anne was calm and gentle, which she always is.

Here, in an uncanny blurring of the distinction between fiction and reality, the author reenacts the role performed by her newly celebrated fictional surrogate, inheriting Jane's excitement and reliving her restraint as headache, sickness, and embarrassment. Like Jane's response to Blanche, Brontë's internal drama masters and exceeds, in complexity, interest, and above all, emotional seriousness, the external scene that occasions it. In this edgy encounter with the London beau monde, the brilliance of the throng becomes a foil for the transcendent display of the provincial author's (self)consciousness. What is remarkable in this account is its delicate balance between a scrupulously half-shamefaced exhibitionism and the tremulous yet invincible *inwardness* it nonetheless affirms.

Where the gaze of her publishers and the "elegant young ladies" who accompany them threatens to turn Brontë into a spectacle, she transforms her own conveniently deglamorizing "spectacles" not only into a powerful instrument of vision but also into a protective barrier behind which a private drama of contemplation may take place unobserved. Thus shielded, she is free to "fe[el] pleasantly excited" but, more important, to "smile...inwardly," quietly appropriating much of the "superciliousness" she ascribes to her sophisticated, but only superficially perceptive, beholders. By means of an ingenious reversal, not unlike that practiced by Jane Eyre in her surveillance of Blanche Ingram, the mere snobbery associated with "fine ladies and gentlemen" gets introjected and refined as the "genuine" (paradoxical, spiritual, virtually inexpressible) loftiness of the "high-made" "country spinster," as Brontë calls herself elsewhere.

Even the possibility of humiliation risked by the acknowledgment of "clownishness" gets preempted, thanks to Brontë's absorptive emphasis on her "consciousness" of it. This biographical vignette recalls still another scene from the novel that Brontë had just published.

In this scene, a similar recuperation is performed, but with a telling difference. Soon after her arrival at Lowood, Jane, having dropped and broken her "slate," is first "exposed to general view on a pedestal of infamy" but then, like her model of self-abasement, Helen Burns, "completely cleared from every imputation" of guilt. In a typically Brontëan pattern, humiliation only serves to establish the victim's unfathomable depth of receptivity, which "no language can describe": the degradations of the outside ironically reaffirm the inviolability of the inside.

Yet, despite the well-known autobiographical nature of her fiction, as well as the crafty literariness of her autobiographical writings, Charlotte Brontë will take chances in her private correspondence that she spares the central character in her more public work as a novelist. For Brontë's drama of appropriation and reversal unfolds in a literal theater, too palpably social a place, whereas Jane Eyre enacts this scenario under the aegis of *displacement:* all of her "theatergoing" and all of her "acting" occur either within the overtly disciplinary space of the schoolroom or within the covertly disciplinary space of (someone else's) home. Where Charlotte Brontë hides behind her spectacles in an actual *site* of spectacles, her fictional creation hides behind surfaces in settings less apt to invest them homonymically with a compromising glitter.

The "treacherous slate" that Jane accidentally breaks is only one of many such surfaces, although its fracture and symbolic reconstitution prove exemplary: hoping to "escape notice" by using it to "conceal [her] face", the heroine finds herself betrayed by the very object that should have protected her; but instead of branding her as a "liar", as Brocklehurst would have it, her "obtrusive" exposure and consequent shaming produce the opposite effect of wiping the slate clean, restoring to Jane the medium on which she may hence inscribe the indescribable signs of her integrity. And since the slate—a surface whose associations with pedagogical compulsion, happily enough, clear *it* from any suspicion of borrowed glamor—is both what one writes *on* and what one hides *behind*, self-inscription is identified with self-effacement, thereby allowing the autobiographer to elude any "imputation" of theatricality. Writing, we are asked to believe, even writing about oneself, is not like acting: it is what one does *instead* of acting.

The form of "restraint" typically adopted in *Jane Eyre,* then, appears less voluntary, and less ambiguous, than that imposed in the passage about the "spectacles," just as writing forgoes its associations with the social luster of professional authorship—especially *successful* professional authorship—to assume instead the protective covering of (home)work.

If less ambiguous, however, this strategy is nothing if not paradoxical, for while the relative abjection of Jane Eyre seems to bar her from "society" in the seductive, specialized sense of a pleasure-seeking elite, it would also have the enabling effect of exempting her from society as a whole.

In order to examine more closely the process thanks to which Jane can say, equivocally, "I appeared a disciplined and subdued character", let us return to Jane's surveillance of Blanche, paying particular attention to the way Brontë frames and thus, oddly enough, detheatricalizes it. It is important to recognize that, by placing Jane "behind the window-curtain"—by having her "shr[i]nk...into the shade", like Fanny Price—Brontë discreetly draws a veil in front of the heroine's performance, occulting its rivalrous histrionics and offering it instead as further evidence of an otherwise inarticulable inwardness.

Indeed, if the entire episode of the Ingrams' visit threatens to become an Austenian comedy of manners, Brontë neutralizes that danger through an equally Austenian countermeasure, according to which the heroine, furtively but avidly consuming the all-too-glittering spectacle of aristocratic role-playing, thereby demonstrates the vast, even inestimable capacity of her own consciousness· (It is this kind of *gourmandise,* one suspects, that has earned Brontë her reputation for what Matthew Arnold, albeit disgustedly, called "hunger, rebellion, and rage." Throughout this episode, whenever Jane might seem to be standing in front of a curtain (whether "literally" or "figuratively"), the narrative recontextualizes her so that she ends up standing *behind* one. As the Ingrams and their party approach the house, Jane watches them from the window, "taking care to stand on one side, so that, screened by the curtain, I could see without being seen".

When she comes downstairs to introduce Adèle to the guests, Jane is relieved to be screened once again:

Fortunately, there was another entrance to the drawing-room than that through the saloon where they were all seated at dinner....The crimson curtain hung before the arch: slight as was the separation this drapery formed from the party in the adjoining saloon, they spoke in so low a key that nothing of their conversation could be distinguished beyond a soothing murmur.

Yet Jane's inability to overhear their conversation actually has the same effect as her unimpeded visual consumption: in both cases, what is ultimately secured for her is a saving opacity. And that *her* opacity is both the antithesis and the double of *their* meretricious brilliance becomes clear a few paragraphs later:

A soft sound of rising now became audible; the curtain was swept back from the arch; through it appeared the dining-room, with its lit lustre pouring down light on the silver and glass of a magnificent dessert-service covering a long table; a band of ladies stood in the opening; they entered, and the curtain fell behind them.

As soon as this "band of ladies," having made a lavishly lit entrance, stands in front of the curtain, that curtain looks very much like a curtain on a stage, and the ladies appear bathed in all the culpable "lustre" of the will to dazzle: for a brief but resonant moment, the decorative match between the "crimson-carpeted staircase" of the opera house and the crimson curtain of the private home hints at the larger and more problematic resemblance between public theater and an unstably "domesticated" theatricality. As long as it is Jane, however, who stands in the same spot, both she and the backdrop look quite different: far from setting her *off,* as a foil does a jewel, the curtain sets her *apart,* marking her distance from and inaccessibility to the resplendent company on the other side.

Like Charlotte Brontë's spectacles and the young Jane Eyre's slate—like a whole series of Brontëan surfaces, for that matter—the curtain validates the self not by revealing it but by obscuring it. Always a consumer (rather than an object to be consumed), Jane will not perform the "ladylike" function of being served up like some temptingly unwholesome "dessert." Even though she and the "band of ladies" occupy the same position in front of the curtain, Brontë manipulates this "screen" so that, in the space of a single page, it serves—or appears to serve—two radically incompatible purposes. By virtue of the author's scenic legerdemain, an anamorphic illusion splits the screen-as-enhancing-backdrop from the screen-as-protective-cover, thereby disrupting any visible continuity between the "ladies" who stand *flamboyantly* before the former and the governess who stands *meekly* before—which is to say, behind—the latter.

This is by no means the only place in the novel where Brontë stages as a distinction, even as an opposition, what might easily look like a similarity. In the novel's crucial opening scene, Jane is punished for her want of a properly "sociable and childlike disposition, a more attractive and sprightly manner", by her exclusion from the Reeds' family circle:

A small breakfast-room adjoined the drawing-room, I slipped in there. It contained a bookcase; I soon possessed myself of a volume, taking care that it should be one stored with pictures. I mounted into the window-seat: gathering up my feet, I sat cross-legged, like a Turk; and, having drawn the red moreen curtain nearly close, I was shrined in double retirement.

If not crimson, this curtain is at least red, and its power to induce a corresponding blush of embarrassment in the would-be "unsociable" text has not gone unexploited. In a recent reading of *Jane Eyre*, Gayatri Chakravorty Spivak performs an adroit deconstruction of this scene, uncovering it as precisely a theatricalization of selfhood: grounded in this "scene of the marginalization and privatization of the protagonist," the subsequent narrative may proceed to naturalize "[t]he battle for female individualism" as it "plays itself out within the larger theater of the establishment of meritocratic individualism, indexed in the aesthetic field by the ideology of 'the creative imagination.' " Rather like Jane Austen when she surfaces as the disruptively parodic Mrs. Norris, Spivak unpacks that ideology by deploying the theatrical metaphor in a frankly deidealizing way.

Nor are she and Kucich, who also emphasizes Brontë's histrionics, the only critics to have insisted on pulling back the curtain that Brontë draws in front of her protagonist. Terry

Eagleton, in his demythifying book on the Brontës, also seeks, in the aggressively noisy manner of the finale of *Mansfield Park,* to show theatricality writ large in a work that endeavors tirelessly to write it small. Eagleton anticipates my questioning of the heavily advertised contrast between Jane Eyre and a character like Blanche Ingram:

Jane, who shares Blanche's liking for "devilish" men, knows better than she does how they are to be handled—when to exert her piquant will and when to be cajolingly submissive.....Jane moves deftly between male and female roles in her courtship of Rochester; unlike Blanche, who is tall, dark, and dominating like Rochester himself, she settles astutely for a vicarious expression of her own competitive maleness through him. She preserves the proprieties while turning them constantly to her advantage, manipulating convention for both self-protection and self-advancement.

While they have very different critical styles and even different political agendas—one traditionally "Marxist," the other more ambitiously "Marxist-feminist"—both Eagleton and Spivak direct the corrosive trope of "theatricality" against what they see as a certain (petit-)bourgeois success story. Instead of joining Gilbert and Gubar in celebration of "plain Jane's progress," these two critics read that narrative as an allegory of the brilliant career of bourgeois or bourgeois-feminist ideology in general, a career whose success has depended in large part on its ability to mask or dull its very brilliance.

Both, therefore, take us behind the scenes of this exemplary tale, exposing Brontë's painstakingly achieved antitheatrical illusion so as to reveal what goes on behind the scenes—on the far side of the curtain—as an elaborate, highly tendentious scene in itself.

It should be clear by now that my own approach to the novel is closer to the demystifying school of Brontë criticism than to the celebratory one. But my aim in acknowledging and describing these prior interpretations has not been merely to take my place in line, a place that all too easily becomes a hiding place, a place *behind*. If it is important not to "cover up for" Charlotte Brontë by covering up theatricality along with her, it is equally important not to cover oneself in the prestigious mantle woven and worn by previous unmaskers. As we have seen, a certain unmasking is already dramatized in the novel itself: but what is most instructive about Jane's desire to "pluck the mask" from Blanche, just as Brontë would "raise the gilding" from her own miniaturized Vanity Fair, is that the ensuing act of demystification, precisely because of the "excitation" it induces in the demystifier, has to subject itself to "ruthless restraint."

As we have also seen, the ruthlessness of this restraint affects both the object and the subject of demystification, although we have devoted more attention to the latter, since potentially violent self-discipline continues to seem somewhat anomalous in a novelist who invokes images of "open country" and "fresh air" to advertise her art.

As for the literary critic, it ought not to surprise us that his or her "ruthlessness" should find an external object, whether in the canonical text, in its author, in its protagonist, or in some composite scapegoat: as popular usage implies, "criticism" has a certain reputation for being mean. In its relentlessly prosecutorial style, Eagleton's reading, for one, epitomizes this destructive tendency—a tendency perhaps less obvious to academic critics than to those outside the profession. For though many of us are intermittently or vaguely aware of the aggressivity that informs our work in general, we may ignore not only the *ceaselessness* of its ruthless excitations but also the professional deformation whereby we restrain or repress them, to say nothing of the ruthlessness with which we do so. Indeed, our very ignorance of that deformation betokens the thing it both "actively" disregards and "passively" fails to know.

If these quotation marks would blur the hierarchical distinction between a deliberate *act* of ignoring and an involuntary *state* of unknowing, this is because I want to bring contemporary demystifying critics—who, in their apparent self-possession, might recall the reserved but savvy, ironic, and newly empowered Charlotte Brontë we glimpsed at the opera—a little closer to that even less glamorous and even more carefully guarded avatar of "the writer," the governess named Jane Eyre. For if Jane represents the writer *disciplined,* it is hard to tell whether that discipline is self-discipline or rather the effect of certain imperious external constraints, whether it is administered willingly or unwillingly, consciously or unconsciously. Indeed, as we have seen, Brontë's disciplining of the self that writes ought the peculiar consequence of transforming what to look like a subjection to social control into what looks instead like a savingly asocial or at least antisocial condition.

Likewise, those of us who practice a deidealizing literary criticism most eloquently attest our embeddedness in the social precisely when, "accepting" the restraints of our discipline, we discreetly withdraw from the scene of our own readings. Critics' techniques of withdrawal can be as sophisticated as those practiced by, or upon, Brontë's heroine.

Eagleton's reading may itself be a study in the "competitive maleness" he identifies in Jane, yet its deftly self-distancing effect of analytic *mise en abîme* at the same time renders it an impressive exercise in the art of "vicarious expression" he attributes to her as well. Spivak, for her part, thematizes the veiling of her own authorial performance as a pragmatic refusal to theatricalize the "author" of the novel along with its protagonist: she chooses "rather strategically to take shelter in an essentialism which, not wishing to lose the important advantages won by U.S. mainstream feminism, will continue to honour the suspect binary oppositions—book and author, individual and history."

And it is no doubt clear that my dilation upon other critics' defenses has served a dilatory and defensive purpose in its own right. One might argue, moreover, that this chapter's relative generality or even diffidence thus far with respect to the specific social—for example, sexual and class—determinants of Jane's behaviour has served as a not-so-reliable screen for certain rather undelightful social aggressivities of my own. Yet I hope that it will not seem merely defensive if I suggest, first, that this diffidence is in large part a temporary response to the necessity for a preliminary analysis of Brontë's own evasion of social specification, and, second, that the interpretive ruthlessness it would occlude is itself a response to my fear that, as a teacher who writes, as a disciplined subject, far from being safely superior to Brontë's literary governess, I am in fact insufficiently differentiated from her.

In the next section of this chapter, I will attempt to specify the social role that, precisely by virtue of its Brontëan "unsociability," the demystifying school of literary criticism has in common with the "disciplined...character" known as Jane Eyre. It might be objected that, even if this analogy demonstrates a structural affinity, it may seem to overlook the obvious difference between the overwhelming "subjectivity-effect" of Brontëan discourse and the constitutive facelessness of most academic criticism.

Yet I hope that what follows will be justified by its delineation of a performative dimension that academic "objectivity" might share, surprisingly enough, with Brontëan "subjectivity." For if we can see what it is that *effects* that "subjectivity," we may be able to see not only how effectively it responds to social pressures, but also how closely the decorum of criticism maintains an active repression not unlike Jane Eyre's. If, in our more or less ruthless unmasking of that unmasker in the text, a certain transferential logic apparently compels us to repeat the double gesture whereby Jane catches others in the act of theatricality while at the same time concealing the traces of her own theatrical implication, we can at least attempt to analyse that logic, to interrogate the motives that sustain us in this productive inconsistency.

We can ask, that is, not only how a curtain gets drawn in front of a certain drama of reading, but also why and on whose account it may be useful, as Spivak suggests, thus partially "to ignore the lessons of deconstruction." Obviously, not all dramas of reading are the same, and the annals of recent criticism would no doubt show that there are many ways of "ignoring" deconstruction while seeming to honour it. The point is not to totalize diverse readings of Brontë's novel, much less to collapse those readings into the equally spurious totality of the different readings performed *in* the novel. Rather, I hope to consider some of the strategies that governesses who write may share with other teachers who, in different ways, take up the pen to inscribe theatricality in the novel.

In the middle of the Ingrams' stay at Thornfield, the theatricality that suffuses the episode finds its most "direct expression" in the charades that the company performs. "They spoke of 'playing charades,' " Jane tells us, "but in my ignorance I did not understand the term".

As is the case with Jane's other professions of "ignorance," and with the professional "ignorance" or self-effacing "restraint" commonly assumed by professors of literature in their role as writers of criticism, we are confronted not with the inertness of a mere lack or negation but with a powerfully signifying opacity.

Positing a gap at the level of cognition, this assertion of "ignorance" comes heavily charged with performative potential. Though Jane's "ignorance" excuses her from participating in the charades, as Rochester invites her to do, it provides her with the leading role in a far more important, if more covert, play. A few pages before Jane recounts the stages of her "ceaseless surveillance," we join her in a less obviously anxious phase of her spectatorship, watching the charades along with her.

What is most striking about this lengthy and thematically pregnant passage is not Jane's response to it but rather her apparent *neutrality:* the narrative here consists primarily of description, forgoing the evaluative and meditative exfoliations that characterize so many other passages in the novel.

This relative neutrality indicates, of course, that Jane's countertheatrical screen is already in place. But the obscurity thus procured for her—an obscurity that Jane would rather have us read as *obtuseness*—has an uncanny analogue in the obscurity generically inherent in the charades themselves: spectator and spectacle are linked in a complicity that Brontë manages artfully to dissemble, mainly by diverting our gaze from the narrator and fixing it instead on the *tableaux vivants* executed in front of her.

So subtle is this distraction that, unless the reader pays particular attention to architectural details that the critical eye is trained merely to scan as so much stage direction, he or she will not notice that the stage for this performance is nothing other than the drawing-room in which Jane has been stationed so as to seem quintessentially *nontheatrical*.

"The drawing-room, as I have before observed, was raised two steps above the dining room"; we have probably *not* observed, however, that it was Jane, before it was the dazzling band of ladies, who loomed on such a platform, and that it was she, not they, who thus stood poised for unveiling within the confines of the room's implicitly dramatic arch. At any rate, when the curtain rises, now enlisted in an avowedly (if amateurishly) theatrical enterprise, it discloses three consecutive, elaborately mounted tableaux: the first representing "the pantomime of a marriage" between Rochester and Blanche; the second, a small triumph of orientalist *mise en scène*, depicting the same two characters as "Eliezer and Rebecca" beside a well; the third displaying a "begrimed" Rochester in a prison cell. At the end of this sequence, the members of the audience solve the charade, whose three scenes denote "Bridewell Prison."

As if to proffer further evidence of her "ignorance," however, Jane does not pause to underscore the semantic implications of this signifier; instead, when the other spectators ascend the stage to perform their own charade, she continues to watch Rochester and Blanche, who, though now spectators themselves, remain spectacularized as a result of Jane's increasingly excited and ruthless—but at the same time supposedly naïve and out-of-it—vigilance. Indeed, a generalized interchangeability of spectator and spectacle seems by now to be one of the defining features of both Brontëan and Austenian theatricality. Yet, we have also seen how much of Brontë's (and, to a somewhat lesser extent, of Austen's) energy goes into the masking of the heroine's participation in these reversals.

In the passage in question, it is precisely Jane's muteness with respect to the charade's meaning that deflects attention from any similarity between that nonresponse and the "dumb show" enacted before our eyes, or between her inscrutability as an observer and the "darkness" (cosmetically as well as hermeneutically guaranteed) of the charade itself. The rules of the game require that the "diviners" become actors in their turn, but Jane appears exempt from this otherwise obligatory transformation of cognition into performance. Just as Brontë severs the connection between opacity and the blinding glitter that might resemble it too closely for comfort, so she forestalls any recognition of the symmetrical relationship between Jane's illegibility and that of the enigmatic tableaux: whereas the latter are made to suggest a potentially uncontrollable *excess* (of meaning), the former is manipulated so as to look like an antithetical and merely static *lack* (of interpretation).

The danger readily illustrated for Jane is that she might end up like the interpreters in the audience, forced into excessive performance herself: "interpretation," after all, is also another name for "acting." In playing dumb, however, Jane in fact does something quite specific, albeit without appearing to do anything at all. What Jane's "ignorance" does is nothing less than to articulate the rhetorical and social topography of the novel. For this "ignorance" is itself articulated or internally divided. On the one hand, it functions as an index of class inferiority, marking Jane's distance from the "showy" aristocrats in whose sophisticated games she must not participate.

On the other hand, insofar as she *chooses* not to participate, it may be inferred that Jane's "ignorance" affords her a certain privilege as well. If "ignorance" stands out as one of the novel's favourite signifiers for *social* repression or restraint, it also belongs to an apparently antithetical set of valuations, in which negativity turns into a virtue, in which privation gets cathected as a positive force. That is, the very minimalness of Jane's social literacy, and the attendant exiguity of her social surface, become the ground for her *rhetorical* authority, an authority signaled early in the novel when, with a kind of grudging admiration, another character says of the young heroine, "I never saw a girl of her age with so much cover". Figured as "so much cover," Jane's density, which we have identified as a certain obtuseness, can be transvalued as a kind of protopoetic compaction analogous to the Freudian dream-work, with its "complex" effects of condensation, displacement, and overdetermination.

"You can't judge a book by its cover": Jane's "ignorance" renders her both unknowing and, more honourifically, unknowable; it can associate her both with unconsciousness—construed rather flatly as a lack of information or experience—and with the unconscious—construed much more generously as an active, if occulted, source of meaning and energy. Jane's bookish cover adumbrates the subversive potential that lies hidden within the socially and psychologically repressed, a potential all the greater for being "linguistic" rather than "real." Emblematically, when Rochester calls Jane "inexplicable" and "uncanny", the prestigious resonance of these epithets cancels out the negativity of their prefixes.

Invested with an aura of textuality that befits a titular heroine, Jane Eyre challenges us to penetrate her cover, to join Rochester in thinking, "An unusual—to me—a perfectly new character, I suspected was yours: I desired to search it deeper and know it better". And when, under such (implicitly violent) hermeneutic pressure, Jane proudly proclaims, "But I have a veil—it is down", she is trading on the conventional wisdom that detects in victimhood and repression a blessing in disguise. Because of its cunning mobilization of "ignorance," *Jane Eyre* is indeed one of the major sites of the convention—central to modern ideology, political and literary—that dissociates rhetorical (and ontological) power from social power, producing a chiasmus in which the inferiority of oppressed or marginalized groups virtually guarantees their latent, but all the more disruptive, eloquence, while the politically and economically powerful, trading eloquence for elegance, surrender their linguistic hegemony and assume a corrupt idiom that is itself "merely" conventional.

Under this chiastic dispensation, the episode of the

charades, for example, can never become an effective locus of what a "subversive" literary criticism might wish to see as Derridean free play.

However seductively "textual" it may seem, this potentially disseminative interlude is reduced to the status of a trivial pursuit: textuality has been dissociated from theatricality, the former imbued, oddly enough, with an almost logocentric inexpressibility and depth—as in, "I desired to search it deeper"—and the latter deflated, rendered superficial and frivolous. Like the private theatricals in *Mansfield Park*, the charades end up signifying nothing more subversive than the fabled vacuity and/or promiscuity of the upper classes, who represent "social exchange" at its most mindless. In contrast, Jane's wise "ignorance" at once saves her from this linguistic fate and affiliates her with the mystifyingly exalted community of those who, could they speak, would utter the *parole pleine* of truth and authenticity.

For if Jane is flanked on one side by Vanity Fair—by "a world of self-marketing Célines and Blanches"—she adjoins on the other side the more figurative but therefore more formidable community of the dispossessed and the incarcerated—the world most aptly symbolized by Jane's "truest and darkest double," The Madwoman in the Attic. As Gilbert and Gubar's canonizing title implies, Bertha is indeed the internalized—the interned—character par excellence; and when, in the famous, ominous scene of her nocturnal visit to Jane's room, she throws Jane's bridal veil over her face, the first Mrs. Rochester reminds her successor of the considerable mystique that attaches to those who know how to remain under cover, even when, as in this instance, they are on the loose.

I am suggesting that Jane's inwardness, far from constituting an end in itself, performs a specific kind of cultural work. To say that Jane functions as an ideological placeholder would exaggerate, but not misstate, her representational role. By cultivating an inaccessible interiority, Jane ultimately and crucially protects not herself but the larger chiastic rewriting of power relations that her "ignorance" makes possible. That the demand for this intermediacy issues not only from within the novel but, perhaps more importunately, from extratextual sources may become clear if we consider a contemporary review of *Jane Eyre,* a review that is also a telling discussion of the lot of the Victorian governess. The reviewer, Elizabeth Rigby, writes:

The line which severs the governess from her employers is not one which will take care of itself, as in the case of a servant. If she sits at table she does not shock you—if she opens her mouth she does not distress you—her appearance and manners are likely to be as good as your own—her education rather better; there is nothing upon the face of the thing to stamp her as having been called to a different state of life from that in which it has pleased God to place you; and therefore the distinction has to be kept up by a fictitious barrier which presses with cruel weight upon the mental strength or constitutional vanity of a woman.

As we will see when we turn to Rigby's specific remarks on *Brontë's* governess, her compassion does not preclude the most stringently prescriptive attitude toward its objects. For though she laments the "cruel weight" resulting from the very groundlessness or arbitrariness of "the line which severs the governess from her employers," what concerns Rigby about this "fictitious" distinction is less the suffering its peremptoriness imposes upon the former than the danger to which its tenuity exposes the latter.

"The distinction *has to be* kept up": otherwise, the "employer" addressed both as the *destinataire* ("you") and as the real subject of this discourse might find himself—and more important, the "ladies" of his social class—uncomfortably close to the marketplace from which the governess has emerged. As M. Jeanne Peterson, Mary Poovey, and Nancy Armstrong have shown, the Victorian governess virtually embodied the deconstructibility of her culture's opposition between "lady" and "prostitute."

An irremediably vexing symptom of tensions within middle-class life, "[s]he was educated to be a 'nosegay' to adorn her 'papa's drawing room,' and as a governess she had sold herself as an ornament to display her employer's prestige."

What makes the governess so unwelcome a presence within the middle-class home is her accentuation not of the pathetic disparity between her intended fate and her real one, but rather of the more painful *affinity* between "nosegay" and "ornament" as tropes of quasi-theatrical ostentation. Constantly threatening to uncover the precariousness of the polarization of idealized female domesticity on the one hand and dreaded female commerce on the other, the governess always already plays an intermediate role—a *disturbingly* intermediate role as deconstructive thorn-in-the-side—that necessitates her ideological refashioning in a more *reassuringly* intermediate role as emblem of interiority. Almost intrinsically a site of "social exchange"—a figure for the transgressive circulation of social meanings—the governess must be reconceived in a way that re-covers her and that thereby covers up her exacerbating potential.

If she cannot help occupying a liminal position in the class and gender system of Victorian culture, then perhaps that position can be buttressed or hypostatized so as to separate the identities it might otherwise conjoin.

Thus, Rigby's apparently empathetic discourse, regretting the "fictitious barrier which presses with cruel weight upon the mental strength or constitutional vanity of a woman," simultaneously constitutes both that barrier and the woman whose task is henceforth to "keep it up."

And if, in bearing, internalizing, and so eventually *becoming* this ruthless restraint, the disciplined governess must repress the "vanity" of her theatrical (i.e., female) nature, the compensation for this pressing upkeep is a ceaseless excitation of her "mental strength," which impresses upon her the profundity of the subjectifying (i.e., female) work she performs, and brings comfort to the "employers" whose homes she thereby defends.

Admittedly, it might appear rather odd to view Jane Eyre's pivotal "ignorance" as consistent with the kind of disciplinary fiction dictated by Rigby. After all, the product of the former—a triptych with Bertha on one side, Céline, Adèle, and Blanche on the other side, and Jane in the middle—does not seem ideally congruent with the aim of the latter—a hierarchy with the "lady" on top, the "prostitute" on the bottom, and the long-suffering governess in the middle. The two models appear to have nothing more in common than the same medial figure. Rigby in fact disliked *Jane Eyre,* denouncing its heroine as "the personification of an unregenerate and *undisciplined* spirit" (emphasis added). Nor is it particularly difficult to understand this hostility: in unmasking Blanche as a "bad" actress—as a more respectable, home-grown version of Céline—Brontë's heroine inscribes the very confusion that Rigby would prohibit.

But before we decide that Brontë's deconstructive unmaskings are automatically "subversive," let us consider—as Rigby does not—the way in which they might actually promote Rigby's project. I would argue that, while one might want to read it as a gesture of defiance, Brontë's fictional work goes a long way toward constructing the fictitious barrier Rigby prescribes; the novel's debunking of certain binary oppositions may thus serve as a kind of alibi.

Indeed, Brontë's defensive strategy is even shrewder than Rigby's. For where Rigby, though reinforcing the boundary that barely differentiates the governess from her employer, would thereby merely hold the line between the still more unsettlingly similar categories of (domestically theatrical) "nosegay" and (commercially theatrical) "ornament," Brontë redraws the social map by superimposing on the vulnerable opposition between home and marketplace what looks like a more radical opposition between an interior now defined as "psychological" and an exterior now defined as "social."

That is, since Blanche Ingram (the "lady") already bears too great a resemblance to Céline Varens (the "prostitute"), Brontë deconstructs both of them into the same inferior category, and provides, on the far side of the governess, the heavy ballast of the id-like Bertha.

That Bertha is "demonic" rather than "ladylike,"

moreover, hardly detracts from her stabilizing power: her very extremity testifies to the vastness of the psychic space capable of containing her. And contain her is just what Jane Eyre does, constituting, by virtue of her own "depth," a barrier behind which the Madwoman lurks as the internalized or repressed "truth" of the redomesticated female subject. Rigby would defend upper-middle-class and would-be upper-middle-class women on the basis of social privilege alone, a privilege she knows to be threatened by its beneficiaries' lack of any corresponding physical, intellectual, or psychological distinction: she admits that, in "appearance," "manners," and "education," the governess is likely to be equal if not superior to her employers.

Brontë, however, places *her* governess at the frontier of a brave new world of female subjectivity, a world that can include not only the demonic Bertha, at its furthest limit, but also, in its great normative middle distance, the same women Rigby protects, though less effectually, without benefit of Brontë's empowering cover of redefined and expanded "privacy."

Brontë's governess, then, figures not an alternative to confinement but a better *form* of confinement, one that offers both shelter and a semblance of liberation. A novel that seems to organize itself into a series of rooms and houses, *Jane Eyre* may be said to comprise three main symbolic spaces, which we can call "Gothic," "Brontëan," and "Austenian," to give a more authoritative sound to the madwoman/governess/prostitute triad. And if the Brontëan enclosure, characterized by the dense psychic layering that makes it a barrier as well, nonetheless seems compatible with effects of "open country" and "fresh air," this is because Brontë positions her heroine strategically between the unspeakably "dark" recesses inhabited and personified by Bertha Mason, and the discreditably "glittering" exteriority inhabited and personified by Blanche, Céline, Adèle and company.

Polarizing two distinct sets of literary conventions—on the one hand, "the dark images of the Gothic," in Raymond Williams's phrase; on the other, the "worldliness" epitomized by Jane Austen—the Brontëan heroine is thus also confined and implicitly conventionalized by them, if only through metonymic contact.

And yet, the structure so produced persists in looking like an *escape* from structures and conventions and constraints—in short, from the sorts of alterity that usually count, in modern critical parlance anyway, as "the social." To be sure, the intermediate space that Brontë maps out seems to exhibit a distinct antigravitational tendency toward the Gothic attic. But Brontë's psychologizing appropriation of that place and of the literary tradition it emblematizes, an appropriation that critics have recognized for some time now, is "novel" only in the sense that a novel, as *Mansfield Park* has shown us, is itself a conventional structure in which a theater lies concealed. The Brontëan middle, and the disjunction it signifies, are as socially determined, and as socially performative, as both the Gothic upstairs and the more overtly stagy Austenian downstairs.

Nowhere is Brontë more effective in her public relations, of course, than when she persuades even her most socially sensitive critics that her fiction furnishes an essentially private site in which, as if for the first time, "passion" can be either "directly expressed" (Williams again), or, as Kucich would have it, *indirectly* expressed but with an even more antisocial result. As I have been suggesting, *Jane Eyre* can perform its ideological duty only if it disguises that performance. Early in Jane's relationship with Rochester—who incarnates social power in this novel and who also, it turns out, is himself a master of disguise—that imperious employer gives her a lesson both in the task she will be expected to carry out and in the proper means of domesticating or effacing it.

In this virtually primal scene of instruction, Rochester tells Jane the story of how Adèle came to be "transplanted" from France to England. It is this narration, as we have noted, that particularly scandalized Victorian readers. Rigby, for example, complains of how Rochester "pours into [Jane's] ears disgraceful tales of his past life, connected with the birth of Adèle."[] But just as the transplant in question intends a homeopathic effect, supposedly defending the world of the novel against the theatricality that Adèle represents, so this narrative-within-a-narrative goes out of its way to declare its innocuousness. Rochester, in fact, pauses in the middle of his story to reassure Jane of her immunity from it: "I know what sort of mind I have placed in communication with my own: I know it is one not liable to take infection". Always a quick learner, Jane echoes her teacher's "knowledge" when, musing on his story, she remarks that "there was probably nothing at all extraordinary in the substance of the narrative itself".

If Rochester has greater faith in Jane's "mental strength" than Rigby has, his disciplinary procedure requires that premise as fundamentally as Rigby's ideological fiction needs the support that it too presses into service; and while the placidity of Rochester's pupil and the tremulousness of Rigby's governed governess may seem incommensurate, Jane, as we have seen, is indeed capable of the agitation—what Rochester in fact forecasts for her here as "whirl and tumult, foam and noise"—that, in complementing her outward calm, proves her interiority to be so usefully receptive.

The "substance" of Rochester's narrative is his affair with Céline Varens. Rochester tells Jane of how Céline betrayed him and abandoned Adèle, whom he subsequently rescued from "the slime and mud of Paris." In narrating his discovery of Céline's faithlessness, Rochester stages his spectatorship in a way that seems to anticipate Jane's equally vengeful acts of consumption. Waiting for his "opera inamorata" one night on the "balcony" outside her boudoir, he sees her returning to her hotel with another man. "Prepar[ing] an ambush," he "draws the curtain" in front of the balcony window, through an aperture of which he may thus, like Jane, "see without being seen." But that Rochester is in fact demonstrating the necessary *difference* between himself and Jane is signaled by the conspicuous absence from his surveillance of any of the voyeuristic titillation that animates hers.

For whatever "excitation" he may have been feeling subsides at the very point where he would seem most susceptible to it—as soon, that is, as he begins to witness the spectacle of his betrayal and ridicule: "They [Céline and her lover] began to talk; their conversation eased me completely: frivolous, mercenary, heartless, and senseless, it was rather calculated to weary than enrage a listener". And if the frivolity of the scene is matched by the boredom of the spectator—if Rochester refuses to get excited—he exempts himself equally from the rigors of restraint. For he responds to this potentially enraging experience not only by coming out into the open, but then by concluding this particular charade with a brisk finesse all the more pointed for the bad acting that serves as its foil:

Opening the window, I walked in upon them; liberated Céline from my protection; gave her notice to vacate her hotel; offered her a purse for immediate exigencies; disregarded screams, hysterics, prayers, protestations, convulsions; made an appointment with the vicomte for a meeting at the Bois de Boulogne. Next morning I had the pleasure of encountering him; left a bullet in one of his poor etiolated arms, feeble as the wing of a chicken in the pip, and then thought I had done with the whole crew.

It turns out, of course, that Rochester cannot quite dismiss "the whole crew": instead, he is forced to transplant the noxiously Parisian Adèle into what he (rather misleadingly) calls "the wholesome soil of an English country garden". Yet insofar as Rochester persists in denying that he is Adèle's father, this transplant neatly figures appropriation as disavowal, and inscription as erasure.

And if the graft in question thus has a dismissive effect after all, that effect derives not so much from the aristocratic insouciance of Rochester's irony as from the domesticating receptivity of Jane's "mind," whose capacity for assimilation his didactic narrative has been seeking to establish.

For in this lesson, Rochester has implicitly but forcefully been impressing upon the governess the need for her governance, not just of her "protégée", Adèle, but also of the mind he has posited in her, and therefore of the potential promiscuity of social exchange—of the social in the most dangerously inclusive sense—that his own Byronic circulation appears to signify. Jane dutifully notes of this and other "conferences":

I, indeed, talked comparatively little, but I heard him talk with relish. It was his nature to be communicative; he liked to open to a mind unacquainted with the world, glimpses of its scenes and ways (I do not mean its corrupt scenes and wicked ways, but such as derived their interest from the great scale on which they were acted, the strange novelty by which they were characterized); and I had a keen delight in receiving the new ideas he offered, in imagining the new pictures he portrayed, and following him in thought through the new regions he disclosed, never startled or troubled by one noxious allusion.

As an upper-class man, Rochester obviously has greater mobility—and less anxiety about it—than does, say, an upper-class woman. Not so differently from a writer like Rigby, however, Rochester still insists on the necessity of a fictitious barrier to hold "the world" in place, to regulate the flow of social meanings.

What better barrier than his newly employed governess, who, equipped with a disciplined, densely structured mind, positively "delight[s] in receiving," and absorbing, all the "tumult" that the narratives of his Byronic theatricality can "open to" her. Indeed, Jane sees herself not as a captive audience but as an expansive consciousness privileged to capture the "novelty" that informs Rochester's "scenes." Subsuming these scenes "in thought," containing these tableaux by "imagining" them, Jane affirms the psychological novel's ability to suppress the "corrupt" and "noxious" associations of the material it incorporates.

For though Jane denies even the corrupt *content* of Rochester's stories (to say nothing of their corrupting *influence*), we may prefer to view that denial as part of a cover-up, in whose distinctive methods Rochester himself has been giving her careful on-the-job training. In narrating for Jane the "frivolous" but admittedly "slimy" scene of Céline's unmasking, for instance, he has also allegorized for her edification, and thus for the strengthening of the social order itself, the appropriately antiseptic, antitheatrical—one might even say "novelizing"—response to it. As if to drive home the lesson he has been teaching, moreover, Rochester, in the middle of recounting this meretricious French melodrama (or is it a farce?), "portrays" what thus becomes a kind of scene within a scene; and the embedded scene not only has the same infectious potential as the foreign affair, but indeed strikes dangerously close to home:

He ground his teeth and was silent: he arrested his step and struck his boot against the hard ground. Some hated thought seemed to have him in its grip, and to hold him so tightly that he could not advance—

We were ascending the avenue when he thus paused; the hall was before us. Lifting his eyes to its battlements, he cast over them a glare, such as I never saw before or since. Pain, shame, ire—impatience, disgust, detestation—seemed momentarily to hold a quivering conflict in the large pupil dilating under his ebon eyebrow. Wild was the wrestle which should be paramount; but another feeling rose and triumphed: something hard and cynical; self-willed and resolute: it settled his passion and petrified his countenance: he went on—

"During the moment I was silent, Miss Eyre, I was arranging a point with my destiny. She stood there by that beech trunk—a hag like one of those who appeared to Macbeth on the heath at Forres. 'You like Thornfield?' she said, lifting her finger; and then she wrote in the air a memento, which ran in lurid hieroglyphics all along the house front, between the upper and lower row of windows, 'Like it if you can! Like it if you dare!' "

An inscription of the novel's Gothic subtext, this passage also records the theatrical implications of that subtext, which the novel frames more often as its buried, repressed, incarcerated "truth," as a signified so private and internal as to *transcend* theatricality, intimating instead a realm of peculiarly logocentric écriture, of unspeakable textuality. Indeed, if—to borrow Gilbert and Gubar's admirable pun—Bertha Mason has to be shut up, this is because the novel cannot risk the contradiction of too obvious or too frequent a staging of its deepest and "darkest" secret; and if the witch of Thornfield nonetheless manages the occasional escape, what these sorties display more crucially, as we have seen, is Jane's ability—far greater than Grace Poole's—to front for and thereby recontain her. As Rochester's pupil and narratee, Jane is in fact being trained in this recuperative function. What completes the lesson, however, is not so much Rochester's Macbeth-like exchange with his "destiny" as Adèle's interruption of it, or rather the exemplary use to which Rochester puts that interruption:

Adèle here ran before him with her shuttlecock.

"Away!" he cried harshly; "keep at a distance, child; or go in to Sophie!" Continuing then to pursue his walk in silence, I ventured to recall him to the point whence he had abruptly diverged—

"Did you leave the balcony, sir," I asked, "when Mdlle Varens entered?"

I almost expected a rebuff for this hardly well-timed question: but, on the contrary, waking out of his scowling abstraction, he turned his eyes towards me, and the shade seemed to clear off his brow.

A certain "abruptness" indeed renders the passage itself oddly resistant to naturalistic interpretation. Paternal (or, as Rochester insists, nonpaternal) resentment is not enough to account for the "harshness" with which he "rebuffs" Adèle. Adèle's sudden appearance, moreover, seems as unmotivated as the verbal violence that greets it.

I would argue that her interruption acts, in its own almost comically contingent way, as a kind of shuttlecock in its own right, providing an accidental though no less unwelcome link between the inscription of Céline on the one hand and the inscription of (and by) the "hag" on the other.

Intruding on Rochester's quasi-Shakespearean scene, and issuing from the tonally and thematically disparate story of the actress-prostitute who is her mother, Adèle figures the threat of a relay between the very rhetorical registers the novel strives to segregate. As a result of such a relay, it might become difficult, if not impossible, to distinguish between the Gothic and the Austenian, between the psychological and the social, between the internal and the external, between the unconscious and the "calculating," between the uncanny and the frivolous, between the demonic and the merely "mercenary."

For despite their respective excesses, it is not so much any intrinsic content that makes both the story of Céline and the dialogue with the hag so potentially harmful; rather, the real danger lies in the possibility that they will infect *each other*.

Hence Rochester's command:

"Keep at a distance, child; or go in to Sophie!" In ordering Adèle to *go in*, he prepares her for the domesticating discipline he is busy teaching her teacher. That the object of his anger is female should not come as a surprise, since the object of his instruction is female as well. Rochester makes an example of Adèle, repelling her for having enacted the very boundary-crossing that her governess, as formed by his pedagogy, must prevent, precisely by upholding the fictitious barrier of her own inwardness. And the arbitrariness of that weighty charge is merely hinted at by the apparent arbitrariness with which Rochester treats Adèle.

Again, though, Jane learns her lesson well. "Recalling" Rochester from his Gothic-Shakespearean seizure to the story of Céline, she need not fear the same treatment Adèle has just received, since the very recalling re-marks—rather than compromises—the boundary in question. Jane has understood the responsibilities of her "post"—or, more specifically, her responsibilities *as* post, as both support and marker. Indeed, the pupil's progress is registered immediately and gratifyingly on the teacher's face, as "the shade seemed to clear off his brow."

Through this clearing, Jane's readiness for her appointed work finds its index on her master's closely watched, heavily meaning-laden countenance. I would suggest, moreover, that the precondition for—or the necessary counterweight to—the novel's insistent and intensive representational heightening of the worldly, if world-weary, Rochester is precisely the heaviness and density of Jane's internalizing discourse.

The point is not just the obvious one that Rochester is on display only because Jane's first-person narrative has produced him; rather, I am arguing almost the opposite case, that the social power for which Rochester stands has in a sense produced or called forth the narrative *in* or *on* which he stands. *Jane Eyre* is thus a kind of command performance that, rigorously veiling its performative exigencies and efficacies, militates not only against a possible slippage of class boundaries within the division of female symbolic labour, but also against an inordinate confusion or extravagance of meanings within a certain world of male social exchange as well.

In other words, the theatrical glamorization of a wealthy and powerful man like Rochester depends upon the antitheatrical subordination of a poor and powerless woman like Jane Eyre. For example, if Rochester's fantasm of "lurid hieroglyphics" already threatens a parodic or hyperbolic collapse of Gothic inscription into the "hysterics" of the bad boulevard drama that frames it, and if that framing itself sets the stage for contamination, Rochester can indulge with impunity in these deconstructive flirtations, because, after all, he has trained the governess to keep up the very distinctions that, as his class and gender entitle him to do, he plays at breaking down.

It is he who owns the shuttlecock, and who determines both its frolicsome appearance and its abrupt disappearance. He knows, that is, that after the scene of Jane's instruction, she will know how to separate—how to mark the incongruity between—the less clearly disciplinary scenes that he has been combining in an almost "carnivalesque" way. We have already noted the docility of the words with which she begins this cleanup operation:

As he had said, there was probably nothing at all extraordinary in the substance of the narrative itself: a wealthy Englishman's passion for a French dancer, and her treachery to him, were everyday matters enough, no doubt, in society; but there was something decidedly strange in the paroxysm of emotion which had suddenly seized him when he was in the act of expressing the present contentment of his mood, and his newly revived pleasure in the old hall and its environs. I meditated wonderingly on this incident.

"Meditat[ing] wonderingly," Jane thereby in effect reinstates the basis for Rochester's "newly revived" domestic "contentment," a sense of security located narratively, and regrounded discursively, in the space *between scenes.* It is tempting, of course, to relieve Jane of this socially useful but unglamorous work of interposition, so that the novel's apparently "carnivalesque" theatrics may be imagined as extending not only to her but—as if *through* her—to "the reader" as well.

Helena Michie, for instance, writes

Reading *Jane Eyre* is a veritable masquerade in which neither the reader nor the character can consistently tell the difference between mask and reality. Throughout the novel both Jane and Rochester try on a series of disguises and personae that grow more and more complex at the point of apparent unveiling. Jane's "discovery" that Rochester is the gypsy, for instance, only complicates matters and generates new questions about their respective roles. For Jane, even more than Rochester, the novel is a series of costume fittings that focus on the central contradictions between heroine and dependent.

Though, as I began by suggesting, Brontë's novels are indeed far more theatrical than either she or some of her most influential critics would have us believe, I have been arguing for most of this chapter that *Jane Eyre,* at any rate, has to restrain or to conceal its heroine's theatricality.

And if Jane's consequent subjectification provides a cover for the women of the employers' class—women whose domesticity might otherwise seem perilously close to the conditions of social exchange from which it would signify an escape—this subjectification also works to neutralize the more expansive and promiscuous social exchange mythically enacted by upper-class men, whose circulation constitutes not one side of the social map but rather an incessant movement back and forth across it.

What this means in terms of Michie's argument is that Rochester may be seen to "try on a series of disguises and personae" to the precise extent that Jane may not.

Rochester may play the gypsy, but Jane must play the spectator. In that showy set-piece of a scene, he is free to transform his body into a site of contradictions, where the maleness of his scrutinizing gaze collides with the femaleness of his "masquerade," or where the temporary "darkness" of his gypsy persona underscores the permanent "darkness" of both his person and his character, and thus seems to deconstruct the opposition between the psychic "darkness" of Gothic repression (Bertha) and the much less scary hermeneutic "darkness" of the charades (Blanche). But the reason these intimations of heteroglossia seem neither threatening nor particularly liberating is that Jane can be counted upon to resist them: "I believe you have been trying to draw me out—or in; you have been talking nonsense to make me talk nonsense".

Such obdurate perspicacity keeps the focus of the narrative *away* from Jane's "costume fittings" and from the "central contradictions between heroine and dependent," ostentatiously investing Rochester alone with the authority to embody social contradictions yet thereby debunking such contradictions as so much "nonsense."

For if the festive destabilizing of sexual, racial, and generic categories comes oddly to seem the exclusive right of the powerful, the tendentious casting of the "aristocracy" in that role makes "subversion" look even more archaic and innocuous, especially in light of what Gilbert and Gubar call Jane's "unseduceable independence."

To maintain the illusion of this independence from an ultimately inconsequential world of profligate social exchange, Brontë usually *avoids* the analogy between reading and masquerade. The numerous scenes in the novel that centre on the more or less aggressive or painful analysis of others employ textual rather than theatrical metaphors. Significantly, the art form with which the heroine is associated is not acting but painting, which is associated in turn with both writing and "discipline".

And when Jane—under theatricalizing pressure—leaves Thornfield, she assumes not a mask but an "*alias*". Indeed, one could interpret each of her successive displacements in the course of the novel—from Gateshead Hall to Lowood School to Thornfield Hall to Moor House to Ferndean—as a way of extricating her from a situation in which her antitheatrical cover is in danger of being blown.

When, for example, she escapes from St. John Rivers to return to Rochester, she is escaping not just lovelessness and authoritarianism, but an increasingly specular power-play, in which the histrionics of the play threaten to surpass the intensities of the power. Breaking away with the declaration, "*My* powers were in play and in force", she marshals the near-redundancy of "power...in force" to put "play" in its place, and to prefigure her final absorption into the asocial utopia of Ferndean.

By means of such strategies of absorption and displacement—strategies similar to those we have discussed in *Mansfield Park*—Brontë inscribes an even more sophisticated and elaborate technology of the self than Austen does. Yet the fantasy that Michie articulates, whereby, as in Austen's parodic curtain call as Mrs.

Norris, that technology may be undone and the novel may be reconceived—and, even better, experienced—as a masquerade, finds an unlikely source of encouragement in Rigby's exuberantly punitive review of the novel. I have said that Rigby thought the character of Jane Eyre "undisciplined," inadequate for the task of keeping up the fictitious barrier in front of a problematic domesticity. Not surprisingly, this inadequacy manifests itself as a certain theatricality: Brontë's governess might sometimes *look like* "a noble, high-souled woman," but Rigby—perhaps getting back at Brontë for having theatricalized the "lady"—exposes Jane as a "flippant, fifth-rate, plebeian actress."

Against my claim that Brontë's discipline of the governess constitutes an even sturdier barrier than the one Rigby demands, Rigby would insist on the failure of that fiction. And, much as one would censure the appalling class animus that informs Rigby's attack, one must admit that she may have a point. For there is often a sense in which Jane's inwardness borders on—indeed, collapses into—the very staginess or bad acting from which it would distinguish itself. (Presumably, if Jane's acting were better than "fifth-rate," one would not notice it as acting, but would see only the noble, high-souled woman she now strains to impersonate.) "One" somehow knows what Rigby means when she writes, "One feels provoked as Jane Eyre stands before us."

Impelled by an unmistakable ardor of discreditation, Rigby of course adduces her own examples; more decorously and discreetly, we might point to some of the "soliloquies" Jane delivers in the course of the book. Yet, if the "failure" implicit in Blanche Ingram's bad acting proves inseparable from Jane's "success" as a heroine, perhaps we should pause to consider the possible virtues of Jane's own bad acting, before lining up behind Rigby to take potshots at the would-be impostor. We have already noted the Brontëan invagination whereby openness becomes inwardness, but we placed that process under the heading of "restraint." When Rigby remarks that "governesses are said to be sly...but Jane out-governesses them all," she identifies a reversal of that process—a turning outward of the inside—and she indicts it as precisely a refusal of restraint: "little Becky"—Becky Sharp of course, 1847's other famous governess-turned-actress—"would have blushed for her."

It is not always easy, however, to tell whether Jane is outside-in, or inside-out. When Jane resists Rochester's pseudocarnivalesque efforts "to draw [her] out—or in," the obstinacy of her "self"-disciplinary in-folding overmasters the prepositional equivocation. But in other scenes, such as the humiliation or the unmasking of Blanche, where Jane's excitation tends not to seem *fully* complicit with her restraint, a certain effect of "*out*-governessing" suggests that Brontë may be playing a game of *fort/da* with the disciplinary techniques that her work generally enforces.

Without going so far as to call that effect "subversive" or "carnivalesque," we can at least differentiate it from the sort of deconstruction or demystification that ruthlessly restrains or ignores its own performance. There is of course no guarantee that demystification-as-masquerade will not be reenfolded within the disciplinary apparatus.

Yet it may be useful to recall another one of our clusters of metaphors, and to remember that, precisely as a central figure in the chiastic redrawing of the social map, Jane Eyre's compulsory "ignorance" already carries within itself an unpredictable potential for the very social exchange that it works ostensibly to segregate as "prostitution" or to trivialize as "aristocratic" errancy. Chiasmus, after all, is the rhetorical schematization of exchange. The intermediary can be both a protective barrier and a dangerously effective conductor of "antithetical" meanings. Like Jane Eyre, contemporary deconstructive teacher-critics, especially those who profess "strategically" "to ignore the lessons of deconstruction," are positioned, just as "strategically," between what is idealized as a transcendent (though not exactly "Gothic") realm of truth and authority, to which we are thought to have privileged access—one has only to recall recent right-wing defenses of "the canon" and of "the Western tradition"—and what is projected—by left and right alike—as a degrading (though not exactly "Austenian") marketplace. Because *our* intermediate space is both as necessary to the culture and as potentially deconstructive of it as is the intermediate space demarcated and maintained by Jane Eyre, we might learn from her a certain "sly," if not "flippant," way of occupying it.

I am implying not that deconstructive literary critics should simply become more theatrical—whatever that would mean—but that, by recognizing certain parallels between our own cultural instrumentality and that of a Victorian teacher-writer-unmasker like Jane Eyre, we might also recognize certain opportunities—under the very cover of our discipline—to be more socially and politically "provoking" than we sometimes think we are. In its very latency as a critical option, deconstruction-as-performance may have greater power to disturb than does deconstruction-as-cognition. In her dazzling essay on Freud's case history of Dora, Jane Gallop suggests that "for psychoanalysis to be a site of radical contestation, Freud must assume his identification with the governess."

For the governess, unlike the phallic mother (or, for that matter, the madwoman), is not only a troublesome source of sexual demystification, but in herself a demystifying emblem of social, and sexual, exchange. Criticism—especially deidealizing criticism—is often depicted as a stripping away of masks, but the critic—at least the academic critic—also *wears* a mask: the mask of the governess. Not by penetrating or—only somewhat less abusively—by lifting Jane Eyre's cover, but by turning it inside-out so that it becomes visible as a mask, "the reader"—more often than not an alias for the professor of literature—expresses, covertly, his or her desire to "out-governess them all": not merely to act out his or her role in the social script, but to act it *badly*, so as to transform a barrier and a surveillance post into a site, if not of radical contestation, then of an excitation that is not inevitably its own restraint.

Bibliography

A book review of Mansfield Park by John Thorpe of Northanger Abbey

LADY SUSAN, 1793-94 - Tahto ja toiveet (suom. Paula Merensuo)

SENSE AND SENSIBILITY, 1811 - Järki ja tunteet (suom. Aune Brotherus) - films: television drama 1971, dir. by David Giles, television drama 1981, dir. by Rodney Bennett; 1995, dir. by Ang Lee, starring Emma Thompson, Alan Rickman, Kate Winslet, Hugh Grant. "Verbally, the film is nicely nuanced and catches the spirit of the text. The female characters tend to be ironists or dimwits, though many of the latter are good, amusing people who generally mean well. For decades readers have been drawn to the civilized world Jane Austen created in her novels. This film brilliantly transforms that world to the screen and is sure to revive Hollywood's interest in Jane Austen, to the delight of literate viewers." (from Novels into Film by John C. Tibbetts and James M. Welsh, 1999); Kandukondain Kandukondain, 2000, dir. by Rajiv Menon; tv series 2007, dir. by John Alexander

PRIDE AND PREJUDICE, 1813 - Ylpeys ja ennakkoluulo (suom. Sirkka-Liisa Norko-Turja) - film 1940, dir. by Robert Z. Leonard, written Aldous Huxley, Jane Murfin, play Helen Jerome, starring Laurence Olivier and Greer Carson. "While Austen sustains a heightened level of clever dialogue, the screenwriters insert various slapstick scenes such as the squawking parrot, Lady Catherine sitting on a music box, Mr. Collins scurrying on his knees as he proposes to Elizabeth, and the tipsy tendencies of Lydia and Kitty." (from Novels into

Film by John C. Tibbetts and James M. Welsh, 1999); BBC televisio series 1995, dir. by Simon Langton, starring Jennifer Ehle, Colin Firth, Susannah Harker, Crispin Bonham-Carter; 2003, dir. by Andrew Black; Bride & Prejudice, 2004, dir. by Gurinder Chadham, starring Aishwarya Rai, Martin Henderson, Daniel Gillies; television series 2005, dir. by Joe Wright, starring Keira Knightley, Rosamund Pike, Talulah Riley, Jena Malone, Donald Sutherland, Simon Woods, and Matthew McFadyen

MANSFIELD PARK, 1814 - Kasvattitytön tarina (suom. A. R. Koskimies) - films: mini tv series 1983, dir. by David Giles; 1999, dir. by Patricia Rozema; television drama 2007, dir. by Iain B. MacDonald

EMMA, 1815 - Emma (suom. Aune Brotherus) - films: 1932, dir. by Clarence Brown; television drama 1948, dir. by Michael Barry; television drama 1960, dir. by Campbell Logan; 1996, dir. by Douglas Mc Grath, starring Gwyneth Paltrow, Toni Collette, Ewan McGregor; Clueless, 1996, dir. by Amy Heckerling, starring Alicia Silverstone and Paul Rudd; television drama 1996, dir. by Diarmuid Lawrence

NORTHANGER ABBEY, 1817 - Neito vanhassa linnassa (suom. Eila Pennanen) / Northanger Abbey (suom. P. Merjamaa) - films: television drama 1986, dir. by Giles Foster; starring Katharine Schlesinger; Peter Firth, Robert Hardy, Googie Withers, Geoffrey Chater; television drama 2007, dir. by Jon Jones

PERSUASION, 1818 - Viisasteleva sydän (suom. Kristiina Kivivuori) - films: 1955, dir. by Rober Michell; BBC television series, 1995, dir. by Roger Michell, starring Amanda Root, Ciaran Hinds, Susan Fleetwood, Corin Redgrave, Fiona Shaw and John Woodvine; mini television series 2007, dir. by Adrian